Governing the Postal Service

Edited by J. Gregory Sidak

The AEI Press

Publisher for the American Enterprise Institute
WASHINGTON, D. C.

1994

Library of Congress Cataloging-in-Publication Data

Governing the postal service / J. Gregory Sidak, editor.
  p. cm.
  ISBN 0-8447-3892-1.—ISBN 0-8447-3893-X (pbk.)
  1. United States Postal Service—Congresses. 2. Postal service—United
States—Congresses. I. Sidak, J. Gregory.
HE6371.G68 1994
353.0087'3—dc20 94-30975

1 3 5 7 9 10 8 6 4 2

The AEI Press
Publisher for the American Enterprise Institute
1150 17th Street, N. W., Washington, D. C. 20036

ISBN 978-0-8447-3893-2

Contents

Acknowledgments

The ideas in this monograph were shaped by the many questions and useful suggestions offered by participants in roundtable discussions held at the American Enterprise Institute in September 1993 and May 1994. I am grateful for their contribution. In addition, I wish to thank those at AEI who assisted in preparing this volume for publication: Douglas Ashton, Julie Bassett, Kathleen Cox, Scott Darling, Peter Tate Jensen, Joseph Matelis, Steve O'Brien, Anna Rao, and Robert Stup. I am also grateful for the assistance of Diana Furchtgott-Roth and Marvin Kosters of AEI.

J. GREGORY SIDAK

Contributors

MICHAEL A. CREW is professor of economics and director of the Center for Research in Regulated Industries at Rutgers University. He is the coauthor, with Paul Kleindorfer, of *Public Utility Economics* (1979), *The Economics of Public Utility Regulation* (1986), and *The Economics of Postal Service* (1992). He is editor of the *Journal of Regulatory Economics* and has been a consultant on regulatory matters to the Royal Mail and the United States Postal Service.

R. RICHARD GEDDES is assistant professor of economics at Fordham University. His primary areas of research are law and economics, the economics of regulation, and industrial organization. His recent publications and working papers address managerial monitoring and organizational form in regulated industries. He received his Ph.D. in economics from the University of Chicago.

DOUGLAS H. GINSBURG was appointed circuit judge for the U.S. Court of Appeals for the District of Columbia Circuit in 1986. Judge Ginsburg previously served as a law clerk to Circuit Judge Carl McGowan; law clerk to Justice Thurgood Marshall; professor of law at Harvard University; deputy assistant attorney general for regulatory affairs, U.S. Department of Justice, Antitrust Division; administrator for information and regulatory affairs, Executive Office of the President, Office of Management and Budget; and assistant attorney general, U.S. Department of Justice, Antitrust Division. He graduated from Cornell University, receiving a B.S. in 1970, and from the University of Chicago Law School, receiving a J.D. in 1973.

HENRY B. HANSMANN is the Harris Professor of Law at Yale Law School. He received a B.A. in mathematics from Brown University in 1967, a J.D. from Yale Law School in 1974, and a Ph.D. in economics from Yale University in 1978. He taught law, economics, and public policy at the University of Pennsylvania from 1975 to 1983, when he joined the Yale Law School faculty. He is also a member of the faculty at the Yale School of Management. Professor Hansmann's scholarship focuses on the law and economics of enterprise organization.

PAUL R. KLEINDORFER is professor of decision sciences and economics and codirector of the Center for Risk Management and Decision Processes at the Wharton School, University of Pennsylvania. He is the coauthor, with Michael Crew, of *Public Utility Economics, The Economics of Public Utility Regulation,* and *The Economics of Postal Service.* He is associate editor of the *Journal of Regulatory Economics* and has been a consultant on regulatory matters to the Royal Mail and the United States Postal Service.

WILLIAM TY MAYTON is the Simmons Professor of Law at Emory University School of Law. He has published widely on administrative and constitutional law and is the coauthor of *Administrative Law* (1992). Mr. Mayton received his J.D. from Columbia Law School in 1972.

SHARON M. OSTER is associate dean and the Frederic D. Wolfe Professor of Management and Entrepreneurship at the Yale School of Management. Professor Oster specializes in competitive strategy, microeconomic theory, industrial organization, the economics of regulation and antitrust, and nonprofit strategy. She is the author of *Modern Competitive Analysis* (1990). Professor Oster received her Ph.D. from Harvard University.

JOHN C. PANZAR is the Louis W. Menk Professor of Economics at Northwestern University. He received his Ph.D. in economics from Stanford University in 1975. He began his professional career at Bell Telephone Laboratories in 1974 and served as head of economic analysis of the Research Department from 1980 to 1983. While at Bell Labs, Professor Panzar wrote, with William J. Baumol and Robert D. Willig, *Contestable Markets and the Theory of Industry Structure* (1982). He serves on the editorial board of *Information Economics and Policy,* as an associate editor of the *Journal of Regulatory Economics,* and as a member of the board of directors of the Telecommunications Policy Research Conference. His research focuses on the theoretical and public policy issues surrounding multiproduct natural monopolies.

RICHARD J. PIERCE, JR., is the Paul J. Kellner Professor of Law at Columbia University. He has written numerous books and articles on government regulation of industry, including *Economic Regulation: Cases and Materials* (1994). Mr. Pierce received his J.D. from the University of Virginia.

GEORGE L. PRIEST is the John M. Olin Professor of Law and Economics at Yale Law School, where he teaches insurance, products liability, antitrust, torts, regulated industries, and, recently, a course on capitalism. He is a graduate of Yale College (1969) and the University of Chicago Law School (1973) and is the author of a wide number of articles and monographs on product liability, tort law, privatization, and economic analysis. He served as a member of President Reagan's Commission on Privatization and is the director of the Program in Civil Liability at Yale Law School.

PAUL H. RUBIN is professor of economics at Emory University and an adjunct scholar at the American Enterprise Institute. Previously, he was senior staff economist on the Council of Economic Advisers and chief economist of the Consumer Product Safety Commission. He has written numerous books and articles on economics, law, and regulation, including *Managing Business Transactions* (1990) and *Tort Reform by Contract* (AEI Press, 1993). Mr. Rubin is editor in chief of the journal *Managerial and Decision Economics*.

DAVID E. M. SAPPINGTON is the Lanzillotti-McKethan Eminent Scholar in the Department of Economics at the University of Florida. Previously, he served on the faculties of the University of Michigan and the University of Pennsylvania and on the professional research staff of Bell Communications Research. His research focuses on the design of regulatory policy. He has served on the editorial boards of the *American Economic Review*, the *Journal of Economics and Management Strategy*, the *Journal of Industrial Economics*, the *Journal of Regulatory Economics*, and *Information Economics and Policy*. Mr. Sappington received his Ph.D. in economics from Princeton University.

J. GREGORY SIDAK is a resident scholar at the American Enterprise Institute and senior lecturer at the Yale School of Management. He served as deputy general counsel of the Federal Communications Commission from 1987 to 1989 and as senior counsel and economist to the Council of Economic Advisers from 1986 to 1987. He is coauthor, with William J. Baumol, of *Toward Competition in Local Telephony* (MIT Press/AEI Press, 1994) and has published numerous articles on antitrust, telecommunications regulation, corporate governance, and constitutional law.

Introduction

J. Gregory Sidak

During the 1980s, the policy debate over the United States Postal Service stalled. Much intellectual effort had previously been devoted to attacking the postal monopoly and demonstrating the benefits of privatizing the Postal Service. But privatization was never seriously considered in the political arena, even at the height of the Reagan administration, and subsequent political changes have made the prospects for such a policy even more remote.

Since the late 1980s, however, the growth of fax machines and new telecommunications and transportation services has effectively privatized significant portions of the Postal Service's business and raised doubts about whether the service can remain viable in its current form. In addition, new research on the appropriate scope and design of regulation in other (mainly privately owned) network industries has invited a reexamination of how the government's mail service is regulated.

The American Enterprise Institute organized the Project on Postal Regulation in 1993 to examine these developments, produce new research on how the Postal Service can be made to function more efficiently in a changing economic environment, and promote a fundamental rethinking of the role of the Postal Service as a public enterprise. The AEI project has focused in particular on these central issues:

• What is the mission of the Postal Service, and how has that mission changed since the Postal Reorganization Act of 1970?

• How does the ownership and governance structure of the Postal Service differ from that of a private, profit-maximizing firm, and how does the difference affect the service's efficiency and productivity?

• How might mailers and competing delivery firms be allowed

to purchase access to unbundled portions of the government's postal network (as customers and competitors can now do, for example, in the telecommunications and electric power industries), and how should such access be priced?

• Why has the debate over public ownership and management of the Postal Service ignored the analogies to government enterprises in centrally planned economies, notorious for their inefficiency and resistance to innovation?

• How might a government-owned Postal Service be commercialized so that private firms might compete more equally for those portions of mail service that can sustain competition?

The six essays in this volume address these and related questions—and introduce a number of fresh academic faces to the study of the law and economics of postal regulation. Presented at conferences held at AEI in September 1993 and May 1994, the essays provoked thoughtful discussion among knowledgeable government officials, business executives, scholars, lawyers, and consulting economists. Their discussions are transcribed here in edited form, along with the prepared comments of expert discussants on each essay. We hope the collection contributes to tangible improvements in the management and regulation of the Postal Service.

1
The Economics of Mail Delivery

John C. Panzar

The most important issue facing postal regulators in the coming years is the opening of the U.S. postal network to increased competition. I do not foresee this happening as a result of a repeal of the private express statutes, nor do I favor a repeal at this time. Rather, I think important efficiency gains can be made through improved use of the existing network of the United States Postal Service. The key lies in establishing a pricing policy that encourages mailers and potential competitors to access this vertically integrated network in a way that minimizes the *total* cost of providing postal services.

The plausible assumption that facilitates the theoretical analysis is that economies of scale are concentrated in the local collection and delivery networks of the Postal Service, with the transportation and mail-sorting functions being characterized by essentially constant returns to scale. This framework bears a striking resemblance to the situation developing in the U.S. telecommunications industry, where the local exchange network is viewed as a "bottleneck monopoly." The basic efficient pricing result has an especially straightforward interpretation in the postal context: mailers should receive a discount equal to the costs they save the Postal Service.[1]

This chapter proceeds as follows. Part one discusses the important technological characteristics of the Postal Service—namely, that it

---

1. The discussion here is not intended to be exhaustive. For a modern theoretical treatment, see MICHAEL A. CREW & PAUL R. KLEINDORFER, THE ECONOMICS OF POSTAL SERVICE (Kluwer Academic Publishers 1992). For papers covering the theory and practice of postal regulation around the world, see REGULATION AND THE NATURE OF POSTAL DELIVERY SERVICES (Michael A. Crew & Paul R. Kleindorfer eds., Kluwer Academic Publishers 1992). *See* Michael D. Bradley, Jeffrey L. Colvin & Marc A. Smith, *Measuring Product Costs for Ratemaking: The United States Postal Service, in id.* at 133; Leonard Merewitz &

is a network industry with relatively low sunk costs. The second part addresses the issue of natural monopoly and concludes that it is unimportant for policy purposes. The third part presents the analysis of postal access pricing, which lies at the heart of the chapter, and comments on more traditional pricing issues and on incentive regulation. The last part concludes with a brief comment contrasting the policy debate in postal regulation with that in telecommunications.

Technological Characteristics of the Postal Service

Network Structure. Like telecommunications, electric power, and the transportation sector, postal service is a *network industry*. This network structure has important implications for the analysis of efficient industry structure in the market for postal services.

The postal network has an obvious hierarchical structure. That is, mail entering the network tends to travel through facilities serving larger and larger geographic areas (*outward* sortation and transportation), until its final destination is contained in a facility's service area. It then begins its *inward* journey, when this process is reversed: mail is transported and sorted at facilities serving smaller and smaller geographic areas until it reaches the letter carrier's route.

There are obvious similarities between postal and telecommunications networks. Since telecommunications is a network industry that has recently been successfully opened to competition, the following description of the postal network will emphasize parallels between the two.

Local delivery networks. Collection and delivery, the beginning and final links in the postal network, provide the same intimate connections to consumers that the local exchange network does in telecommunications. And, as in telecommunications, the terms of access to this local distribution network will prove to be crucial for the successful introduction of competition into the provision of postal services. Also, each of these local networks performs sorting (switching) and short-haul transport (transmission), as well as handling most interactions with the consuming public.

Mark A. Zupan, *Franchise Bidding, Contracting Out, and Worksharing in the Production of Postal Services: Can They Collect, Sort, and Deliver?, in id.* at 69; Cathy M. Rogerson & William M. Takis, *Economies of Scale and Scope and Competition in Postal Services, in id.* at 109; John C. Panzar, *Competition, Efficiency, and the Vertical Structure of Postal Services, in id.* at 91. For a valuable introduction to the policy issues, see GENERAL ACCOUNTING OFFICE, U.S. POSTAL SERVICE: PRICING POSTAL SERVICES IN A COMPETITIVE ENVIRONMENT (1992).

2

Internal studies by the Postal Service indicate substantial economies of scale associated with mail delivery, because the time-consuming activity for a letter carrier is making a stop at a business or residence. Since the number of stops increases less than proportionally with mail volume, substantial economies of scale are associated with the delivery function.

It is equally plausible to suppose that there are substantial economies of scope between delivery and *collection*. These scope economies have two sources. The first occurs any time two or more functions are able to make use of the same increasing-returns production process. Put simply, once the fixed costs associated with a delivery network have been incurred, using that same network for collection avoids duplication of such costs, even if there are no particular cost savings present at the margin. The peak-load structure of postal service also gives rise to a stronger form of economies of scope, both here and elsewhere in the postal network. It seems reasonable to suppose that the (inward) volume of mail to be delivered is the primary determinant of the capacity of a local postal network. This assumption is based on the difference in peaking characteristics of the two types of mail flows. Inward mail tends to arrive at a high rate for a brief period of time, while the flow of outward mail is more evenly distributed over the day. To the extent that service standards require human and physical capacity sufficient to deal with this inward peak, there will be extra capacity available to process outward movements.

Sortation. The sorting that occurs in the postal network performs the same role that switches do in the telecommunications network. It directs mail to the next point on its journey through the network hierarchy. Like telecommunications switching, postal sorting has been the focus of substantial technical change. These changes have affected the vertical structure of postal services by altering the hierarchical location at which key sortation functions are performed. The final step in inward sortation—for example, sorting mail to the order in which a carrier walks his route—has typically been performed by the carrier at the local post office before beginning his rounds for the day. If carrier route sorting is automated using large-scale sorting machines, this function would probably be transferred to regional mail-processing centers, at least for "out of town" mail.

There is also an asymmetry associated with the sortation function that is largely absent in switching. Because the peak demands on facilities and personnel are driven by the inward flow of mail, the costs of a sorting facility are affected differently by the relative mixture of inward and outward traffic. While it seems reasonable to

3

assume that these volumes are essentially balanced in aggregate, this cost asymmetry has important implications for the terms under which competitive service providers are allowed access to the postal network.

Sortation has traditionally been viewed as an activity in which increasing returns to scale are exhausted at small scales of operation. Recent advances in computerized optical character recognition, however, may lead to more mechanization and larger minimum efficient scales for sorting centers.

Transportation. Transportation is an important component of postal costs, and the Postal Service is a heavy user of the nation's highways and airways. Long-distance transportation is generally considered to be a function having essentially constant returns to scale. Short-haul transportation, typically between post offices and mail-processing centers, may exhibit some scale economies resulting from scheduling constraints and the need to operate some less-than-truckload movements. These differences in the structure of short-haul and long-haul transportation costs are reflected by the fact that much short-haul transportation is undertaken by the Postal Service itself, while most long-haul transportation is contracted out.

While they play analogous roles in their respective networks, the postal transportation sector differs significantly from long-distance telecommunications transmission. The latter involves substantial infrastructure investments, typically made by the firms providing the service. In contrast, the transportation of mail is made over publicly provided highways and airways in vehicles that are often leased from private firms. Indeed, a substantial portion of the Postal Service's transport function is contracted out. The thorough integration of postal transportation into the national transportation network, and the substantial role that competition has long played in the provision of postal transport services, limits the strength of the direct analogy between the introduction of competition into telecommunications and postal services.

In other words, the emergence of competition in long-distance telecommunications does not provide a blueprint for the analogous introduction of competition into the market for postal transportation services. Rather, as we shall see, the lessons to be transferred from the telecommunications experience concern the importance of vertical structure and the pricing of network access.

Sunk Costs. Unlike telecommunications and other network industries, the provision of postal service requires relatively little in the way of sunk costs. This is largely due to two factors. First, the provision of postal service requires few specialized facilities. Thus, if forced to exit the industry, a firm would be able to dispose of most of its assets (vehicles and buildings) without serious loss. Second, like the trucking and air transport industries, a postal system's sunk investments (highways and airways) are owned and operated by the public sector. Bruce Owen and Robert Willig have pointed out the low sunk costs in the natural monopoly local collection and delivery function and suggest that some sort of "competition for the market" might be appropriate.[2] Leonard Merewitz and Mark Zupan document the extensive use of franchising and contracting out by the Postal Service.[3] The low sunk costs in providing postal services clearly mitigates the pitfalls associated with such practices.

Institutional Design

Is the Postal Service a Natural Monopoly? The policy debate surrounding postal service has centered on the monopoly enjoyed by the Postal Service by virtue of the private express statutes. An important focus has been on whether this favored position can be justified on the grounds that postal service is a natural monopoly. This is, of course, an empirical question. An economist would like to decide the issue using convincing econometric evidence. Although a large amount of thorough statistical work has analyzed postal costs, it is unlikely that such work will ever support a definitive resolution of the natural monopoly question. The reason is quite simple: there is only one Postal Service. As the experience in the Bell System antitrust case demonstrated, it is all but impossible to obtain convincing econometric evidence on the costs of a multiproduct monopoly using aggregate time series data.

Nevertheless, I argue that postal service is highly likely to be a natural monopoly. This follows as a matter of logic from the (reasonable) assumption that there are substantial economies of scale associated with local delivery networks. If such is the case, the vertical structure of the postal network will "transmit" these economies to the entire end-to-end network, even if there are only constant returns to scale in the transportation and sortation functions.

Why Should We Care? This reasoning also reveals that the natural monopoly characteristics of the postal service network are largely

2. Bruce M. Owen & Robert D. Willig, *Economics and Postal Pricing, in* THE FUTURE OF THE POSTAL SERVICE (Joel Fleishman ed., Aspen Institute 1983).

3. Merewitz & Zupan, *supra* note 1, at 71–75.

irrelevant for policy purposes. The posited natural monopoly in the provision of local delivery services makes that function a bottleneck monopoly. Consequently, an efficient national postal network is best pursued through efficient pricing of access to the bottleneck monopoly.

Should the Delivery Monopoly Continue? There remains the treatment of the local delivery monopoly itself. Even if natural-monopoly cost characteristics are present, there is no guarantee that the Postal Service is cost efficient. Removal of statutory entry barriers would subject it to a market test. Such a policy, however, has its risks. Even if the Postal Service were producing efficiently, there might still be profit opportunities for inefficient, cream-skimming entrants. In addition, the social objectives of universal service at uniform rates may require restriction on entry.

While it is theoretically possible that the national postal service network may be an *unsustainable* natural monopoly, a more likely outcome would be the erosion of the Postal Service's market share due to inefficient pricing policies. The loss of profit contributions from the reduced mail volumes would drive up the prices of remaining services until the Postal Service was left with only high-cost services and regions that no independent operator would be willing to serve.

Of course, a policy of free and open entry may be the only way to push the system to efficiency. Given the risks involved, however, it seems more prudent to reserve this policy as a last resort, to be implemented only after efficient pricing policies and franchise contracting have been fully exploited. These policy tools can provide powerful incentives for the creation of a cost-efficient network.

Regulatory Pricing Policy

Using Competition to Promote Efficiency. The bottleneck monopoly view of delivery services suggests a parallel to the introduction of competition into the market for long-distance telecommunications service. MCI and Sprint became successful competitors in switched long-distance service only after the Bell System was required to grant them access to its local exchanges. This made it unnecessary for them to make the massive fixed and sunk investments required to carry a call the last several miles to a customer's residence or place of business.

While this policy of mandated access removes the need for such clearly wasteful and redundant investments, how does one ensure that efficient entry is encouraged while inefficient entry is deterred?

What, then, is the economic rationale for a policy that requires owners of essential facilities to provide nondiscriminatory access to their competitors?

There is a clear economic efficiency argument for such a policy. The argument is especially compelling when there are no significant economies of scale in providing the service component in question, hence its potential applicability to postal transportation and sortation as part of a "make or buy decision" facing a local collection-delivery monopolist. Ideally, such a firm would choose to provide such a service component itself only if it could not be purchased more cheaply from an outside vendor. For if it could, the monopolist would gain by contracting out this function. Note that this argument is based entirely on the principle of cost efficiency. It does not matter if the monopolist's goal is profit or economic welfare.[4]

Unbundling the pricing of service components. Under constant returns to scale, competition in the market for one service component can be used to decentralize this make-or-buy decision. This decentralization, however, requires the (former) monopoly service provider to unbundle its pricing so that each service component is priced separately. In telecommunications, unbundling has meant separately pricing access to the local exchange network (monthly charge) and usage of the local exchange network (message unit charges). Although unbundling is by no means complete in telecommunications, this process makes it possible for the providers of competitive services to compete for consumers' business on the basis of their efficiency. If all service providers are charged the same price for access *to* and usage *of* the local exchange network, any difference in their costs must be due to differences in their efficiency in providing long-distance transmission. If competition forces prices to costs, then by choosing the lowest-cost carrier, the final consumer ensures that the costs of the telecommunications network are minimized.

In the telecommunications industry, the introduction of competition into the provision of the long-haul transmission service component was accompanied by the breakup of the Bell System, which

4. The discussion in this section is drawn from Panzar, *supra* note 1. Somewhat surprisingly, these principles have only recently been articulated in the telecommunications context. *See* WILLIAM J. BAUMOL & J. GREGORY SIDAK, TOWARD COMPETITION IN LOCAL TELEPHONY 93-116 (MIT Press/AEI Press 1994); William J. Baumol & J. Gregory Sidak, *The Pricing of Inputs Sold to Competitors*, 11 YALE J. ON REG. 171 (1994); Alfred E. Kahn & William Taylor, *The Pricing of Inputs Sold to Competitors: A Comment*, 11 YALE J. ON REG. 225 (1994).

separated the bottleneck monopoly of the local exchange from AT&T's long-distance service. Such divestiture, however, is not required in principle. The end result will be the same as long as the pricing of service components is unbundled and access to essential monopoly service components is priced on a nondiscriminatory basis.[5]

Although an exact list of unbundled service components of a postal system must be compiled by someone more knowledgeable about postal technology than I, it would seem that, at a minimum, it would be necessary to determine unbundled rates for collection, outward sortation, transportation, inward sortation, and delivery. Of course, these rate elements would have to be established for each class and category of service.

In practice, such unbundling would be equivalent to a system of rates based upon the point at which competitors' mail entered the postal network. There would be one rate charged for mail deposited at the local post office presorted to route sequence, another rate for mail deposited at a regional processing center for its inward sortation, and yet another rate for mail deposited at a regional processing center for outward sortation and transportation.

Basic principles for efficient discounts. How could such a system of unbundled service component rates be used to enhance the efficiency of the postal network, public *and* private? The issue reduces to that of determining nondiscriminatory terms of access to the Postal Service's local delivery network.

First, it is necessary to determine the delivery access charge implicitly paid by the Postal Service's nondelivery operations. This analysis is easy to perform if it can be assumed that all nondelivery functions are performed under conditions of approximately constant returns to scale. Then, assuming that the Postal Service as a whole just breaks even, it must be the case that the unbundled rate is equal to the implicit delivery access charge plus the sum of the per unit marginal and incremental costs of all nondelivery functions. Thus, the delivery access charge paid by the Postal Service (to itself) is equal to the bundled rate less the per unit incremental costs of all nondelivery functions.

Under a regime of nondiscriminatory access pricing, the Postal

5. Ameritech has recently made this argument to the Federal Communications Commission. *See* Petition of Ameritech for Declaratory Ruling and Related Waivers to Establish a New Regulatory Model for the Ameritech Region (filed before the FCC Mar. 1, 1993).

Service would pay the same rate for access to the local delivery network as would any of its competitors. This rate is the average cost bundled rate *less* the incremental cost of all nondelivery functions. This rate should be available to any competitor willing to deliver presorted, route-sequenced mail to the loading dock of a local post office. Put in discount terms, the discount paid to mailers that perform all postal functions except local delivery should be exactly equal to the costs the Postal Service would have incurred had it moved the mail through the nondelivery portion of its system.

It should be easy to see that no other policy is capable of ensuring that a competitive mailer, at least as efficient as the Postal Service, has the incentive to enter the market. Clearly, any larger discount would be inappropriate, since it might induce a mailer to undertake to provide the service even though its costs would exceed those of the Postal Service. Similarly, any lesser discount would deter an entrant whose costs were only slightly less than those saved by the Postal Service. Yet, participation by such an entrant would lower the total social costs of postal services.

Expressed this way, it seems as though this efficient access pricing rule allows all the gains of efficient entry to be captured by competitors and their customers. This is not the case, however. Nondiscriminatory access pricing merely requires that the terms of access to the delivery network be equal for both competitors and the nondelivery portions of the Postal Service. The *level* of this nondiscriminatory access charge is determined by the profit needs of the enterprise. Indeed, this is precisely the strategy an unregulated profit-seeking monopolist would employ to ensure cost efficiency and maximize its profit. In fact, under these circumstances, a local delivery monopolist could earn the maximum possible monopoly return, without providing nondelivery services—except where it was the low-cost producer.[6]

The public interest regulated firm would proceed in the same manner to ensure the most efficient possible provision of postal services. Instead of adjusting the nondiscriminatory access charge to extract maximum profits, however, the firm would be regulated to limit the rate to levels required to cover the overhead costs of local delivery networks.

It should also be pointed out that, while access charges should

6. This is a standard result in the theory of vertical integration. The monopolist can extract all the available monopoly rents. The competitors who actually perform any nondelivery function receive per unit rents equal only to the cost advantage they enjoy over their most efficient unsuccessful rival. If all competitors are equally efficient, *none* earns supracompetitive profits.

be nondiscriminatory with respect to service providers, they would vary across classes and categories of mail. If there were separate rates for local and intercity mail, for example, these two classes would undoubtedly be charged different local delivery access rates, even though they would be virtually indistinguishable as they proceeded through the local network. The difference would result from differences in the price elasticities of demand and in the availability of substitutes. As in any application of optimal pricing, the mail class with the least elastic (derived) demand for local delivery would receive the local delivery access rate with the greatest markup over marginal delivery cost.

Toward Economically Efficient Pricing. The previous subsection has presented the theory of postal access pricing at some length because of its novelty and the important role that it has to play in the introduction of competition into the postal network. This focus should not obscure the fact that postal regulation in the United States has also suffered from a tendency to base prices on attributable (allocated) costs without sufficient regard to demand considerations. I agree with the General Accounting Office that a movement to demand-based pricing would enhance the efficiency of the nation's postal network.[7]

Economic theory tells us that economically efficient pricing takes into account demand elasticities as well as marginal costs when determining the prices that maximize consumer surplus while allowing the firm to cover costs. Put simply, services for which the elasticity of demand is high (due perhaps to the existence of competitive substitutes) tend to receive a low markup over marginal costs, while services with inelastic demands tend to receive a high markup over marginal costs. Applying these principles to the Postal Service would lead to lower prices for competitive services such as parcels and Express Mail and higher prices for services such as first-class letters. The resulting prices and revenues should be checked to ensure that they are free of cross-subsidy—that is, that no service (or group of services) generates revenues less than its incremental costs or greater than its stand-alone costs.

Incentive Regulation. The access-pricing analysis presented here was purely normative. I have not attempted to analyze the likelihood that the regulatory process will actually lead to the recommended prices being implemented. In theory, any profit-maximizing firm will have an incentive to implement the efficient postal access prices discussed

---

7. GENERAL ACCOUNTING OFFICE, *supra* note 1, at 8, 54-57.

earlier. Unfortunately, there is no reason to believe that the Postal Service is a profit maximizer. Recently, several foreign countries have moved to privatize their posts in the hope that introducing profit-seeking behavior will improve their efficiency. Some form of enhanced incentives should also be devised for the Postal Service. When this has been achieved, the incentive regulation research of the past decade can also be fruitfully applied to postal regulation.

A Contrast between the Postal and Telecommunications Access-pricing Debates

While the term "access pricing" may not yet be familiar to postal analysts, recent rate cases have certainly addressed the appropriate magnitude of the "pre-sort" discounts offered to mailers who inject partially processed mail at various points in the mail stream. Typically, mailers request a discount equal to the total costs saved by the Postal Service. The Postal Service proposes a much smaller discount, and the outcome is typically a discount of less than 100 percent. Furthermore, the Postal Service should favor this outcome, since a partial discount does not maximize profits.

In telecommunications, however, competitors often demand access to bottleneck facilities at the marginal cost of providing it. (This is equivalent to a final service "discount" of more than 100 percent.) Local exchange carriers argue that the access price should generate the same profit contribution as would result if the utility retained the business. If competition held the final service price to cost, the competitor would receive a discount exactly equal to the cost not incurred by the utility.

The regulatory outcome tends to be between the two: that is, a "discount" greater than 100 percent. In one case, the theoretical benchmark provides a ceiling on the regulatory outcome; in the other case, a floor. Why is that?

Commentary by Douglas H. Ginsburg

Professor Panzar's chapter is tightly reasoned, and it is perilous for someone with little actual knowledge of the facts to question either his methodology or his analysis, which in their own terms are quite persuasive. The thought of reforming postal regulation, however, appealing as it may be, pales in comparison with the idea of abolishing postal regulation. To my knowledge, that idea first surfaced when

11

Chris DeMuth, back for a weekend visit from Washington, asked me as we stood in front of the Harvard Law School what I thought about privatizing the postal system. That he would even ask such a question made his role in Washington seem that much more glamorous.

About a dozen years later, I heard James Miller tell a story that may suggest the origins of the idea. Miller described someone who goes to Macy's in Times Square on a Saturday before the holidays and encounters a mob scene. After a long wait in line to pay for his parcel, the shopper says to the cashier, "My gosh, I have not been here in years. Is it always like this?" The cashier responds, "Oh, no sir. This is the best Saturday we have had in years." The man then takes the parcel across the street to the post office to mail it. There he encounters another mob scene. After again waiting in a long line, he asks the clerk, "Is it always like this on a Saturday?" The clerk says, "Oh, no sir, this is the worst Saturday we have had in years." Most of us who are not engaged professionally in thinking about the Postal Service tend to regard its operations much as Jim Miller does.

It is discomforting to think that the Postal Service is a natural monopoly and that one must make the best of it, either in the way that Professor Panzar described or by some alternative. I hope that we can now question whether the Postal Service is a natural monopoly, whether it need be a natural monopoly, and whether it would be a monopoly if it were not supported by legal protection.

Professor Panzar suggests that the Postal Service is a bottleneck monopoly and that the efficient solution is properly pricing access. He notes two risks associated with the increased competition that would result from legalizing entry.

First, pricing inefficiencies would provide opportunities for inefficient cream skimming even when the Postal Service is producing efficiently. Second, the social objective of uniform service at uniform rates might be precluded in a competitive environment. Should rate uniformity, however, be the foundation on which postal regulation reform would be grounded? I am not certain why it is that postal communication has to be priced in such an inherently cross-subsidizing fashion that the delivery of a letter to the outermost island off the coast is priced the same as the delivery of a letter across town. There are large variations in the cost incurred due to the large variations in the difficulty of local collection and distribution. If we do not insist that telephone service be provided without regard to costs, why do we consider it as a natural law and entitlement that a person should pay no more than anyone else in the country to mail a letter? That may have been an important social goal when communication with the frontier was fragile and incentives were needed both to settle the

West and to make western life accessible for eastern goods, but I do not believe that these once lofty goals are important anymore.

We have already deregulated other network industries, particularly air service and trucking. Initially, there was a great deal of concern that deregulation would result in either prohibitively expensive service or in the complete truncation of service to small communities and remote territories. This does not seem to have happened in any meaningful way.

Because of the risks that Professor Panzar associates with open entry, he suggests that we first institute efficient pricing policies and only after such policies are deemed successful should we repeal the private express statutes. Yet it is possible to do both at once. For instance, this could be accomplished by treating the Postal Service in the same manner in which the Federal Communications Commission treats AT&T. Regulating the Postal Service while allowing others to compete around it would speed the effects of deregulation.

In practice, efficient pricing is impractical because it is beyond our regulatory capabilities. Even though Professor Panzar says that calculating the costs saved or avoided by the Postal Service is a nontrivial issue that would keep lawyers and economists busy in perpetuity, he has still managed to understate the nature of that task. It is questionable whether one could be confident that the resulting rates borne out of extensive study would truly be the efficient set of rates. In a deregulated environment, the result may be continued monopolization, either by the Postal Service or by some new player that provides better service.

The key question is, What presumption do we make at the outset? Should we presume that the Postal Service serves a natural monopoly market or that it is potentially a competitive industry? Professor Panzar observes that we are unlikely to get a very solid answer simply because of the inherent lack of opportunity for comparing the two situations. All we can do is try to analyze the cost data, never comprehending the opportunities that are lost through lack of competition. We can look only at the production inefficiencies or inefficient pricing policies that can be identified in the absence of a competitive benchmark.

One wonders whether the collection and distribution function is likely to indicate the existence of a monopoly. Such an outcome is not at all obvious. On the one hand, this is a retail business that has locations all over the country. Moreover, retailing is generally competitive. It also involves a more intense network for collection and distribution, stopping literally at every home for distribution and at least every several blocks for collection. I do not believe that there is

13

any other enterprise that operates quite like the Postal Service.

On the other hand, when new services arise, like the express services (DHL, Federal Express, United Parcel Service, and so on), we do not see rival firms contracting among themselves for their joint provision of any segment of their respective services. Instead, we see them setting up boxes right across the street from each other. We do not see them centralizing that function in the hands of the most efficient provider. This may be because the function is *not* a natural monopoly, or it may be for other reasons entirely.

Professor Panzar leaves us with a very interesting question: why is the Postal Service not now doing what he prescribes? If the Postal Service were a true profit-maximizing entity, it would act in a more efficient manner, effectively shedding those tasks that its competitors or customers could perform less expensively. The Postal Service, however, is offering less than 100 percent discounts—less than all of its costs avoided—to shippers who use something less than end-to-end service. I am not sure why the Postal Service does not have incentives to maximize its profits. Perhaps there are some legal inhibitions.

If the Postal Service is not doing what could be done to maximize profits in the present, then it is unreasonable to expect that regulation of the Postal Service, aimed at determining efficient prices for each segment of its unbundled services, could ever reach an efficient result. Unless we assume perfect regulation—and Professor Panzar's chapter is pristinely neutral on that subject—and unless we assume that there is some entity or demigod capable of dispensing perfect regulation, it is not clear that his proposal, even though superior in principle, could produce a better result than the existing regime. It is also unclear whether Professor Panzar's proposal could produce the price, output, and quality outcomes of a competitive market.

Commentary by J. Gregory Sidak

Professor Panzar asserts that there are probably substantial economies of scale associated with mail delivery. These economies, he argues, justify retaining the private express statutes while requiring the Postal Service to sell unbundled access to the local delivery network at appropriately determined prices. Since we are seeking to identify questions that warrant further research, I address three issues raised by Professor Panzar's provocative chapter.

First, on the question of the natural monopoly over mail delivery functions, is there a relationship between product quality and

scale economies? Economies of scale in delivery may be endogenously determined by the level of service quality that the Postal Service
selects. The scale economy in delivery comes from the likelihood that
a mail carrier's stop at a single mailbox will result in the delivery of
more than one piece of mail. If mail delivery occurred only once a
week, the likelihood would fall that a stop would be generated by the
delivery of only a single piece of mail (thus yielding no scale economies). Conversely, if mail were delivered twice a day, or on Sundays,
the likelihood would rise that a stop would be generated by a single
piece of mail; thus, it would become more likely that economies of
scale in delivery would not accrue. This relationship, if it exists as an
empirical matter, implies a trade-off between the *frequency* or *urgency*
of delivery and the magnitude of scale economies in delivery.

Put differently, economies of scale in delivery are an increasing
function of the *infrequency* of delivery. The Postal Service can increase
the likelihood of scale economies in delivery by redefining its quality
in terms of slower, non-time-sensitive delivery. It could, for example,
discontinue Saturday delivery. Another way to raise the likelihood of
scale economies in delivery is to change the composition of the mail
stream so that the Postal Service is providing a service that is, to use a
telecommunications analogy, more akin to broadcasting than to
point-to-point communications. The Postal Service could do so by
pricing non-time-sensitive mail (direct mail advertising, for example)
very favorably.

Whether the foregoing production technology actually exists
could be empirically tested. If it does exist, we would have further
insight into why even highly efficient private overnight delivery services might not exhibit the scale economies that are asserted to exist
in the Postal Service. For these reasons, a profitable line of research
would examine the extent to which the quality of service and scale
economies in delivery are interdependent.

Finally, we must not draw incorrect policy inferences from
economies of scale in delivery, assuming for the moment that they do
occur. In particular, the existence of economies of scale in delivery do
not provide evidence of the continued need for a postal monopoly,
for these economies could accrue just as easily to private firms. The
delivery of monthly gas or electricity bills, for example, could achieve
economies of scale by piggybacking on the delivery of direct advertising or newspapers already going to virtually every home in a
neighborhood.

A second and related point is that consumers cannot buy higher-
quality mail service from the Postal Service the way they can buy
higher-quality services from private widgets producers. The delivery

of mail in my suburban neighborhood, for example, is to a group of boxes about seventy-five feet from my home. As far as I know, I cannot pay the Postal Service to deliver to my door. If we accept Professor Panzar's invitation to unbundle mail services, we should consider the possibility that there may be services that consumers would buy that are not currently offered to them.

Furthermore, the current truncation of services offered by the Postal Service relates to the question of economies of scale in delivery. Aggregated mailboxes in new neighborhoods (such as mine), for example, reduce the cost of delivery for the Postal Service but impose a delivery cost on mail recipients, who must walk from their homes (sometimes in the rain or snow) to get their mail. Thus, the economies of scale that Professor Panzar claims exist over the delivery function may come at greater private cost to consumers. If so, they are false economies indeed.

A third issue is universal service. Professor Panzar points out that, if there were free and open entry into mail delivery, there would be cream skimming. As he puts it, the loss of profit contribution from the reduced mail volumes would drive up the prices of remaining services until the Postal Service was stuck with only high-cost deliveries in regions that no independent operator was willing to serve.

Is that really such a bad result? The Postal Service is presumably publicly owned to advance a public policy goal of some sort. If we had open entry but continued public ownership of the Postal Service, then the functions performed by the Postal Service would be revealed by the competitive process to be strictly those that would be infeasible for a profit-maximizing firm to undertake. Once this revelation had occurred, we would have identified, as precisely as economic science permits, the nature and magnitude of the market failure requiring government subsidization of universal service. We could then proceed to address how to fund the attainment of that social objective at lowest cost to taxpayers. The options for financing the revenue shortfall for the provision of unremunerative services are well known to public finance economists. Various tax and subsidy solutions are available.

Discussion

QUESTION: I would like to explore further Judge Ginsburg's comment that it would be better to eliminate the Postal Service monopoly and institute some form of economically rational pricing instead. It is at this point that I believe the analogy to the telecommunications industry breaks down. When the FCC began to deregulate, it knew that there was competition—MCI was already in business. My concern is that, if postal service is left to competition, it will turn out to be a natural monopoly. Elimination of one monopoly will simply result in the transfer of monopoly power from a public enterprise to a private one. What is the harm if we follow Professor Panzar's suggestion of pricing the function rather than, as the Postal Service does now, pricing the product and then discounting it? What is the harm to consumers if there is some margin of error in the calculation of the unit cost? What is the harm to competition? My guess is that, if we badly miscalculate, then no competition will enter the market and the prices will have to be reviewed.

JOHN C. PANZAR, Northwestern University: If you are questioning the terms of calculating the particular values of the access price, then that is a good point. I presented the discussion in the way I did because postal parlance talks in terms of discounts. But if you were pricing the access directly, as long as it was nondiscriminatory across providers, a miscalculation of one or two cents high or low will have no effect on competition. The only result will be that the monopolist will or will not make money. If you were calculating the discount and you were one or two cents off in terms of avoided postal costs, however, then you would be either discouraging efficient competitors or encouraging inefficient competitors. There is a lot to be said for just pricing access. But the discount focus has a long history in postal rate cases.

HENRY B. HANSMANN, Yale Law School: Judge Ginsburg said that cream skimming is a problem only if services are incorrectly priced. I accept that as being true. If local delivery is a natural monopoly and we eliminate the private express statutes that forbid competition, then we are not going to interfere with the Postal Service's monopoly as long as it can price its services correctly. The problem is one of adverse selection. As was stated, if you cannot accurately discriminate among different types of mail, then the customers will discriminate for you. The low-cost customers in any given price range will exit the system and patronize a private cream-skimming operation, leaving the Postal Service with the high-cost elements. Then the Postal Service will increase prices to cover costs, which leads to more adverse selection. Is this a serious problem in practice? Is it the case in practice that you cannot pick a set of prices that will avoid adverse selection problems, thereby forcing you to maintain a monopoly?

DOUGLAS H. GINSBURG, U.S. Court of Appeals for the District of

Columbia Circuit: It is hard to think of cream skimming as a phenomenon apart from cross subsidies built into the price structure. If you want to have uniform prices, whether it is over an inexpensive route or an expensive route, then there will be cross subsidies and opportunities for cream skimming. You have to determine whether you really want to wring the subsidies out of the system if you are going to take a risk of cream skimming. We saw the same thing with business versus residential telephone service: the price of residential service had to go up when these subsidies became unsustainable because business customers had competitive alternatives.

SHARON M. OSTER, Yale School of Management: Professor Panzar, I take it from your analysis that the principal source of the returns to scale are at the local collection and delivery level. If that is correct, then you might well imagine an alternative solution: the creation of local monopolies, again much like telecommunications, rather than one single monopoly with many local installations. Those of us interested in incentives and organizational issues would prefer the existence of multiple local monopolies as opposed to a single nationwide monopoly. In particular, local monopolies tend to be more competitive and innovative if there are others and they can observe each other. You also tend to get more local control, which is typically thought to improve managerial incentives. Is it plausible to consider, as an alternative to the existing single natural monopoly, a series of more localized natural monopolies?

PROFESSOR PANZAR: It is certainly plausible to think of it that way. In my analysis, I focus on the local post office just as I would on the local telephone exchange. In theory, you could easily have more than one. Access-pricing theory is agnostic on that point. The postal people, just like the people of the old Bell System, undoubtedly have network reasons for why it is necessary to have only one entity interconnecting all these local exchanges. The Bell System made these arguments for many years, and I am sure that there are analogous postal arguments.

JUDGE GINSBURG: These arguments were not all unfounded to the extent that network standards had to be maintained and prescribed. That function was simply retained on a network basis, a national basis, through such entities as Bellcore, and through FCC regulations.

QUESTION: I was struck by the juxtaposition of the two anecdotes: Judge Ginsburg's regarding the busy day at Macy's versus the busy day at the post office, and Mr. Sidak's query as to why you could not get delivery through a door slot instead of seventy-five feet from your home. Perhaps we have not quite figured out whether the Postal Service is supposed to be a retail business or a collection and delivery business. Certainly a throng of people buying a lot of merchandise would bring joy to a retailer; but to a collection and delivery operation, if everyone was standing in line, it would indicate that there was something wrong.

JUDGE GINSBURG: I thought Mr. Sidak's example was a terrific one. Actually, he gave two. First, he cannot buy door-to-door service because, under the postal regulation, the mail goes only to the street. Second, there is only daily service, and increasingly less of it. You cannot sign up for twice-daily service. And you cannot say, "I'll pay less to receive twice-weekly service," because you do not pay on the receiving end. This high degree of uniformity and standardization that has become normal in the Postal Service—even the postal box has to conform to postal regulations—is emblematic of the potential loss in consumer satisfaction, consumer surplus, and consumer welfare that we associate with the old integrated telephone system.

Under the old system, before the breakup of AT&T, you could buy only a Western Electric telephone. And, arguably, because of the way in which the rate base was compensated versus labor, you could buy only an indestructible Western Electric telephone. Many are still working. Many of them will be dug up by archaeologists hundreds of years from now and will probably still give a dial tone. The system was engineered in this way. It was not done this way because of some indwelling necessity, but because of regulatory incentives. When the norm was relaxed, when suddenly you no longer had to have a Western Electric phone on your desk, it turned out that there was a big demand for three-dollar phones from Korea—phones that, if dropped, would break. "Breakable" was not in the lexicon of the old AT&T. Although there is now a huge array of telephones, this aspect went unquestioned under the old Bell System.

There are many aspects of postal service that we all take as unquestioned, two of which Mr. Sidak raised. What we do not know is what we are losing in competitive alternatives if we could either eliminate or scale back the monopoly to the smallest necessary extent.

J. GREGORY SIDAK, American Enterprise Institute: We might also be understating the true cost of monopoly mail delivery. As Professor Panzar states, we need to look at the sum of the public and private costs of mail delivery. When it is snowing and I have to go out to my mailbox to collect my mail, there is a cost that I must incur. This cost would be even more for an older person who does not like to navigate the snow.

COMMENT: One of the problems of the current system is the rigidity. There are two reasons for this. First is the consumer: the end recipient does not pay. The second reason relates to what Professor Panzar is talking about.

JUDGE GINSBURG: It seems to me that the proposition that demand will call forth the supply is a "no-brainer" regardless of the application. Take another industry—forget customer-premises equipment—and you will see the same thing happening. No one imagined the array of different quality levels of brokerage service once commission regulation was dropped or the way in which trucking firms would specialize into different niches once the rigidity of regulation was removed.

QUESTION: Why isn't some firm competing with the Postal Service? I see a UPS truck go down my street every afternoon.

COMMENT: That depends upon what you are mailing. You do indeed see a UPS truck going down your street every day and it carries parcels. I am mailing a very different product. Indeed, I am mailing a variety of products. Some do not hit every address, some UPS would prefer not to handle, some UPS might be willing to pick up. But there is an enormous diversity in the mail stream, and Professor Panzar's focus on the problem of the uniform rate is well taken. But even in classes that come much closer to his model, in terms of the Postal Service's and the Postal Rate Commission's willingness to disaggregate to some degree, there is still enormous diversity. The categories are very broad, and there is a concern that there will simply not be a delivery system, or that a delivery system will come into being while I wait for ten or twelve months (or years)—paying exorbitant rates in the meantime. That is a risk that mailers are very reluctant to take, which is why I think that we should proceed by pricing it correctly and then begin to pull away.

JUDGE GINSBURG: The ten-to-twelve month transition problem that you mention is an interesting and real problem, although probably a manageable one if there is enough advance notice—if something does not just happen overnight, as it never does. To say that delivery services would not come forward at the end of that period is to say that you simply are not willing to pay enough. The point about the complexity of the mail is important. Here the telecommunications example is not very useful, but the trucking example is very appropriate because of the large variety of specialized freight and the different transportation needs that freight has in temperature, fragility, timeliness, shape, weights, and so on—thousands of variations.

QUESTION: To a certain extent, the telecommunications world is consuming the postal world. I am not aware of any business that sends first-class mail anymore. It is all done by fax machines or Federal Express. To what extent do you regard telecommunications industry developments as a hedge? I understand the concern: if we get rid of the monopoly, we end up with a disaster on our hands. Does the presence of the communications industry—which is invading the postal world—give you any reassurance?

I would have thought that fax machines and electronic mail would have brought about improvement in the Postal Service. I think the telecommunications industry has had little, or perhaps a negative, effect, or maybe no particular effect. Maybe it is just that first-class mail is deteriorating on its own. But do you see the electronic alternatives as some form of insurance?

COMMENT: Some years ago, someone tried to do a study on the cross elasticity between telephone and first-class rates. It failed. I think they may be completely unrelated markets.

QUESTION: Even with fax and electronic mail?

COMMENT: Since that time, much new information suggests they have certain markets in common. Ever since the advent of the telegram, volume has been diverted.

COMMENT: Yes, there is no question that some volume is being diverted. But that does not provide any comfort for those who find the electronic medium in the delivery of messages either unsuitable or prohibitively expensive for their purposes.

MR. SIDAK: Does that not also suggest something about universal service? Would it not be cheaper to give everyone in Alaska a fax machine at some point?

COMMENT: I do not believe the fax machine would deliver their groceries.

21

MR. SIDAK: Yes, but neither does the Postal Service.

COMMENT: But we do.

COMMENT: And rubber tires.

MR. SIDAK: Pardon me.

JUDGE GINSBURG: Can we get that service down here?

COMMENT: You have to talk to Senator Stevens about that.

QUESTION: There might be places like Alaska, where the private carriers would not go. But I notice when I order clothes from catalogs, they list shipping and handling as $3.50—which points out that maybe the transaction cost of figuring who lives out on County Road 612 is not worth it. You may lose a quarter on that person every now and then, but what shipper wants to handle a list of 575 different prices? I think that this notion that uniform pricing is a big block to deregulation may be false.

MICHAEL A. CREW, Rutgers University: In a similar way, perhaps the concern that some services are not supplied and that some services are bundled together may not be warranted. Also, the cross subsidy may not be a big issue except for Alaska.

Let us take the services that are not supplied. Mr. Sidak, do not expect the Postal Service or any other large business to offer the kind of service you mentioned. But there is a market that will provide this service for you—twelve-year-old kids will take the mail from your box to your door—likewise your paperboy. What kind of paperboy do you have now? Do you have the Panzar-type who would take the paper to your doorstep? Or the type who flings the paper from a car to your driveway? This is an example of how the old Panzar-style paperboy is not supplied anymore and how subservices are all bundled together. It is inevitable. I do not drive at night. So I asked Ford Motor Company if I could get a discount for a car without any headlamps, but they would not do it for me.

How do postal services mitigate the cross-subsidy effect? One way is that they offer a lower standard of service to the outlying districts. The United States Postal Service will deliver the mail overnight within a certain area, but beyond that it could take two or three days. The same applies for postal services the world over. The British Postal Service figures that it has a lower reliability of service for delivery in the north of Scotland than it does in the London area, where it is less costly to deliver. This factor and the transaction cost issues raised make the cross-subsidy problems less significant than they may have first appeared.

JUDGE GINSBURG: As Professor Crew stated with newspaper delivery, the baseline service that you get when you subscribe has changed over the years. If you are willing to pay extra, the delivery boy will bring the paper to your door. But you cannot buy additional service from the Postal Service—if you try to pay the letter carrier extra it is probably a felony. The question is not whether one can imagine a demand that is being unserved. Rather, the question is whether one is going to give it a test and see whether the imagination of other people is greater than our ability to anticipate.

QUESTION: Under what conditions should the Postal Service remain regulated if it did not have a statutory monopoly? Under what conditions would the Postal Service—and only the Postal Service, as opposed to the Postal Service and its competitors—need to be regulated if it has foresworn its monopoly?

JUDGE GINSBURG: In the closest analogy, in the interest of providing an opportunity for new competitors to enter without fear of predatory pricing or other exclusionary practices, AT&T was subjected to continued—although somewhat relaxed—regulation by the FCC. Since the incumbent firm starts off in the competitive market with something approaching 100 percent of the market, it is not unreasonable to shield competitors for a few years from what might otherwise be anticompetitive behavior.

QUESTION: Why have we not reformed or abolished postal regulation? From a technological point of view, it makes sense to deregulate parts of the Postal Service and open them to competition. It is hard to conclude on the basis of common sense that the Postal Service is a natural monopoly. Local delivery is probably the only part that could be considered a natural monopoly of any sort. If we are interested in reform, why have we not had it yet? What are the political and organizational reasons that have driven us to a situation where postal deregulation seems unlikely? I am not too concerned, however, because I think in another twenty years, if the Postal Service is not deregulated, it will be eliminated through faxes and other delivery services—unless there are very strict statutes forbidding private companies from providing these services.

23

PROFESSOR PANZAR: Politically, the Postal Service is perhaps the largest employer in every country. These usually have a lot of political power. This is why you have private express statutes almost all over the world.

COMMENT: There is another political reason Judge Ginsburg identified. There is a real possibility that what is now twenty-nine cents will be thirty-five or forty cents in a competitive market. As a result, 535 senators and representatives will not vote for deregulation. That is the problem. The uniform rate was deliberately conceived when Congress reorganized the Postal Service in 1970. It was not an accident; it was a political decision. There are uniform rates for books, also for the same kind of political considerations. You have a peculiar beast here. It is an economic enterprise still perceived, at least by those who make political decisions, to be a social enterprise. At one time, I thought that it was also intended to be the employer of last resort. I do not think that is true anymore.

QUESTION: Another factor is that "the establishment of Post Offices and Post Roads" was originally a function of Congress. For several hundred years, Congress has jealously guarded that prerogative and considered the postal system its own creature.

COMMENT: And even today the Postal Service cannot close a post office in a small town without getting permission from the regulators.

JUDGE GINSBURG: With all the knowledge assembled in this room, I would be very interested in knowing why the Postal Service advertises the sale of stamps.

COMMENT: Because people do not use them all.

COMMENT: We would like you to save them.

COMMENT: It is to encourage stamp collecting, not waste. People value Elvis stamps.

JUDGE GINSBURG: People are collecting them, then, not just losing them?

MR. SIDAK: Is there an estimate of how much revenue stamp collecting brings in each year?

COMMENT: It has a name—PHOP, postage in the hands of the public. The accountants report it each year. The Postal Service values it somewhere in the neighborhood of $200 million in net revenue per year, out of $50 billion.

MR. SIDAK: I would like to solicit half a dozen questions that merit further research. Does anyone have any suggestions?

QUESTION: Is there a political demand for averaging? Each rate case is seen as a single case—the twenty-cent stamp case, the twenty-nine-cent stamp case. If there were a more differentiated set of products, that number would be different. Yet the household may be more attentive to the price of the stamp than is warranted by its total postal bill—that is, by the total amount that it spends on postage. The FCC imposed a two-dollar subscriber line charge a few years ago. That amounts to what a household pays on postage, and yet it went by much more quietly than a new stamp price. Is there a demand for averaging?

MR. SIDAK: What about the issues raised by Professor Panzar concerning scale economies? Can the econometricians in this room frame a question?

COMMENT: I wonder about the assumption that there are economies of scale in distribution. We know that there are economies of scale in distribution in telecommunications, electricity, and gas for two reasons. First, because of environmental reasons, we do not want a whole host of wires or pipes running from house to house. Second, the physics of electric wires and pipes favor one, large physical unit. But postal delivery implies people, automobiles, and small trucks. It is not obvious to me that it is much more expensive having more than one mail carrier going down the street.

QUESTION: Would not two mail carriers walking down the street together cost roughly twice as much as one person?

COMMENT: It is not obvious to me; I do not know how much extra it would cost.

COMMENT: We have different newspaper delivery boys—whole rows of them coming down the street delivering different papers. It is not obvious to me that they are sacrificing economies of scale.

25

FRANK A. WOLAK, Stanford University:[1] One aspect of a regulated firm that is often ignored is that the structure of the regulatory process does not necessarily imply that the firm will produce its output at minimum cost. If a firm is going to be compensated based on some observable performance characteristic, then it will attempt to make that characteristic as large as possible. This implies that in most cases the firm will not produce its output in a minimum cost fashion.

Second, if we believe that the introduction of competition will reduce the total cost of production, then there must be some way to compensate the losers from the benefits accruing to the gainers. That is where the major issues lie in situations of deregulation. I believe that every successful deregulatory action has accomplished this sort of competition.

MR. SIDAK: And by the "losers" do you mean consumers as well as producers?

PROFESSOR WOLAK: Yes.

JUDGE GINSBURG: The big losers have been labor. All these dinosaurs are sheltered workshops for labor unions. We saw it happen with pilots, teamsters, and communication workers.

QUESTION: There seems to be a difference of opinion on the role of intermodal competition. One view is that faxes will eliminate the Postal Service in twenty years; the other view is that faxes are not a relevant alternative for certain types of services. It would be useful to marshal some empirical evidence on that issue. It seems to be quite important to see whether the fax machine or other innovations are possible alternatives to the Postal Service. They may have very important consequences, or perhaps for certain classes of activities they may have no consequences. This may help us to understand what we should be focusing on. Maybe the intermodal competition will affect certain classes of products but not other classes of products.

QUESTION: In a recent decision in the District Court in Alexandria, it appears that the regional Bell operating companies will be allowed to enter entertainment distribution in their own territories in competi-

---

1. Frank A. Wolak of Stanford University is writing a monograph for the AEI Studies in Postal Regulation concerning the Postal Service's performance as a monopolist.

tion with cable networks.[2] At the same time, they are the beneficiaries of the monopoly of the local service network. Do you think that an analogous situation will occur if the Postal Service has a monopoly over a network and still competes with others?

PROFESSOR PANZAR: The cable-telco case is a bit different for several reasons. First, there are sunk costs involved. Second, I believe that both of those industries are natural monopolies in the strictly technical sense. But that does not mean that there will not be competition. If two firms are willing to incur the costs, there can be competition.

QUESTION: Are you anticipating that the cable company is allowed to enter telecommunications?

PROFESSOR PANZAR: Yes, that will probably unfold. The decision mentioned will probably hasten permission. I see the postal situation to be somewhat different—more an issue of cream skimming at first. If the market were opened to competition, all the high-valued, low-cost letters would be scooped up pretty quickly. Then the question becomes, What is the government going to allow the Postal Service to do in response?

QUESTION: Do you think that third-class mail would be scooped up faster than the first-class mail? I do. The density that advertising mail would give to a potential competitor's profit is greater than what he might derive from trying to figure out which was the valued first-class mail that would bear a premium.

PROFESSOR PANZAR: That could be right, but somebody will arbitrage the difference. What then will we allow the Postal Service to do in response? Then the antitrust authorities and the Postal Rate Commission would begin to play a role. The situation would get interesting, to say the least.

Judge Ginsburg started with a very closely specified premise that the Postal Service will be a protected monopoly. He then went on to suggest some of the pricing issues. I do not see anything inevitable about the postal monopoly except in Congress. Technological change, the logic of competition, and the diversion of mail volumes all suggest that the postal monopoly's days are numbered, although mail volumes continue to increase.

---

2. Chesapeake & Potomac Tel. Co. of Va. *v.* United States, 830 F. Supp. 909 (E.D. Va. 1993).

QUESTION: Are faxes more competitive with telephone or mail? Stated in economic terms, what are the cross elasticities between the demands for mail and fax, and the demands for telephone and fax? Everybody thought the computer would put the Postal Service out of business, but it accomplished quite the opposite effect. It made the production of hard copy very cheap. For example, we all got our registration materials for this conference through the mail.

PROFESSOR PANZAR: I believe the postal monopoly is doomed, but not the Postal Service. I do not think that mail will disappear. People have been saying that for a hundred years, but it continues to increase, despite all these diversions.

QUESTION: What type of empirical test would determine whether the letter monopoly should be continued?

PROFESSOR PANZAR: I cannot imagine a test that I would find conclusive based on the data available. I do find convincing the time-and-motion studies that the Postal Service has done on the additional stops required as a function of volume of mail. I also believe the conclusions that the elasticity is about .6, but with rather substantial increasing returns. But fifteen years ago, when I worked for Bell Labs during the antitrust case, I used to think that econometricians would provide conclusive evidence to preserve the unified Bell System.

QUESTION: The time-and-motion studies can suggest some sort of technological economies of scale, but they do not attack the monopoly overall. Costs can be higher in total if they fall when you add more stops.

PROFESSOR PANZAR: If you pay more than the market wage, then even your downward sloping average cost curve will be a lot higher.

QUESTION: Professor Panzar, are you deliberately resisting a market test? I agree with your econometric analysis. But others think that we should open the markets and see what happens.

PROFESSOR PANZAR: Interesting things would certainly happen if you did that. How will you control the competitive situation, however, that emerges down the road—or is not controlling it one of the options? In terms of antitrust regulation, it is not clear to me that the FCC's residual regulation of AT&T in this environment makes a lot of sense. It is not clear who the agency is protecting—MCI or AT&T?

The one constituency that it is not protecting is consumers.

QUESTION: What if you had no regulation and simply had to trust the antitrust laws? Would you still be nervous?

PROFESSOR PANZAR: Yes, a little bit. The antitrust laws essentially have to do with the judicial process. What I was trying to describe is the regulatory model. You have to determine whether or not the postal delivery network is an essential facility.

MR. SIDAK: But reasonable access to an essential facility is not the same as mandatory access. The level of obligation on the dominant firm may be different.

JUDGE GINSBURG: The facility ceases to be "essential" if, even though it does nothing, another firm or two enter.

COMMENT: The question of economies of scale is an important one. We should look beyond the current service and cost structure of the Postal Service because, even if the Postal Service is doing what it does the cheapest way possible, postal service may still be provided in other, less costly ways.

Another issue implicit in the discussion is the question of universal service and cross subsidies. Admitting that there is some degree of cross subsidy, it is not clear that a rational Postal Service, even if it were allowed to provide any level of service it desired, would not offer universal service. The extent to which the Postal Service is made to carry a public-service burden for serving rural areas—whether at a uniform rate or not—has never really been quantitatively identified. It would be a great service to the debate for this task to be accomplished. I suspect that when the smoke clears, you would reassure a lot of rural congressmen.

QUESTION: Let me pick up on the comment regarding residual regulation or the future of regulation in a reorganized postal firm. If there is a monopoly, what nonmonopoly services should the monopolist be allowed to offer, and how should the pricing of the nonmonopoly services be regulated? This issue has arisen in telecommunications, electricity, and natural gas pipelines. It is assumed, for example, that natural gas pipelines are a natural monopoly. They are also used to provide the service of selling natural gas.

In response to Mr. Sidak's request for questions that merit further research, I suggest two:

• How should the pricing of that competitive service be regulated?

• And, what should be the pricing method for the ancillary nonmonopoly services offered by the Postal Service?

2

The Postal Service as a
Public Enterprise

Sharon M. Oster

In 1970, when the Postal Reorganization Act was passed, the goal of its architects was clear: to make the mail service a more businesslike operation. But while the new structure was indeed more businesslike than the old government agency it replaced, it was still far from a pure business structure. In fact, the act created a hybrid governance structure with characteristics from all three sectors: for-profit, public, and nonprofit. While the 1970 act gave the United States Postal Service a number of the managerial instruments of the private sector, it left the service with a set of incentives and controls more like those found in the nonprofit or public sectors. This chapter is a preliminary exploration of some of the issues raised by this mixed system.

Governance Structures

The Postal Service is a government corporation, broadly along the lines of the Tennessee Valley Authority. It is a hybrid form. Like public agencies and most nonprofits, the government corporation is designed to serve a public purpose, not a private one. In common with government agencies and nonprofits, government corporations have no stockholders and cannot directly redistribute any surpluses they earn. Indeed, it is generally believed that government corporations, like nonprofits and government agencies, should not be consistently earning large surpluses.

The government corporation, however, does share some characteristics of the private firm. Most significantly, it is intended to cover its costs with revenues generated from commercial activity, without relying on either public agency tax dollars or charitable donations. Finally, in negotiating with suppliers and its work force, the government corporation is intended to have the freedoms associated with the for-profit business.

In the past decade, we have come to appreciate the fact that an optimal governance structure is contingent on the goals with which we are most concerned and the characteristics of the markets in which we are operating.[1] Thus, questions we may wish to ask are, How well does this hybrid form fit the facts of the Postal Service's business, and how well does it allow the service to go about the business of delivering the mail in a cost-effective way?

To what kinds of activities are for-profits, nonprofits, and government agencies best suited? For-profit businesses are generally thought to perform quite well in terms of productive efficiency and, under competitive conditions, to be allocatively efficient. In competitive situations, for-profit businesses produce goods and services that individuals want at the least cost. These businesses, though, do rather poorly in balancing complex public and private goals, as the large literature on socially responsible businesses suggests.[2]

Public sector organizations—both those operated as government agencies and those that are heavily regulated enterprises—have advantages in their ability to manage multiple goals and constituencies. In public goods or markets with natural monopoly characteristics, public sector organizations may also be preferable in allocative efficiency. The failure of the public sector in productive efficiency, however, is well known.

Nonprofit organizations dominate for-profits in their ability to manage multiple, complex private and social goals. Indeed, it has been argued that the nonprofit form arises in part as a way to add diversity to the menu of public goods produced in response to heterogeneous tastes.[3] For goods or services in which quantity or quality is not observable (thus making institutional trust important), nonprofits may also have advantages in allocative efficiency.[4] Thus,

1. The most influential and far-reaching work in this area has been done by Oliver Williamson. *See* OLIVER E. WILLIAMSON, THE ECONOMIC INSTITUTIONS OF CAPITALISM (Free Press 1985); OLIVER E. WILLIAMSON, MARKETS AND HIERARCHIES: ANALYSIS AND ANTITRUST IMPLICATIONS (Free Press 1974).

2. For a sympathetic discussion of private business grappling with public values and issues, see R. EDWARD FREEMAN & DANIEL R. GILBERT, CORPORATE STRATEGY AND THE SEARCH FOR ETHICS (Prentice Hall 1988).

3. The original work done in this area was Burton A. Weisbrod, *Toward a Theory of the Voluntary Nonprofit Sector in a Three-Sector Economy, in* SUSAN ROSE-ACKERMAN, THE ECONOMICS OF NONPROFIT INSTITUTIONS (Oxford University Press 1986).

4. *See, e.g.,* Henry B. Hansmann, *The Role of Nonprofit Enterprise,* 89 YALE L.J. 835 (1980).

relief efforts, social services, and medical care may all be produced effectively in the nonprofit sector. Nonprofits, in contrast, lacking the discipline of an equity market or clear, quantifiable criteria for success, are often accused of being productively inefficient.[5] They tend to do somewhat better, however, particularly in labor costs, than the public sector, principally because of their businesslike ability to negotiate.[6]

In short, the different governance structures are more or less able to deliver various goods and services and are each deficient in one way or another. As a result, a number of scholars have suggested blending the various structures to try to take advantage of the strengths of each. Broadly speaking, the blending of structures can take one of two forms. The most common form is what I call the *vertical blend*. Organizations with different governance structures cooperate in the delivery of goods and services by assuming different roles in the production process. For example, the U.S. defense industry delivers its products and services through a process that uses the funding and planning capacity of the public sector with the production process of the private sector. The delivery of much of the social service output in this country comes from funding by various government levels to nonprofit organizations. Here the nonprofit organizes production. For example, nonprofit organizations produce their fundraising output with the help of for-profit solicitation firms. In the typical vertical blend, the attempt is to exploit the ability of one sector to be efficient in production, while using the ability of the other to accomplish complex public goals.

An alternative way to deal with the fact that each of the three common governance structures has its limitations is to create a new governance structure, which *horizontally blends* some of the features of the public, private, and nonprofit form. The Postal Service is an example of a horizontal blend. Given that most of the costs of mail delivery are labor cost—as much as 80–85 percent of the operating budget is wages and benefits[7]—the management of these costs was modeled

5. *See, e.g.,* David Easley & Maureen O'Hara, *The Economic Role of Nonprofit Firms*, 14 BELL J. ECON. 531 (1983).

6. *See, e.g.,* Estelle James, *How Nonprofits Grow, in* THE ECONOMICS OF NONPROFIT INSTITUTIONS, *supra* note 3.

7. "Personnel compensation and benefits (including interest on unfunded liabilities) accounted for 80 percent of Postal Service total expenses in 1993." 1993 U.S. POSTAL SERV. COMPREHENSIVE STATEMENT ON POSTAL OPERATIONS 39. For the fiscal year ended September 30, 1993, compensation and benefits amounted to $38,447.7 million of $46,192.6 million in total operating expenses (excluding restructuring costs), or 83.23 percent. 1993 U.S. POSTAL SERV., ANNUAL REPORT OF THE POSTMASTER GENERAL 16.

after the for-profit system. In some ways, then, the Postal Service has been given access to the labor negotiation tools available to the private sector. This is in considerable contrast to the earlier requirement that the Post Office use the Civil Service system. As for goals, though, the Postal Service is most like the nonprofit sector; it is intended to cover its costs, and thus not be a drain on the Treasury, but not to earn large surpluses. In contrast with the for-profit system that operates at least in theory to maximize profits, the Postal Service has a vaguer, multipart goal to provide reliable mail service while breaking even. As for control, the Postal Service has a management structure considerably removed from the political patronage system of the Post Office and thus more like that of the profit-making firm. Still, the Postal Service suffers from far more congressional oversight than the typical for-profit or even nonprofit firm.

There are a number of open questions about the current system that relate directly to this broad area of governance structure. First, what are the advantages of the current blended system over the more common vertical blend? Second, can one expect the Postal Service to use effectively the private sector management flexibility that it has available to it, given that it lacks private sector profit-maximizing goals and is controlled to a large extent by Congress? A study by Douglas Adie on the wages and benefits in the Postal Service suggests that, at least for the first decade, the businesslike instruments available to the service did not appreciably solve the problem of overpaid workers.[8] Is this inherent in the structure? Finally, to what extent are current operating problems experienced by the Postal Service—in particular the continued deficits—the result of the incentive and control systems built into the service?

In looking at some of these issues, we may find evidence from the nonprofit sector helpful. Nonprofits also have available many of the instruments of the for-profit sector without the private sector's profit-maximizing incentives. How well have nonprofits done in achieving efficiency in their operations?

As indicated earlier, theoretical work suggests that shirking and waste may come to dominate the nonprofit sector as a result of the combination of ambiguous criteria for success and the lack of strong profit motives.[9] It may well be, however, that for many nonprofits the break-even constraint and the threat of failure are as powerful motivations as the lure of profits is to the typical for-profit manager. Indeed, Walter Powell and Rebecca Friedkin have argued that many

8. Douglas K. Adie, *How Have the Postal Workers Fared since the 1970 Act?*, *in* PERSPECTIVES ON POSTAL SERVICE ISSUES (Roger Sherman ed., AEI Press 1980).

9. Easley & O'Hara, *supra* note 5.

nonprofits are highly responsive to their environments because they live so close to the edge financially.[10] Moreover, many nonprofits operate within highly competitive environments, and there is some evidence that this competition may push them toward more effective management.

For most nonprofits, and for the Postal Service as well, labor costs dominate the operating budget. How efficient are most nonprofits in attracting and managing labor? There is clear, well-executed work, done principally by Anne Preston, that suggests that nonprofits on average pay less for workers than for-profits do, even holding constant the human capital of those workers.[11] On this evidence, it would appear that nonprofits outperform for-profits, despite the absence of the profit motive. This wage advantage, though, appears to be driven by ideology. That is, nonprofits can pay less primarily because their workers are committed to the social principles to which the nonprofit is dedicated. Thus, nonprofits are driven to lower wages not by managerial acumen and persistence, but by the commitment of the workers they hire. Moreover, this commitment discourages shirking among these nonprofit workers, even in the absence of economic incentives.[12]

What lessons, useful in understanding the Postal Service, can we learn from the nonprofits about the ability of an organization to use private sector management techniques in the absence of strong profit motives? First, we observe that one force driving the nonprofit to efficiency is the force of competition and the threat of failure. Nonprofits can, of course, go bankrupt; and, indeed, the failure rate among nonprofits is quite high. For the Postal Service, competition is intermittent, depending on the product. And although the existence of deficits clearly creates political pressure on managers in the Postal Service, the threat of outright bankruptcy is low.

10. Walter W. Powell & Rebecca Friedkin, *Organizational Change in Nonprofit Organizations, in* WALTER W. POWELL, THE NONPROFIT SECTOR (Yale University Press 1987).

11. Anne E. Preston has written a number of articles tackling this issue from different perspectives. *See, e.g.,* Anne E. Preston, *The Nonprofit Worker in a For-Profit World,* 4 J. LAB. ECON. 438 (1989).

12. Interesting work on the role of worker sorting and ideology in nonprofits comes from Dennis R. Young, *Entrepreneurship and the Behavior of Nonprofit Organizations: Elements of a Theory, in* THE ECONOMICS OF NONPROFIT INSTITUTIONS, *supra* note 3. Recent work analyzing the role of incentive compensation in nonprofits, picking up on the role of ideology, is Richard Steinberg, *Profits and Incentive Compensation in Nonprofit Firms,* NONPROFIT MGMT. & LEADERSHIP, Winter 1990, at 137.

Second, we observe that, in the nonprofit sector, ideological commitment to a mission in part substitutes for the economic incentives used in the for-profit world to reduce shirking. But it is hard to argue, at least at the present time, that mail delivery is a career to which postal workers are drawn for ideological reasons. Indeed, the movement away from Civil Service may have reduced the ideological appeal of the business. Thus, one of the advantages many nonprofits have in reducing inefficiency in the labor market—the draw of ideology—is not likely to be present in the Postal Service.

In sum, the Postal Service may well have more trouble implementing private sector management techniques than the nonprofit sector has, principally because of incentive issues. Another source of difficulty may come from the control side. In particular, the Postal Service is subject to considerably more control from Congress than the typical nonprofit is. This, too, may make it hard to implement managerial reform, particularly since reform typically brings with it both winners and losers. We will pursue this theme further as we next examine the nonprofit mail subsidy.

Subsidies for Nonprofit Mail Carriage

Charitable, educational, and other nonprofit organizations pay considerably reduced rates for postal service. Under the Postal Reorganization Act, the authority to decide who gets reduced rates and under what conditions is a congressional matter. And, indeed, recent congressional discussions to limit favorable rates have met with strong political response, including heavy lobbying from nonprofit groups. It is interesting to examine the current organization of the political response as a way to explore—at a more micro level—the operations of this quasi-governmental business.

Congress supports reduced postal rates for nonprofits as a matter of public policy. Reduced-rate carriage is thus a service that the government wishes to procure from the Postal Service business, much like the delivery of a program to help the homeless is a service that local governments wish to buy from the nonprofit sector. But the current transaction involving the reduced rate for nonprofits is actually quite different from the usual government-nonprofit negotiation. In most nonprofit-government transactions, the nonprofit has the opportunity to reject the government's business. When the Department of Mental Retardation offers a social service agency a contract to establish a group home, that agency can choose to reject the contract should the price or other characteristics of the contract be unattractive. The Postal Service, however, has an obligation to carry the reduced-rate mail, *even if the payment offered by Congress is grossly inadequate.* In this sense, the Postal Service has less bargaining clout than the typical nonprofit partner. But Congress also lacks the option of bargaining with a variety of possible vendors, an option that we typically see in nonprofit-government transactions. Thus, both parties to the transaction have less flexibility than is typical. With this background, we can examine what has happened in the past few years with the subsidy for nonprofit reduced-rate carriage.

The Bush administration strongly supported efforts to reform the structure of the nonprofit rate benefit and thus to reduce the tax burden from the program. As a way to enforce reform, President Bush requested an appropriation for the Postal Service in 1993 that was substantially below the subsidy requested by the Postal Service to cover the costs of this activity. Indeed, while the postal subsidy was $970 million in 1985 and $470 million in 1992, President Bush requested only $121 million in 1993.[13] At the same time, increased competition in the nonprofit world has arguably increased the pressure on the postal system to expand the carriage of nonprofit mail. Thus, the size of the postal appropriation was a matter of political maneuvering, rather than a response to the costs of the service provided by the Postal Service. Moreover, in responding to this price cut, the Postal Service did not have the option available to most businesses of refusing to sell its services at the price offered. It is up to Congress to decide who gets the reduced rates and under what conditions; the Postal Service must deliver the service at whatever price Congress authorizes. In this market, price does not play its usual role of signaling the costs of production, since the Postal Service is not permitted to behave in a businesslike way in response to the price offered. In this respect, the Postal Service operates under many of the constraints faced by the railroads before deregulation facilitated route abandonment.

What options are available to the Postal Service in this situation? First, to the extent that the price does not cover the costs of the service, the Postal Service can borrow money and charge future customers—both nonprofit and commercial—for the shortfall. Or it can try to wheedle the money out of Congress in the future. In the former case, prices will be distorted in other markets served by the Postal Service. In the latter case, the Postal Service is essentially lending money to the Treasury. Moreover, the Postal Service clearly has no incentive to serve the nonprofit mailers well. Needless to say, under these conditions, the Postal Service has come out in favor of reducing

13. *Treasury/Postal Bill Survives Battle*, CONG. Q. ALMANAC 627 (1992).

the size of the rate subsidy given to nonprofit mailers.[14] Given the price that Congress is willing to pay for preferred rates to nonprofits, this is not a business the Postal Service finds attractive. But the only way it can extricate itself from this unprofitable venture is through the political process. Clearly, this is a very different situation from the one usually faced by a nonprofit or commercial business in an unattractive market.

Conclusion

In contrast with much of Europe, the United States has had little experience with government corporations. Two examples worth contrasting with the Postal Service are Conrail and the Tennessee Valley Authority. By most reckonings, TVA has been relatively successful in its business of generating low-priced energy in support of economic development in that region of the country.[15] Conrail, in contrast—the federal government's attempt to run a railroad system—was widely viewed as a disaster. Much of the success of TVA has been attributed to the energy and professional commitment of its engineers and managers. In many ways, TVA, like many nonprofits, has been able to capitalize on ideological and professional appeal as a way to reduce problems of shirking by workers. Conrail, with its larger and less professionally committed work force, had considerably more difficulty in labor management. Both TVA and Conrail were monopolists in many of their markets, but TVA could measure itself against the yardstick of a number of comparable utilities, while the comparative operations for Conrail were less clear. Finally, it can be argued that Conrail— saddled with old equipment and a unionized labor force in a market being nibbled away by alternative modes of transportation—had a much harder problem to solve than did TVA, which was blessed with

14. "Former Postmaster General Tony Frank, Deputy Postmaster General Michael Coughlin and postal board chair Norma Pace all have told Congress that neither the USPS nor regular-rate payers should be expected to suffer if Congress decided not to fund fully the preferred-rate subsidy. If the nation no longer could afford to pay for nonprofit organizations' postal rate preferences, they argued, then nonprofit-rate mailers should be required to pay the same rates as others. Any subsidy from the USPS or regular-rate payers was deemed unacceptable." Gene A. Del Polito, *Are Special Charity Rates Doomed?*, DM NEWS, Oct. 26, 1992, at 22.

15. For an early, but excellent account of TVA, see DAVID E. LILIENTHAL, TVA—DEMOCRACY ON THE MARCH (Harper 1953).

cheap hydroelectric power in a less labor-intensive business.

Unfortunately, the Postal Service looks more like Conrail than TVA. The work force is large and unionized and does not appear to be ideologically committed to the profession. Competitive yardsticks for many businesses are still unavailable, at a time when competition erodes many of the Postal Service's more lucrative markets. Finally, the problems with which the Postal Service began its life and the legacies from its time as a public agency make it look much more like Conrail than TVA.

Commentary by Henry B. Hansmann

Sharon Oster's chapter is a helpful overview of some of the organizational problems the Postal Service faces and offers some sensible conclusions as well. I would like to build on her observations, in particular on her comparison of the Postal Service with other kinds of limited-profit organizations, such as nonprofit firms and utilities.

Why was governmental ownership the organizational form chosen for the Postal Service? There are several possible answers. It may be a response to monopoly. Alternatively, government ownership may be used to cross subsidize across classes of consumers for the benefit, say, of rural consumers or nonprofit mailers, or it may be used to provide a secure form of employment for constituents. I will assume here that the latter possibilities are secondary functions that are merely epiphenomena of governmental ownership and that we are principally talking about solving a monopoly problem.

The two other organizational forms besides governmental ownership that we routinely use in the United States to deal with the problem of monopoly are regulated for-profit firms (investor-owned firms) and consumer cooperatives. The use of nonprofit firms for this purpose is uncommon. Instead, nonprofit firms are used in more competitive sectors of the economy where problems of poor information on the part of the consumers make it difficult to police the quality and quantity of a given service.[1] This is not the problem with the Postal Service; its problems are due to its operation in a monopolistic market. Consequently, it is hard to draw strong conclusions about the Postal Service by comparing it with firms in the nonprofit sector.

1. *See, e.g.,* Henry B. Hansmann, *Ownership of the Firm*, 4 J. Law, Econ. & Org. 267 (1988); Henry B. Hansmann, *The Role of Nonprofit Enterprise*, 89 Yale L.J. 835 (1980).

Let us consider the alternative organizational forms available and consider whether those forms are possible alternatives for the Postal Service. Even if we do not think that the Postal Service can be converted to another form of ownership, it is still useful to analyze those forms to see whether they offer any insight into how we might reform the Postal Service while staying within the context of its governmental ownership structure.

The first option is to deregulate the system by selling it to a for-profit firm without regulation. Professor Oster has advised us that this would not necessarily lead to productive efficiency. After all, look at General Motors or IBM, which are fairly small firms compared with the Postal Service. A widely held business corporation the size of the Postal Service may not be a model of productive efficiency, especially if it operates within a very sheltered market.

Consumer co-ops are, however, a very common way of dealing with public utility monopolies. In fact, it might be useful to think of the Postal Service as a consumer co-op: the Postal Service is like a municipally owned utility, with the public as its consumers and owners. A problem with this analogy, however, is that Congress has other agendas and other organizations to monitor, and thus it does not police the Postal Service as closely as might the board of a true consumer co-op. More important, Congress is responsive to more than just the interests of postal consumers. It is also responsive to producer interests and labor interests, especially to those of the people who work for the Postal Service. To some extent, the government runs the Postal Service as if it were a worker co-op as well as a consumer co-op, consequently serving two sets of clients whose interests are completely diverse. Workers want to charge the highest prices possible for the least amount of service, and consumers want the reverse. This divergence of interests leads to a fragmentation of goals.

Could we run the Postal Service as a pure consumer co-op? I think not. The consumers are too numerous and the volume of the transactions of the Postal Service too large to give individual consumers an interest in policing the enterprise. Moreover, an effective consumer co-op requires one clear homogeneous class of consumers who all share the same interest. Consumer co-ops are not often found in urban areas that exhibit highly fragmented, conflicting groups of consumer interests. But consumer interests are highly fragmented in the Postal Service. Perhaps, for example, a few mass mailers could gain control of a Postal Service co-op and divert its operations for their own purposes, running up the first-class rate and running down the mass-mailing rates.

In short, it seems unlikely that we would fare better if we had a consumer co-op rather than the kind of removed consumer co-op that government ownership effectively confers.

Another point is that effective consumer co-ops are typically highly federated. There are some enormous consumer co-ops; many are Fortune 500 corporations. They tend to be federated with a number of local offices. A farm supply co-op, for example, has local stores that are owned by local farmers; these stores federate into regional and then international groups. This creates an intensely interested group of consumers who monitor these firms. The Postal Service could be effectively run by its consumers only if we could construct a similar federated order.

Professor Oster asked whether this could be done. Could you split off activities of the Postal Service to create a federated structure? Could post offices exist at the state or city level? It is hard to draw comparisons with the breakup of the Bell System because it had already broken itself up into local operating companies before the divestiture. Antitrust officials simply mimicked AT&T's subsidiary system. The problem with the Postal Service is that it does not have that kind of subsidiary system. This fact may be a strong indication that a federated system would not work, perhaps because of strong network effects.

Alternatively, we could transfer ownership in the Postal Service to a for-profit firm and regulate it. The firm would serve the interest of its investors while rate regulation would serve the interest of consumers. There are several problems with this arrangement, however. If improperly devised, regulation will create wasteful incentives. For instance, too little or too much investment results when regulators set the rate of return too high or too low. More important, the Postal Service is a very complex service, more so than other industries to which we apply rate-of-return regulation. The Postal Service is more complex than railroad passenger service, and we did not do a very good job with that. As Professor Panzar noted, there are terrible problems of attaining information for the regulatory agency concerning the cost of different kinds of service. There is also the possibility that the regulatory agency will use its powers to cross subsidize certain constituents to serve political ends. Thus, we are forced to consider the question of who appoints the regulatory agency and who would be likely to pursue an agenda different from the Board of Governors of the Postal Service. In short, a simple regulatory model does not look attractive here because of the complexity of the service.

Let us now consider the true nonprofit form. Reforms have moved the Postal Service increasingly toward a pure nonprofit. That is, the Postal Service is not a profit-maximizing entity but instead is supposed to break even. At the same time, it is also more independent of the government than it once was. We could, however, go further, giving the Postal Service even greater autonomy from Congress and bringing it even closer to a pure (nongovernmental) nonprofit firm. This would be advantageous in terms of increasing its independence from the political agenda of Congress. It might also be possible to remove the worker interest at this point, depending on how the board was structured. Yet the efficiency implications of this structure are not clear. Professor Oster notes that nonprofits can operate efficiently. In hospital care, for example, nonprofits compete very well in productive efficiency. But, as Professor Oster observes, there is competition in most of these industries—with the product market serving as a good disciplinarian.

Nonprofits can price discriminate very effectively. (Consider the recent Ivy League price-fixing case.) The government, in contrast, does not like to price-discriminate; it likes to set uniform prices and classes of service for a variety of reasons that come from the political process. Nonprofits are not subject to that constraint. So we might solve this problem by cutting the Postal Service loose from the government, the result being that the Postal Service would be more responsive to the kinds of price-discrimination schemes that Professor Panzar discussed. That is, the more independent we make the Postal Service, the more likely it will be able to price discriminate, which is probably a good thing.

As the Postal Service is allowed to be more and more independent from the government, however, we encounter another serious problem: capital allocation. Nonprofits are very slow to accumulate capital. Consequently, when there is a large increase in demand, nonprofit firms do not exhibit a rapid supply response. Worse, when demand slackens, the nonprofit firm does not disinvest. Invested capital is embedded, and it does not come out. Nonprofits will continue to run prices down as long as there is something left. We have watched just such a scenario unfold in hospital care. Interestingly, governmental firms seem much better at pumping money in and at taking money out. For example, the government was responsible for most of the investment that built the capital stock of the hospital system after World War II. In the 1960s, we moved to demand-side subsidies; consequently, there was room for for-profit firms to enter the hospital sector, and the government firms pulled back. Ultimately, we dissolved most of the governmental hospitals in the country. But nonprofits, in contrast, have not exited the industry, I think because capital gets embedded in those firms. The more we move toward a true nonprofit form (a really independent but non-profit-maximizing Postal Service), the more we will encounter capital allocation problems. Will we be able to pump capital in or to take capital out in an effective way? Or will we merely create a firm that grows and grows?

The other side of the capital allocation issue is that, if Congress exercises the power to decapitalize the industry, then it incidentally can exercise political control in a manner that may be unacceptable— power such as serving the interests of suppliers of inputs to the Postal Service or the interests of certain classes of consumers that we do not want other classes to subsidize.

Professor Oster observes that nonprofits often keep wages down. She suggests that it is owing to the ideological commitment of its workers. This may be true. But it may, alternatively, be because nonprofits were exempt from the labor laws until twenty years ago and unionization has been slow to catch up with them.

What about simply reforming the existing system of governmental ownership? What I have said about nonprofits is relevant here. We could try to give the Postal Service more independence, but we should be aware of the costs, especially capital allocation. Another question is how to appoint management. From our consumer co-op analogy, there is much to be said for actually giving consumer interests as much responsibility as possible in appointing directors, subject to the concern that these consumers have mutually conflicting interests. (If different classes of consumers were to appoint or elect the board directly, we might observe a very fractious board that would eventually compromise or just get mired in controversy.) Maybe, in any case, we should try to appoint a board that at least understands that it is the fiduciary of consumers, not the work force.

Professor Oster also points to other governmental analogies, such as the Tennessee Valley Authority. I wonder whether the reason TVA is effective is that, as Professor Oster suggests, its workers are highly ideologically motivated. TVA is clearly responsive to some very strong, concentrated, and clear consumer interests. It distributes electricity to a group of local distributing co-ops, for-profits, and governmental utilities, all of which have a strong interest in having TVA keep the price per kilowatt hour very low. But the Postal Service does not have quite so organized a constituency to monitor it. Thus the question becomes, How do we build that kind of consumer activism into the Postal Service? That question leaves us with few encouraging options, which in turn brings us back to the earlier question: how do we alter the governance of the Postal Service to make it more responsive?

Discussion

QUESTION: Comparing the productivity of the TVA with a regulated monopoly does not tell us much, since monopolies are not famous for being especially efficient. And I have trouble coming up with a service that has greater ideological motivation than housing the poor. But when I look toward a politically constituted authority to provide the management for public housing, I see horrible inefficiency. If ideological desire leads to an efficient nonprofit, then a lot of people would agree that public housing should be very efficient. But unless I am mistaken, the public housing authorities are grossly inefficient in many ways. In this discussion, we also talked about the postal regulations and how, maybe, there are some people being subsidized. There is a notion that we should not expect everyone to pay the full rate. It sounds as though we are providing income redistribution instead of postal service, and I wonder if that is very efficient. For the poor who cannot afford to pay the full price of mailing their letters, is there some other way of achieving income redistribution other than through the Postal Service?

SHARON M. OSTER, Yale School of Management: Public housing is an interesting example. A lot of nonprofits actually have some of the same goals, albeit at a much more local level. People donate tremendous amounts of their labor to accomplish essentially some of the same things—for example, Jimmy Carter and Habitat for Humanity. So there seems to be some sorting of the dedicated into the nonprofits and the undedicated into the government. Or perhaps something happens when someone becomes part of a government bureaucracy that transforms the dedicated into the slothful. I am not sure which is accurate.

Returning to the issue of local control, I do not think it is surprising that a big bureaucracy cannot motivate its workers as well as a small operation. It is an interesting question whether the government can have *any* highly motivated workers. The example that most sociologists use for motivated government service employees is the Forest Service. Maybe economists just do not know anything about rangers in the woods, however, and that is why economists assume that they are ideologically committed. Professor Hansmann's observation about the local control associated with small operations is quite a good one. It could be that with public housing consumer control is not sufficiently local and concentrated to push the organization toward efficiency.

QUESTION: Could it also be that they are regulated—that is, the people who run the public housing authority are put together by a political process, whereas Habitat for Humanity is not?

PROFESSOR OSTER: Right.

HENRY B. HANSMANN, Yale Law School: I am not sure that the difference is simply between governmental and nongovernmental organizations—that somehow the government attracts slothful people and nonprofits do not. As Professor Oster's last comment suggested, small governmental operations are quite efficient. It is very hard, for example, to find any strong evidence that municipal utilities are less cost efficient than investor-owned utilities. The problem comes in scale. Part of the problem with public housing is that the federal government is responsible for an enterprise that has essentially no important economies of scale. In housing, the efficient size is only some hundreds of units. But giving the national government control of housing necessitated creation of a large bureaucracy that connects each local housing project to Congress and the Executive Branch. As a result, we have many additional layers. Naturally, a nonprofit that has to manage only its own little housing project will be more effective.

The Postal Service does not have the same problem. Because the Postal Service must be run as an integrated system, the bureaucracy is already in place. We do not have to build anything extra to have the Postal Service report to the federal government, because it must necessarily be organized on a scale comparable to governmental agencies in any case.

3
Socialism, Eastern Europe, and the Question of the Postal Monopoly

George L. Priest

The prospectus of the AEI postal regulation project indicated that I was to "bring up to date . . . well known research on the history and goals of the postal monopoly." The term "well known research" is a reference to an article of mine published in the *Journal of Law & Economics* in 1975.[1] After a lengthy description of the colorful history of the Post Office, that article ended with what I regarded as a devastating critique of the postal monopoly as a mechanism of economic organization, revealing the monopoly's great failings and proving that no rational person could support its continued existence. In fact, the economic arguments of that article were quite familiar, especially to readers of the *Journal of Law & Economics*, where the arguments appeared in articles published throughout the 1960s and 1970s criticizing antitrust law, regulation, and other governmental controls on economic activity.

The extraordinary changes in economic organization in this country and the world over the past two decades would certainly require that most *JLE* articles of that period be updated extensively. In the United States, we have seen a revolution in antitrust law with the Supreme Court's basic adoption of the Chicago School approach. We have also seen the triumph of the deregulation movement in transportation, telecommunications, the airlines, and power. We have observed changes in the nature of government regulation that few could have predicted in 1975, from the actual death of a regulatory agency (the Civil Aeronautics Board) to the recent auctions of the airwaves. The changes in economic organization around the world have been even more outstanding. We have seen the collapse of commu-

---

1. George L. Priest, *The History of the Postal Monopoly in the United States*, 18 J.L. & Econ. 33 (1975).

nism and of the socialist states in the former Soviet Union and its Eastern European satellites as well as the rapid decline of socialism in all other forms of its existence in the world, with broad-scale privatization from Britain to New Zealand.

Despite these extraordinary changes in economic organization since 1975, however, it is not in the slightest degree difficult to bring my article up to date: there has been no change whatsoever in the U.S. postal monopoly, and my article has had no influence, or exactly the same influence it possessed before its publication. I cannot claim that a zero coefficient of the variable "influence over time" is atypical of articles of mine. But the more important and quite serious question that I would like to address is why those economic arguments— which seem to have been exceptionally influential in the contexts of antitrust law, of regulation, even of socialist organization—have had so little influence in the context of the postal monopoly.

The link between changes in antitrust law and regulation in the United States, the decline of socialism around the world, and articles published in the *Journal of Law & Economics* (including articles on the postal monopoly) is deeper than one might think. In essence, the changes in economic organization over the past two decades reflect the fact that the subjects of attack in the *JLE*, for the most part, no longer exist. There can be no question that the cumulative attack in the *JLE* on the Supreme Court's historical interpretation of antitrust law strongly influenced the change in academic opinion, leading and encouraging the Supreme Court to adopt the Chicago School approach. Similarly, few can doubt the *JLE*'s influence on the deregulation movement of which it provided the principal academic support. Those many articles remain classics of the field and are well known and treasured by all of us.

Readers who focused chiefly on antitrust and regulation, however, may not have noticed that sprinkled throughout issues of the *Journal of Law & Economics* during the 1960s and 1970s were articles of a more overtly ideological nature critical of socialism and dedicated to the triumph of liberty. The attack on the prevailing antitrust jurisprudence and on regulation was only part of a larger ideological project initiated by Aaron Director and continued by Ronald Coase aimed against socialism and governmental control in all forms. The political content of the *Journal of Law & Economics* is less apparent today and may not exist. That journal and economics as a discipline have been captured by scientists and effectively neutered in terms of express ideology. During the 1960s and 1970s, however, the political content was frequently overt and in many other cases, even in articles now remembered only for their scientific aspects, lay only slightly beneath the surface.

Perhaps the best and most surprising example I might choose to illustrate this point is the single most prominent article ever published in the *Journal of Law & Economics* and the most frequently cited article, whether in economics or law, Ronald H. Coase's "The Problem of Social Cost."[2] The article is chiefly remembered—even by those who know it well—for its lessons about the importance of transaction costs and the potential for bargaining around legal rules. Many others will recall its introduction of the concept of reciprocal harm. Today, the article seems somewhat long-winded for the purpose of presenting even these profound points. The modern reading, however, reflects another illustration of capture by scientists and the suppression of an author's deep political ambitions. Those seemingly long-winded and now largely forgotten portions of the article contain a powerful political argument against socialism and governmental interference in the economy. Indeed, I suspect that Coase aspired for his article to become a classic, not in the analysis of liability rules, but in the field of public finance.

Remember those long discussions of Pigou and what Coase called the Pigovian tradition? Why the attention to Pigou? Certainly not because Pigou had written anything about transaction costs. Coase's broader point—ignored today by most in the field of law and economics—was that Coase's law of reciprocal harm invalidated Pigou's prescription that government, which is to say socialist government, could correct society's externalities through taxes, subsidies, or, surely, liability rules. According to the law of reciprocal harm, there are no externalities; the concept has no coherent meaning. It follows that there exists no basis for the government to interfere in economic life on the grounds of affirmatively correcting a misallocation of resources. This is the point of Coase's somber conclusion in the final section of the article entitled "A Change of Approach," which mentions nothing about transaction costs but presents a summation of the implications of Coase's analysis: "problems of welfare economics must ultimately dissolve into a study of aesthetics and morals."[3]

The ideological scrubbing of political economy in general and the political economy of the *Journal of Law & Economics* to reformulate them into the neutral science of economics has edited out for the modern reader and from the less modern reader's memory the deep political content of "The Problem of Social Cost." In a different

---

2. Ronald H. Coase, *The Problem of Social Cost*, 3 J.L. & ECON. 1 (1960).

3. *Id.* at 43.

library, Coase's article would be shelved next to Hayek's *Road to Serfdom* in the section, Classics in the Criticism of Socialism. This reading of "The Problem of Social Cost" may be unfamiliar to some, but it makes sense of what to a biographer of Coase might otherwise seem only evidence of eclecticism. How many remember the project to which Ronald Coase turned immediately after writing "The Problem of Social Cost"? Again, perhaps surprising given the modern reading of that article, it was not to the analysis of liability rules in tort law nor to trespass or nuisance law to examine the importance of transaction costs. Coase turned his attention to the postal monopoly.[4]

I have described earlier the extraordinary influence of the *Journal of Law & Economics* on American antitrust law and the deregulation movement, deriving from the editorial ambitions of Aaron Director and Ronald Coase. I have also described Ronald Coase's individual influence. The Federal Communications Commission auction of some portions of the electromagnetic spectrum—first proposed by Coase in his 1959 article, "The Federal Communications Commission"[5]—is only the most recent example. This broad intellectual project, in my view, has also influenced the collapse of communism and the decline of socialism throughout the world. The rigorous and systematic academic approach toward governmental interference in the economy surely stiffened the resolve in the West in favor of free markets and competition and undermined in the East the conceptual basis of a planned economy.

Despite these triumphs, however, neither this great intellectual movement of our time nor the specific work of scholars of the stature of Ronald Coase has had any appreciable influence on the U.S. postal monopoly. As described, it took the FCC thirty-five years to adopt Coase's proposal in the pages of the *Journal of Law & Economics* to auction the airwaves, but it has been fifty-five years since Ronald Coase first condemned the postal monopoly and thirty-three years since he

---

4. R. H. Coase, *The British Post Office and the Messenger Companies*, 4 J.L. & ECON. 12 (1961). Coase had been interested in the problem of the postal monopoly for many years. *See* R. H. Coase, *Rowland Hill and the Penny Post*, 6 ECONOMICA 423 (n.s. 1939); R. H. Coase, *The Postal Monopoly in Great Britain: An Historical Survey in* ECONOMIC ESSAYS IN COMMEMORATION OF THE DUNDEE SCHOOL OF ECONOMICS 1931–1955 at 25 (J. K. Eastham ed., 1955).

5. 2 J.L. & ECON. 1 (1959). Twenty-two years ago, as a student in one of Ronald's seminars, I remember asking him after a class session in which we had discussed his airwave auction proposal why government regulators had not immediately adopted it. He responded that it would take 30 years for an idea like that to become successful. A pretty accurate estimate—it took 35 years.

did so in the pages of the *Journal of Law & Economics*[6] (and nineteen years since my article following his). The U.S. postal monopoly remains unmoved.

Certainly, there have been changes in Postal Service operations over these years, even changes in the direction of privatization and enhanced competition. For example, today, virtually all long-distance transport is contracted out; rural delivery is almost uniformly contracted out. Other markets have been largely given up by the Postal Service—parcel post, overnight mail, as examples—abandoned to private carriers. But these changes have not resulted from a rethinking of the postal monopoly and an embrace of competition, but from the necessity of controlling costs in a political climate simultaneously jealous of postal subsidies and hostile to postage increases. The underlying support for the postal monopoly remains as strong today as ever.

Given broad-scale deregulation in the United States and the decline, if not collapse, of socialism around the world, we ought to view the survival of the Postal Service in its current form and the retention of the postal monopoly as very surprising. The Postal Service remains today as the most significant example of socialism in the United States. We know from theory and the American public knows from the success of Federal Express, Purolator, and other competitors that there is no inherent reason for a government monopoly of the delivery of written communication. My article showed that the historical reasons for the survival of the monopoly were not strong. One might honestly defend a governmental postal service to maintain contact among the separate colonies or even to maintain a link to the Western frontier, but the argument becomes somewhat less plausible where the Union appears secure, the continental United States is largely settled, and the public demands delivery as fast as possible of 171.2 billion pieces of mail per year.[7]

The U.S. Postal Service today embraces almost all the aspects of socialism rejected in Eastern Europe and in the privatized Western economies. Some have called the Post Office the employer of last resort. That is not entirely correct. An AEI study of some years ago estimated that postal workers' salaries were 21 percent greater than competitive rates, with long queues of aspiring applicants.[8] This is not a practice typical of an employer of last resort. That wage scale does

6. *See* Coase *supra* note 4.

7. 1993 U.S. POSTAL SERV., ANNUAL REPORT OF THE POSTMASTER GENERAL 26.

8. Douglas K. Adie, *How Have the Postal Workers Fared since the 1970 Act?* in PERSPECTIVES ON POSTAL SERVICE ISSUES 74 (Roger Sherman ed., AEI Press 1980).

indicate, however, substantial subsidies to the work force, characteristic of socialized management. In the same vein, the Postal Service possesses the largest unionized work force in the country and one of the few in which union membership has continued to increase over the years, rather than decline, as has been true in almost all privately managed industries.

The Postal Service has many other socialized features. Its predecessor, the U.S. Post Office, had a long and noble history of nondiscrimination or, perhaps more accurately, lesser discrimination in employment than private employers. Historically, a far greater proportion of blacks have worked in the Post Office than in any comparable private sector. Moreover, the operational commitment of the Postal Service to the principle of universality—universal delivery at a uniform price, whatever the required subsidy—is surely characteristic of a socialized governmental, rather than private, enterprise.

In addition to these aspects of socialized operations, the Postal Service is enmeshed in governmental regulations and control to a level unimaginable for a private entity. Indeed, when these relationships are revealed, the legal implications of removing the postal monopoly, not to mention of privatizing postal operations entirely, are of substantial significance. Though not often emphasized, our socialist Postal Service provides the underlying legal basis for a wide range of governmental regulatory activity. For example, the control of obscenity in the United States consists in small part of local governmental raids on topless bars and the like but in major part of federal prosecution under statutes prohibiting the dissemination of obscene materials through the mails. The federal criminal count of mail fraud is a central component of federal controls over a broad array of illegal business activities. Without counts for mail fraud or for engaging in other illegal activity by using the mails, the application of racketeering laws might be limited to the prosecution of actual organized crime. In addition, the Postal Service provides an important, though usually concealed or denied, source of access for the FBI and other law enforcement agencies. As has been true in other countries and over the history of postal operations around the world, the government investigates citizens by intercepting their mail, a practice that might become much more difficult where alternative private carriers are routinely available and surely more difficult in a fully privatized postal system.

Finally, I do not know how many of you have spent much time in an urban post office, but it is a remarkable institution. Perhaps exactly because it and its workers are shielded from competitive pressures, it often more closely resembles a welfare office than it does a retail business. The services often provided include wrapping up box-es, providing advice and counsel, helping to organize the lives of citi-zens who wait patiently in long lines, often because they have little else to do. Services of this nature could not possibly survive in a fully privatized system. If the Postal Service is viewed as a welfare office, Douglas Ginsburg's anecdote about the postal worker's dismay at the Christmas rush becomes much more comprehensible.

There has been discussion of the impending demise of the U.S. Postal Service or of its inevitable obsolescence as it is progressively supplanted by electronic mail, facsimile transmission, or private overnight delivery, such as Federal Express. Certainly, there have been large increases in recent years in the use of electronic transmis-sions as well as in private overnight delivery. But we will not soon witness the disappearance of the Postal Service. Federal Express, for example, has increased its deliveries from 178 million pieces in 1988 to 435.6 million in 1993, an estimable increase of 257.6 million pieces.[9] Of course, it is extremely difficult to estimate electronic mail and fac-simile use, though we all know that the increases over the past few years have been extraordinary. Has the Postal Service begun to shrink in response? Hardly. The proportions will not be equivalent because of the large differences in absolute volume.[10] But from 1988 to 1993, the total volume of U.S. Postal Service deliveries *increased*, not decreased, and increased from 161.0 billion to 171.2 *billion* pieces. However admirable Federal Express's increase in deliveries from 1988 to 1993 of 257.6 million, the Postal Service's 10.2 billion increase in deliveries over the same period equals 38.8 times the Federal Express amount. Perhaps it might be thought that the Postal Service gains occurred principally in third-class or other services not requir-ing immediate delivery: not the case. Over the same period, 1988–1993, the Postal Service recorded an increase in first-class mail deliveries of 7.5 billion, 29.1 times the respective increase of Federal Express. The Postal Service's priority mail service—two days, two pounds—also increased over this period, from 436 million pieces in 1988 to 664.3 million in 1993, an increase of 228 million, almost as large as the increase of Federal Express.[11] Federal Express and elec-

9. These are fiscal year figures. Telephone interview with Becky Mosbey, Annual Report Department, Federal Express (Nov. 3, 1993).

10. In my oral remarks at the Conference, I mistakenly compared differ-ences between changes over time in first-class and total mail volumes. The numbers in the text are now correct.

11. 1988 statistics of United States Postal Service deliveries are taken from 1991 U.S. POSTAL SERV., ANNUAL REPORT OF THE GENERAL 55–56 and 1993 statis-tics from 1993 U.S. POSTAL SERV., ANNUAL REPORT OF THE GENERAL 31–32. I am grateful to Robb Stup of the American Enterprise Institute for research.

tronic transmission are surely growing rapidly, but public demand for the delivery of written communications appears to be growing even faster. There are few grounds upon which to predict the demise of the U.S. Postal Service.

Nevertheless, the lack of serious debate over the elimination of the postal monopoly or the broader privatization of the Postal Service remains puzzling. That the Postal Service is the greatest example of socialist enterprise in the United States is uncontroversial. Given the debate raging over socialism all around the world and the fall of socialist states in Eastern Europe and the Soviet Union, how can there be no debate in the United States over the Postal Service? Indeed, let me bring the issue closer to home by attempting another analogy. The Postal Service in its current form and structure closely resembles AT&T before its breakup: sheltered from competition, committed to principles of universal service maintained by whatever necessary cross-subsidization; and sluggish with respect to innovation and expansion. Few today would dispute that the breakup of AT&T was a seminal event in telecommunications, unleashing an extraordinary flowering of new and innovative services to the benefit of all Americans. If the Postal Service resembles AT&T, and if the breakup of AT&T and the consequent introduction of competition in telecommunications generated benefits recognized by all, why is there not greater support for either the breakup of the Postal Service or for the introduction of new competition with it?

The argument that I put forward is that the debate over the postal monopoly and the privatization of the Postal Service can be distinguished from the debate over socialism around the world and even from the appreciation of the benefits of the breakup of AT&T because it remains, today, a debate dominated by economists and chiefly by economic arguments. The debate over socialism was entirely different: it was not fidelity to the Chicago School analysis of the relative inefficiency of public to private management that led millions of East Germans into Czechoslovakia and the West. Similarly, regardless of the academic grounds for the breakup of AT&T, the public embrace of modern telecommunications does not stem from the closer identity of price to marginal cost. Put less elliptically, it is only when the debate over the postal monopoly and the privatization of the Postal Service is reoriented away from pure economic analysis and toward the new and expanded innovations and services that can be expected to result that progress will be made toward these reforms.

In a perverse sense, my 1975 article and its lack of subsequent success prove the point. In describing the history of the postal monopoly in the United States, the article showed that economic arguments were never very important to support or justify the monopoly. The Constitution, of course, does not compel a postal monopoly; it does not even compel a federal postal system. The Constitution only gives Congress the authority to establish post offices and post roads; it is not obligatory that the Congress do so. From the earliest days, however, the Post Office and the postal monopoly were justified as central elements of a democratic state. In the first instance, the Post Office and its monopoly were justified by the ambition of unifying the country. The extension of the mails to the far reaches of the land was viewed as important to the creation of the new democracy. Consider the following discussion in Congress in 1789 defending the institution of the Post Office, the extension of post roads, and the subsidized delivery of mails (here newspapers):

> Wherever the newspapers had extended, or even the correspondence of the members [of Congress], no opposition has been made to the laws, whereas the contrary was experienced in those parts to which the information had not penetrated. And even there, the opposition ceased as soon as the principles on which the laws had passed were made known to the people.[12]

The central idea expressed in this passage is that the Post Office serves as an implement of democracy, providing information to the inhabitants and transforming them from potential rebels into well-informed citizens, loyal because appreciative of the sound basis for governmental decisions.

Of course, after some decades of peaceful existence, the notion that it was necessary to subsidize newspaper delivery to maintain public order diminished to some extent. Remnants of the argument, however, remained. Indeed, especially with the expansion of the country during the first half of the nineteenth century, there was the broadly held belief that the Post Office served to maintain ties between the urban East and the Western frontier, binding all citizens to the country by making their disparate experiences known to all, unifying the country, as it were, spiritually. For example, from the debate in 1844 over the private express statutes, here are the words of Congressman George W. Hopkins, chairman of the House Post Office Committee, explaining why it was necessary to create the Post Office, why it must maintain a monopoly, and why it must charge uniform postal rates nationwide:

12. Priest, *supra* note 1, at 52 (quoting 3 ANNALS OF CONG. 254 (1791).

The obligation was assumed in our national compact to content the man dwelling remote from towns with his more lonely lot; to assure the immigrant who plants his new home on the skirts of the distant wilderness or prairie, that he is not forever severed from the kindred in society that still share his interests and love; to prevent those whom the swelling tide of population is constantly pressing to the outer verge of civilization from being surrendered to surrounding influences and sinking into the hunter or savage state. These are the considerations which the advocates of the right of individual enterprise to the conveyance of the mails disregard.[13]

It was predicted that, if the private express statutes were not reenacted and made watertight against competitive incursions, the price of delivery on the frontier would rise from five cents to twenty-five cents—an increase of five times. That increase, twenty cents, was equal roughly to one-fifth of a day's wage in 1844, a considerable amount. Still, the proposition that, but for twenty cents per letter, the sturdy immigrant would sink into the savage state is a remarkable proposition.

In my 1975 article, I criticized these various arguments on familiar economic grounds: these values can be attained without monopoly; a monopoly introduces distortions; even if the society wants to support frontier (unprofitable) delivery, there is no inherent reason to subsidize it through a tax on urban delivery, rather than through tapping some other source of revenue; allowing competition will create incentives for greater responsiveness, enhancing consumer welfare. These arguments, familiar though they are, have been largely disregarded in the years since 1975, just as they were largely disregarded in 1844 and in 1789. Throughout the history of the Post Office, Congress has embraced a different set of values. The value of universal service has been embraced since before the Revolution. The uniform pricing value is not of equal vintage, though it could be concluded that Congress has moved progressively toward its achievement. In 1844, Congress approved a two-tier price structure—five cents for local delivery; ten cents (not twenty-five) for delivery to the near-to-be savage on the frontier. It was only in the 1920s that the uniform rate value became fully established.

Of course, many continue to raise chiefly economic arguments concerning Postal Service operations. It is strange that we would

13. *Id.* at 65 (quoting H.R. Rep. No. 477, 28th Cong., 1st Sess. 1, 2 (1844)).

believe that these arguments are likely to have more success today than in 1844 or 1789. As suggested in the passage above, Congressman Hopkins estimated in 1844 that the subsidy for frontier delivery equaled five times the cost of first-class urban delivery. Despite the magnitude of such a subsidy, Hopkins and his colleagues in Congress endorsed it. Can we imagine that postal subsidies today amount to five times the cost of first-class delivery? The cost differential among first-class delivery within the continental United States must be very small. Federal Express, for example, itself employs a uniform pricing structure within the continental United States, suggestive of small geographical cost differences. Perhaps the first-class subsidy approaches that magnitude for delivery to some remote parts of Hawaii or Alaska (indeed, the subsidy probably exceeds five times in some Alaskan communities since the Postal Service serves frequently as the only delivery mechanism among Arctic villages). But the dollar magnitude of the subsidy to Alaskan and Hawaiian delivery is trivial among the totality of Postal Service costs.

If Congress was willing to override cost subsidies of this magnitude in 1844, how can we imagine that neoclassical economic arguments concerning costs—despite our fervent belief in them—will lead Congress to eliminate the postal monopoly or privatize the Postal Service today? In my view, to reform the Postal Service, it will be necessary to move beyond the calculation of subsidies, beyond the magnitude of cost savings, beyond the mechanics of efficiency, and even beyond the analysis of organization and form. However important these concepts and the values underlying them may be to economists, public policy regarding postal operations, just as public policy regarding the great revolutions against socialism in Eastern Europe and around the world, is motivated by a set of values related to the political commitment to freedom and democracy.

The stakes of the revolutions of Eastern Europe extend far beyond comparative changes in gross national product. Similarly, the stakes of the elimination of the postal monopoly or the privatization of the Postal Service extend far beyond reducing cross-subsidies and increasing per capita labor productivity. The principal effect of all the great changes in economic organization that we have witnessed over the past decade—including the revolutions in Eastern Europe, the breakup of AT&T, and the broad deregulation of trucking, airlines, telecommunications, and power—has been to free the forces of innovation and experimentation to develop new and previously unimagined freedoms, products, and services. Each of the countries that has abandoned socialism, like each of the deregulated industries in the United States, is fundamentally different today from before, because it possesses infinitely new possibilities that have grown up from the removal of centralized control.

It is difficult to imagine now the capacity for technological innovation and growth with respect to mail delivery that might result from the elimination of the postal monopoly or the privatization of the Postal Service. Perhaps that inability to imagine the future is a reason that academics rely chiefly on neoclassical implications involving costs and factor distortions in analyzing the implications of competition and privatization. But there is no reason to doubt that the extraordinary flowering of new products and services that attended the introduction of competition in telecommunications will be equaled following the introduction of competition in the delivery of written communication by the elimination of the postal monopoly and the privatization of Postal Service operations.

One must admit that there are obstacles to leading a revolution in the delivery of written communication by invoking little more than if-only's and what-might-be's. In my view, the opponents of the postal monopoly have remained at an overwhelming disadvantage because none of their arguments possesses a political saliency of the same magnitude as the invocation of the values of national unity and the promotion of democracy. It is unusual that this is so. The dissemination of written communications is of principal importance to a democracy. What is odd is that the opponents of the postal monopoly (including myself) have allowed the statist supporters of the Post Office and Postal Service to command that higher ground, despite our belief—and it is a straightforward implication of economic analysis—that competition and privatization will lead to better and cheaper forms of letter communication than any form of socialist organization.

The critics of the postal monopoly and the proponents of Postal Service privatization must embrace the values, not simply of cost reduction and superior factor allocation, but of the role of competition in letter delivery as the best mechanism for achieving the democratic values of enhancing the ability of the citizenry to communicate among itself. This suggests a change or, at least, an addition to the empirical studies that might be conducted to show the advantages of eliminating the monopoly and privatizing the Postal Service. Theory teaches that—in the context of a socialized postal system engaging in some level of cross-subsidization and, through enforcement of the monopoly, suppressing innovation—there will develop "an underground postal system" where citizens or corporations avert Postal Service restrictions to provide better delivery service at lower prices. Activities of this nature ought to be identified, studied, and exposed because they represent efforts by citizens to enhance communication abilities by evading Postal Service restraints. Studies of this nature will be just as important as calculations of cross-subsidies and factor distortions because the achievement of better and cheaper forms of letter communication is, without question, of tremendous value in a democracy. The strongest argument in favor of elimination of the monopoly and of privatization of the Postal Service is that the citizenry and thus democracy in America can be made better off by freeing the forces of innovation and experimentation to empower the discovery of new methods of delivery that advance communication.

The lesson of 200 years of the postal monopoly is that those who seek to eliminate the monopoly or privatize solely on the basis of the virtues of lowering costs, reducing subsidies, and increasing productivity will lose the battle to those who portray postal operations as serving democracy. Sadly, my 1975 article proves this point in two ways: in the historical sections that show that noneconomic arguments have always prevailed and in the abject failure of the economic arguments that were the centerpiece of the article itself. It is clear in my view, thus, that the most fervent defenders of the role of postal delivery in promoting democracy must be the critics of the monopoly, not the reverse. Supporters of the monopoly and of the socialized features of Postal Service operations must be portrayed—as I believe they are in fact—as the enemies of true democracy who seek, through advocacy of the principle of universality, to tax the communication of all of us, stifling innovation and experimentation and burdening the communication of the citizenry to subsidize particular mail classes or high-cost routes.

This is not to say that anyone proposes eliminating the federal Postal Service. The elimination of the monopoly and even the privatization of large areas of Postal Service operations need not compel the elimination of subsidies to newspapers, magazines, nonprofit mailers, Alaskans, Hawaiians, citizens needing welfare office help, or other current high-cost beneficiaries, including current Postal Service employees. Privatization and elimination of the monopoly, however, will compel a different understanding of these features of modern Postal Service operations. Some set of current Postal Service operations may be appropriately regarded by Congress as entitlements. The U.S. Postal Service may well be retained to achieve these ends: to provide residual delivery service to remote areas not served by private carriers; to deliver other forms of mail—say, newspapers and magazines—at rates lower than for-profit carriers can offer; and to provide welfare-like services in urban offices. Even if these services are retained, there is a tremendous advantage in viewing them as entitlements and evaluating their continued provision against the provision of other government benefits. Moreover, there will prove to be an even greater advantage in funding these entitlements through other revenue sources, rather than taxing written communication to the detriment of democracy.

What I propose is a shift in the grounds of debate. Proponents of privatization and of the elimination of the monopoly must defend these goals by invoking the values of democracy, enhanced communication among citizens, and innovation. Such a shift compels those who would defend the monopoly and the socialized Postal Service themselves to invoke cost as a defense. It is difficult to contest that democracy in America will be enhanced by any policy that improves the possibilities of written communication among the citizenry. The only available grounds of opposition are that to privatize and to end the monopoly will require the government to spend a lot of money to continue its subsidies of advertisers, magazines, employees, and perhaps Alaskans and Hawaiians. Such a shift in debate, I believe, will have important effects on the future of the postal services in America because, as we all know from the history of the postal monopoly in the United States, cost arguments of this nature have never met success.

4

The Missions and Methods of the Postal Power

William Ty Mayton

For the Post Office, the reorganization of 1970 was proclaimed as an end of history. Congress intended this reorganization to end a history of deficits, inefficiency, and inequity in postal operations. But reorganization has not ended that history. Just six years after the reorganization, the new Postal Service was, as a Senate report noted, technically bankrupt, and Congress was forced to rescue the service with a special $1 billion appropriation.[1] And so the postal history and the forces that produce it go on.

The Constitution provides for the "postal power." This chapter surveys the origins and development of this power and its most recent deployment in the Postal Reorganization Act of 1970. In this survey, we might well keep in mind a remark of Postmaster General Winton Blount during debate on the 1970 reorganization: "I think we need to straighten out as a matter of semantics the term public interest."[2] Indisputably, postal services benefit the whole community and are therefore in the "public interest." The confusion, though, has come from the long-standing assumption that the public interest requires government control of the mail.

The first two parts of this chapter briefly cover the English and colonial backgrounds of the Postal Service. The next part addresses the establishment of the "postal power" under the U.S. Constitution,

---

1. S. REP. NO. 94–966, 94th Cong., 2d Sess. 1, 43 (1976), *reprinted in* 1976 U.S.C.C.A.N. 2400, 2431. The special appropriation was carried out by the Postal Reorganization Act Amendments of 1976, Pub. L. No. 94–421, 90 Stat. 1303 (1976).

2. *Hearings on Postal Modernization before the Sen. Committee on Post Office and Civil Service*, 91st Cong., 1st Sess. 254 (1969) [hereinafter *Postal Modernization Hearings*].

followed by a discussion of the first defense of the statutory monopoly held by the Post Office. Next, the historical missions and methods of the postal power are described. The final part discusses the Reorganization Act of 1970 and the forces that produced it.

Early Postal History

The useful history of the U.S. postal power probably starts with the British mail. The complete history of postal systems, though, begins earlier. The postal motto—"Neither snow, nor rain, nor heat, nor gloom of night stays these couriers from the swift completion of their appointed rounds"—is adapted from Herodotus.[3] He was describing the postal system of the Persians, who had established a string of relay stations at 14-mile intervals across their empire. By horseback, messages moved along that route at better than 200 miles a day. The system was reserved for matters of state (military and diplomatic correspondence) rather than private correspondence. The next large postal system seems to have been the Romans' *cursus publicus*. As with the Persians, this system was reserved for state matters and was built on relay stations, which were known as posts (from *positus*, meaning "stationed").

During the Middle Ages, organized communication systems again emerged, but not necessarily on a governmental model. Merchant cities (such as those of the Hanseatic League), banking houses, and universities all variously used private messenger services. Messages were carried in small metal bags known as *malle*, hence the term *mail*. The most famous continental system was a private service that the Emperor Maximillian chartered in 1493 and the von Taxis family operated. For a fee, this system carried private as well as public correspondence, and did so rather well. The von Taxises' post "blanketed much of central Europe and the lowlands with relay stations, equipped them with fine horses, established regular schedules for their post riders, and made their post a model of efficiency."[4] The rise of the nation-state, however, eventually ruined this service as a transnational operation.

"The English post," as it has been said, "might conceivably have originated out of private or business correspondence organized by some private individual desirous of meeting the growing demand."[5]

---

3. CARL SCHEELE, A SHORT HISTORY OF THE MAIL SERVICE 83 (Smithsonian Institution Press 1970).

4. WAYNE E. FULLER, AMERICAN MAIL: ENLARGER OF THE COMMON LIFE 5 (University of Chicago Press 1972).

5. HOWARD ROBINSON, THE BRITISH POST OFFICE 6-7 (Princeton University

But it did not. Considerations of state security, and then later the possibility of Crown revenues, moved the English system to that of a government monopoly. This development is significant to the United States, for "[t]he framers must have had in mind the fact that for 150 years, both in Britain and in the colonies, the postal service had been a monopoly of the government . . . ."[6]

In England as in Europe, as government, cities, merchants, banks, churches, and universities developed at the end of the Dark Ages, so did organized communication by means of letters. But again, this organization was often no more than a somewhat systematic use of messengers. Henry VIII established the first permanent government postal service when he appointed a Master of Posts in 1516. This official managed a sketchy system of post roads with posts (relays) established at prescribed points.

Under Queen Elizabeth, efforts were made to establish the post as a government monopoly. Popish plots and the like were in the air, and treasonable correspondence could, it seemed, be more easily limited by government agents concentrated in a single system of communication. As said in a Parliament report, "With respect to correspondence conveyed by messengers other than their own, the Monarchs viewed it with great suspicion . . . . The frequency of disputed successions to the Crown, and the constant jealousy entertained of the Court of Rome, will assist in explaining their desire to prevent such correspondence."[7] One of the more significant private systems eliminated by these new measures was the Merchant Strangers' Post, which carried commercial correspondence both domestically and across the English Channel. For reasons of "good order" (state security), the Crown in 1591 established a monopoly respecting overseas postal operations. After Queen Elizabeth, the postal monopoly, for domestic and international correspondence, was continued as a Crown monopoly during the reigns of James I and Charles I.

After the English Civil War and under Cromwell, the post office was for the first time subject to parliamentary scrutiny and was a matter of public inspection and debate. Parliament announced that it was open to advice for improving the system "for the best interests and ease of the people."[8] Complaints and suggestions were received

Press 1948).

6. JOHN HALDI, POSTAL MONOPOLY: AN ASSESSMENT OF THE PRIVATE EXPRESS STATUTES 7 (American Enterprise Institute 1974).

7. ROBINSON, *supra* note 5, at 7 (quoting Secret Comm. on Post Office, House of Commons 4 (1844)).

8. *Id.* at 40.

respecting the quality and costs of mail delivery. Some suggestions were rather concrete; they consisted of petitions by entrepreneurs who specifically promised better service at lower rates, should they not be barred entry to the market by the government monopoly.

These petitions show that these entrepreneurs understood that the mail was a common good. At the same time, they understood that the mail did not have the qualities of a "public good" that only government could deliver. Instead, postal service was, as they knew, a good that private firms could and would provide. For instance, Clement Oxenbridge and Francis Thompson together promised to provide regular mail delivery and cut postage in half and were confident of a "freeness in law" that would permit this private enterprise. They described the service they proposed:

> [A] work both acceptable to the State and beneficial to the people, to contrive the abatement of these excessive rates; and thereafter maugre all oppositions and abuses of the monopolizer and his interest, they at first dash ventured on postage at the rate of 3d a letter beyond eighty miles, and 2d a letter within or to eighty miles; and to make return three times weekly.[9]

Parliament and Cromwell did reorganize the system but not so far as to terminate the monopoly. Probably the same idea as before, of using the postal monopoly to curtail sedition, was at play.[10] Apparently, Parliament was also interested in securing, as it did, monopoly rents for the Commonwealth. In any event, Parliament established new standards (specifying post roads and frequency of delivery), set new postal rates, provided for the free carriage of government mail, and continued the monopoly.

Parliament did not, however, entirely forgo the private sector option. By contract, Parliament let the operation of the system to the highest bidder. In return for his bid (in the form of an annual fee) and his management, this private contractor kept the postage he collected. (In the first auction, John Manley was the high bidder among seven bidders, with an offer of £10,000 annually.) In the annual fee, Parlia-

---

9. *Id.* at 42.

10. In 1657, Parliament established a postal system for the British Isles as a whole. A purpose of this unified system was to "discover and prevent many dangerous and wicked designs which have been, and are daily contrived against the Peace and Welfare of this Commonwealth, the intelligence whereof cannot be well communicated but by letter." *Id.* at 46, quoting II Acts & Ords. Interregnum 1110–13 (C. Firth & R. Rait, eds. 1911).

ment collected its monopoly rent. The contractor could not increase postal rates nor reduce service below the floor that Parliament had established. His gain was the amount by which his net revenues exceeded the annual fee, and this potential was his incentive to operate the system efficiently.[11]

Because of the Restoration, we cannot know whether the auction of the postal monopoly might have led to an efficient regulatory regime. After the Restoration, the Crown resumed control of the postal monopoly and, in the Charter of 1660, retained the monopoly in the form set by Parliament under the Commonwealth—but with a significant change. Charles II discontinued competitive bidding for the postal contract and commenced the practice of awarding the contract as a form of patronage. (As it turned out, the postal system in North America was first established according to the method of Charles II, when the Crown commenced postal service here as a monopoly and as an act of patronage.) Once the postal monopoly was awarded as a matter of patronage, this award no longer included a particular allowance (the auction to the lowest bidder) for competency and efficiency as it had under Cromwell. Instead, the Crown's allowance was for friendship, alliances, and flattery. In theory, patrons who had been awarded the postal monopoly (interested as they would have been in profits) should themselves have allowed for their incompetency by hiring good managers. But apparently they did not; the judgment of postal historians is that the British post was then not well managed.

The English postal monopoly was not airtight. For instance, commercial carriers of commodities would also carry private letters among their goods. The Penny Post—established by William Dockwa in London in 1680 as a private service—was instituted not as an illegal evasion but as a (presumably) lawful avoidance of the monopoly. This private service was hugely successful. Its innovations include d same-day delivery at a uniform rate of one penny. Other innovations were insurance (for items properly packaged) and the postmark. The responsive service of the Penny Post is shown in this directive respecting postmarks:

> The Undertakers have provided the stamps aforesaid to Mark the Hour of the Day on all Letters when sent out . . . and Persons are to expect their letters within one hour . . . . Letters coming too late at night shall be by Seven next

---

11. See George Priest, *The History of the Postal Monopoly in the United States*, 18 J.L. & ECON. 33, 36–37 (1975). See also STEPHEN G. BREYER, REGULATION AND

morning sent out, and Delivr'd by Eight and sometimes sooner . . . .[12]

This private service was as profitable as it was efficient. And so the Crown opposed Dockwa. The Duke of York, who stood to share the profits of the Penny Post if it were taken over by government, sued Dockwa for infringing the government monopoly. Dockwa argued that his service was so new and different as to constitute an "invention" excepted from the Crown monopoly under the Statute of Monopolies. The king's brother won the suit, however, and the Crown took over Dockwa's Penny Post.[13]

The British Post Office in North America

Organized postal service in North America was established under a patent granted in 1691 to one Thomas Neal, who paid a nominal amount for that privilege: six shillings and eight pence per year. Neal did not have a promising background; he was the Crown's "groom porter" (a manager of court games such as cards and dice), and he never set foot in North America.[14] He did, however, procure an agent of some ability: Andrew Hamilton, a Scottish merchant, who, after seven years in the colonies, had become governor of New Jersey. Under the patent, postal rates were the same as those set for England or such other rates "as the planters and others will freely agree to give for their letters or packets upon the first settlement of such office or offices."[15]

For the North American post, Hamilton established a general plan, in the form of a bill, that he presented to the various colonies. This bill provided for a general post office in the principal town in each colony, the postmaster of which Hamilton was to appoint. Each colony was to "ascertain and establish such rates and terms as should tend to quicker maintenance of mutual correspondence among the neighboring colonies and plantations, and that trade and commerce

---

ITS REFORM 286 (Harvard University Press 1982).

12. ROBINSON, *supra* note 5, at 73.

13. *Id.* at 74.

14. "Neal seems to have been one of those parasitic creatures who manage to bask in court favor and to batten upon sinecures. He was at one time or another, and to a large extent simultaneously, master of the mint, groom porter . . . , conductor of government lotteries, patentee of the postal service in North America, and commissioner of wrecks on the coast of Bermuda." William Smith, *The Colonial Post Office*, 21 AM. HIST. REV. 261, 261 (1916).

15. *Id.*

might be better preserved."[16] Government mail, however, was to be carried free.

Also, Hamilton's plan established the postal service as a government monopoly. But such a monopoly met resistance. In the colonies, the whole practice of awarding business monopolies as patents to Crown favorites was generally and heartily disliked.[17] Indeed, Virginia had proposed that "no person need employ the post office should other more convenient or cheaper modes of conveyance be available."[18] Still, as the Post Office was established in North America, it began as a monopoly along British lines.

Hamilton's work resulted in an operational postal system, consisting of weekly deliveries over a line of posts from Maine to Philadelphia. For the first six years, 1693–1699, the system suffered deficits that fell upon Neal.[19] In 1699, Hamilton traveled to England to join Neal in asking the Treasury to extend the monopoly to include overseas mail and to increase postal rates. During the course of the appeal, the British authorities observed that the monopoly seemed essential to profits and that the monopoly would be better respected by the colonists if supported by the whole majesty of the British government through a Crown monopoly as opposed to a patent monopoly. Neal, weary of losses, leapt at that idea and offered to sell his patent monopoly back to the Crown. After a time, the Crown repurchased the monopoly and operated it, down to the American Revolution, as a Crown monopoly.

It is familiar history that in 1753 Benjamin Franklin became postmaster in North America and thereafter organized the service into an effective and occasionally profitable outfit. At the time of the Revolu-

---

16. *Id.* For a comprehensive history of the British postal operations in North America, see WILLIAM SMITH, THE HISTORY OF THE POST OFFICE IN BRITISH NORTH AMERICA, 1639–1870 (Cambridge University Press 1920).

17. *See, e.g.*, Michael Conant, *Antimonopoly Tradition under the Ninth and Fourteenth Amendments: Slaughter-House Cases Reexamined*, 31 EMORY L.J. 785, 797–801 (1982). Antimonopoly clauses were featured in the charters of some of the colonies and, thereafter, in state constitutions. For instance, the Massachusetts Body of Liberties of 1641 provided: "No monopolies shall be granted or allowed amongst us, but of such new Inventions that are profitable to the Countrie, and that for a short time." THE COLONIAL LAWS OF MASSACHUSETTS 1672, at 35 (W. Whitmore ed., 1890). The 1776 Constitution of North Carolina stated that "perpetuities and monopolies are contrary to the genius of a free State, and ought not to be allowed." 5 THE FEDERAL AND STATE CONSTITUTIONS, COLONIAL CHARTERS AND OTHER ORGANIC LAWS 2788 (F. Thorpe ed., 1909).

18. Smith, *supra* note 14, at 262.

19. However, business improved so that in 1699 revenues covered all expenses except Hamilton's salary.

tion, however, the British postal service was unpopular, and its monopoly often ignored. A reason for this unpopularity was that the British Post was a Crown monopoly that operated with the aim of producing revenue. Intelligently and accurately, the Americans reasoned that such profits, forced from their purses by a coercive monopoly, in fact amounted to an unconsented tax. So, as they objected to the Stamp Act, the colonists objected to the postal monopoly. Also, postage rates were high. Consequently, people avoided and evaded (indeed flouted) the monopoly by private means—such as a traveler headed in the right direction—as such means were available.

The Constitution and the Postal Power

In 1774, William Goddard (a rival of Ben Franklin who, like Franklin and most postmasters, was a publisher) developed plans for a "Constitutional Post" among the colonies. Each colony would form its own postal committees to oversee local operations, and together these committees would select a postmaster general. This plan was to some extent executed. Post stations were established and riders hired, so that in 1775 the new postal system was said to be in operation, with thirty post offices from Maine to Williamsburg, Virginia.[20]

The Constitutional Post was, however, short-lived. Faced with an immediate need to maintain communications with the forces in the field and with the new states, the Continental Congress quickly established a postal system that superseded the Constitutional Post. This first U.S. postal system was established according to this resolution:

> That a Postmaster General be appointed for the United Colonies . . . with power to appoint such and so many deputies as to him may seem proper and necessary.

> That a line of posts be appointed under the direction of the Postmaster General from Falmouth in New England to Savannah in Georgia, with as many cross posts as he shall see fit.[21]

The Continental Congress also set postage rates and provided that any losses incurred by the new post would be "made good" by the Congress.[22] Ben Franklin was appointed postmaster general, and God-

---

20. U.S. POSTAL SERVICE, HISTORY OF THE UNITED STATES POSTAL SERVICE: 1775–1993 6 (United States Postal Service 1993).

21. 2 J. CONTINENTAL CONG. 208–09 (1775).

22. *Id.* at 209.

dard was named surveyor of posts. In the meantime, the British Post folded its operations and at Christmas 1775 quietly departed New York Harbor.

Under the Articles of Confederation, the national government was given the "sole and exclusive right and power . . . of establishing and regulating post offices from one state to the other throughout the United States, and exacting such postage on the papers passing through the same as may be requisite to defray the expenses of the said office."[23] The "sole and exclusive" language did not, as has been thought, vest a monopolistic power in government. Instead, this language simply denoted that the power was a national power held "exclusive" of the various states (as opposed to exclusive of the private sector).

The aspiration expressed in the Articles of Confederation was that the Post Office would be self-sufficient. The articles provided for "exacting such postage as may be requisite to defray the expenses of the said office."[24] But it was not self-sufficient. After the Revolution, the Post Office struggled. The postwar depression and the shortage of hard currency encouraged people to send letters outside the system as best they could, by friends or itinerants or whatever.[25] Also, the frank—the right to send mail free, claimed by postmasters as a privilege of office and by the Continental Congress for itself—was a drain on profits. Therefore, the Continental Congress was forced to subsidize the service.

In 1782, Congress passed a more comprehensive postal ordinance.[26] Among other things, this ordinance established a new system

---

23. Articles OF CONFEDERATION art. IX, § 4, cl. 4.

24. *Id.*

25. *See* FULLER, *supra* note 4, at 37. During the Revolutionary War, the postal service also experienced problems. Writing from Philadelphia, John Adams explained:

> A committee on the post-office, too, have found a thousand difficulties. The post is now extremely regular from north and south, although it comes but once a week. It is very difficult to get faithful riders to go oftener. And the expense is very high, and the profits, so dear is everything, and so little correspondence is carried on except in franked letters, will not support the office. Mr. Hazard is now gone southward, in the character of surveyor of post-office, and I hope will have as good success as he lately had, eastward, where he put the office into very good order.

Letter from John Adams to Thomas Jefferson (May 26, 1777), *in* 9 THE WORKS OF JOHN ADAMS 467 (Charles F. Adams ed., Books for Libraries Press 1969) (1856).

26. An Ordinance for Regulating the Post Office of the United States of America, 7 J. CONTINENTAL CONG. 383 (1800 ed.). *See also* LINDSAY ROGERS, THE

of differential rates based on miles carried, the number of pages of a letter, and weight. The frank was somewhat curtailed. Newspapers, however, were given a favorable fixed rate and free "exchange" privileges—that is, publishers could freely mail their newspapers among themselves. Also, the ordinance established a postal monopoly; it precluded the private carriage of letters or packets by any sort of regularly operating private postal service. Why did the Continental Congress establish a monopoly? Initially, there was a military need, the Revolutionary War. Otherwise, the British practice of operating a presumably self-sufficient government service had prepared the Continental Congress to continue the monopoly. And then, just after the Revolutionary War, there was no visible alternative of a nationwide commercial service.

The Constitution was ratified in 1787. It simply provides that "Congress shall have Power . . . To establish Post Offices and post Roads."[27] This text denotes that the postal power is a national power assigned to Congress. In its brevity, this text also indicates that Congress was delegated the authority to answer questions of whether, for what purposes, and how this power was to be used.[28]

Debate about the postal power was also sparse and does little more than underscore the breadth of the delegation to Congress— except that this debate perhaps indicates that the postal power should *not* be used to raise general revenues. At the Constitutional Convention, the establishment of the postal power as a source of general revenues was proposed. This proposal was that the Constitution's "acts for raising a revenue" include "a postage on all letters and packages passing through the general post office, to be applied to such federal purposes as they shall deem proper and expedient."[29] This revenue-raising feature, however, was deleted. The Committee on Detail simply provided that "[t]he legislature of the United States shall have the power . . . to establish post offices." Elbridge Gerry of Massachusetts moved to add "post roads" to this provision, and the motion was approved.[30] Thereafter, the Committee on Style expressed the

POSTAL POWER OF CONGRESS: A STUDY IN CONSTITUTIONAL EXPANSION 17–20 (Johns Hopkins Press 1916).

27. U.S. CONST. art. I, § 8, cl. 7.

28. The sparse language was also a probable product of the general idea, as expressed by Gouveneur Morris, of "put[ting] nothing into it [the proposed constitution], not very essential, which might raise up enemies." 4 MEMOIR, CORRESPONDENCE AND MISCELLANIES, FROM THE PAPERS OF THOMAS JEFFERSON 506 (T.J. Randolph ed., F. Carr & Co. 1829).

29. 1 MAX FARRAND, THE RECORDS OF THE FEDERAL CONVENTION OF 1787, at 243 (rev. ed. 1966).

30. 2 FARRAND, *supra* note 29, at 308. Two other amendments were offered

postal power in its present succinct form, to wit, "to establish Post Offices and post Roads." In the ratification debate in the states, the Post Office was simply not much of a topic.[31] The only significant reference was that of a possible abuse of the power by the postmaster general, who was alleged to have used his office to interfere with the distribution of newspapers critical of the proposed constitution.[32]

As the Constitution came into force, the postal system, as it had been established under the Articles of Confederation, had about seventy-five offices and 2,400 miles of post roads to serve 3 million people spread over a large territory. This system was continued in that Congress's first postal act simply provided that "the regulations of the post-office shall be the same as they were under the resolutions and ordinances of the [Continental Congress]."[33] Soon, however, there was pressure for "a more energetic system."[34]

A particular concern, as explained by Postmaster General Samuel Osgood, was that the postal system was not generating sufficient revenue. This small revenue was in part laid to a big and sparsely populated country. Osgood wrote that "the disbursed manner of settling the country may operate powerfully against the productiveness of the post-office."[35] Other problems were the frank (which "may

but defeated. "To regulate Stages on the post roads" was suggested but was not reported from the Committee on Detail. *Id.* at 326. Also, Benjamin Franklin proposed that there be added "a power to provide for cutting canals where deemed necessary." *Id.* at 615. This proposal also was defeated. *See id.* at 616.

31. James Madison referred to the post roads provision as "a harmless power . . . [that] may perhaps, by judicious management, become productive of great public conveniency." THE FEDERALIST NO. 42, at 287 (James Madison) (Jacob Cooke ed., 1961).

32. 16 THE DOCUMENTARY HISTORY OF THE RATIFICATION OF THE CONSTITUTION, App. at 560–61 (J. Kaminsky & G. Saladino, eds., 1986). George Washington was also perturbed by the Post Office's action. He wrote to John Jay: "It is extremely to be lamented that a new arrangement in the Post Office, unfavorable to the circulation of intelligence, should have taken place at the instant when the momentous question of a general Government was to come before the People." Letter from George Washington to John Jay (July 18, 1788) *in* GEORGE WASHINGTON: A COLLECTION 409 (William B. Allen ed., Liberty Classics 1988).

33. An Act for the Temporary Establishment of the Post Office, 1 Stat. 70 (1789).

34. SAMUEL OSGOOD, 1ST CONG., 2D SESS., PLAN FOR IMPROVING THE POST OFFICE DEPARTMENT (1790), *reprinted in* American State Papers, Post Office Department (class 7) 5 (Walter Lowrie and Walter S. Franklin, eds., Gales and Seaton 1834).

35. *Id.*

have extended too far") and the fact that perhaps the letter monopoly was not tight enough. For instance, "[s]tage-drivers and private post-riders may have been the carriers of many letters, which ought to have gone in the mail."[36] Profits might be increased, Osgood said, by increasing postage and by shoring up the monopoly.[37]

In 1792, Congress enacted a comprehensive postal ordinance, the first such statute under the Constitution.[38] In the enactment of this statute, much of the debate concerned whether Congress should delegate to the postmaster general the authority to establish post roads or to set postal rates.[39] Congress decided to delegate neither authority. Thus, the 1792 act had a long section that specified post roads and another that set postal rates. Also, the act continued and tried to strengthen the letter monopoly. The act precluded anyone outside the Post Office from carrying letters "[1] for hire or reward, on any established post road . . . [2] whereby the revenue of the General Post Office may be injured."[40] Excepted were letters that pertained to goods transported by commercial carriers and letters sent by "any private friend or special messenger."[41] Because the monopoly by its terms covered only letters and packets (packages of letters), newspa-

---

36. *Id.* In full, the reasons that Osgood cited for this small revenue were:

First. That there may be so few letters written . . . and the disbursed manner of settling the country may operate powerfully against the productiveness of the post-office.

Second. The franking of letters may have extended too far.

Third. Ship letters may not have been properly attended to.

Fourth. The rates of postage may have been too high in some instances and too low in others.

Fifth. Stage-drivers and private post-riders may have been the carriers of many letters, which ought to have gone in the mail.

Sixth. The postmasters may have consulted their own interest in preference to that of the public. *Id.*

37. *Id.* Osgood would have extended the monopoly not only to carrying letters for hire, but also "to all who receive and carry letters, whether with or without hire or reward." *Id.* Osgood added that "[s]ome few exceptions may be found necessary, where masters of vessels carry letters respecting merchandise under their immediate care and letter sent by a special messenger, by a friend, or by a common known carrier of goods." *Id.*

38. 1 Stat. 232 (1792).

39. 3 ANNALS OF CONG. 254 *passim* (1791).

40. An Act to Establish the Post Office and Post Roads Within the United States, 1 Stat. 236 (1792).

41. *Id.*

pers and packages were, as they had been before, outside the monopoly.

Under the Constitution, the first postal power issues of much debate pertained to federalism and to delegation of legislative power. One of these is a modern issue; the other is not. The federalism issue was whether the federal power "to establish post roads" also allowed the federal government (as opposed to the states) to construct such roads (and canals). That debate, of course, has no particular relevance today, because in the meantime the federal government has assumed the authority to subsidize all sorts of domestic works, including roads, by means of its spending power.

The delegation issue concerned whether Congress could delegate the postal power to the postmaster general. The Senate favored a broad delegation of an extensive authority to manage the postal system and to determine its growth by establishing postal routes. The House was opposed. It thought that an undertaking as large and as important as the postal service ought to be managed by Congress in its primary respects, such as determining postal routes, setting rates, and selecting local postmasters.[42] Of course, the local post office was a primary measure of a congressman's success in representing his district in Congress. The House, as we have indicated, won. Thus commenced a pattern of congressional hegemony in postal matters that lasted until 1970 and the Postal Reorganization Act of that year.

From the expanding nation, Congress received numerous petitions for postal routes and services that were dutifully recorded, voted on, and most often granted. Thus, the postal service grew rapidly, and Post Office officials struggled to keep up. As Congress provided for new post roads, these officials had to ensure that post offices were established along these routes, to assume that these routes, which were sometimes no more than forest trails, were passable, and to make and supervise innumerable contracts for the carriage of mail along these routes. In 1792, there were 6,000 miles of post roads and 195 post offices; by 1800, the country had over 20,000 miles of post roads and 903 offices. In 1819, Postmaster General Meigs, assisted by twenty-one postal clerks, opened 8,000 miles of new post roads; the next year he opened 500 new post offices.

This rapid expansion of postal service could be viewed optimistically, as a politically inspired but beneficial forced march, so that, as John Calhoun said, "a citizen in the west will read the news of Boston still moist from the press."[43] Or the expansion could be viewed

42. 3 ANNALS OF CONG. 254 *passim* (1791).

43. WESLEY E. RICH, THE HISTORY OF THE UNITED STATES POST OFFICE TO THE YEAR 1829, at 88 (Harvard University Press 1924).

not so optimistically, as by Thomas Jefferson, who had earlier advised that the Post Office "will be a source of eternal scramble among the members, who can get the most money wasted in their states."[44]

Deficit Financing and the First Defense
of the U.S. Postal Monopoly

The Postal Act of 1792 presumed that the Post Office would be self-sufficient and continued as a matter of course the government monopoly established by the British. Forty years or so later, these features were matters of dispute.

Initially, the Post Office was self-sufficient.[45] But in 1820 the postal system was greatly extended, over long routes in not so populous regions. That year the Post Office finished in the red. Thus began a long-standing debate in Congress: should the capacity of the postal service to generate revenues limit the service, or should the general treasury subsidize the service? The Post Office opposed subsidies; postal officials claimed that such underwriting would throw the Post Office on the Treasury.[46] Then as now, these officials feared that as they lost a measure of financial autonomy, they also lost managerial autonomy.[47]

As we have seen, the Constitution in no way requires the postal monopoly. Congress had continued the British practice, however, and established a letter monopoly as a matter of course as it first exercised its postal power. But some forty years later, in the 1830s and 1840s, the economy was larger and more organized than in 1792. Private firms now had the ability to offer postal service comparable to that provided by the Post Office. Indeed, private firms had commenced to offer a useful mail service. Newspapers needed a faster exchange of information than the Post Office provided. Commodity dealers (for

---

44. *Id.* at 128 (citing letter from Thomas Jefferson to James Madison dated March 6, 1796).

45. Over the years preceding 1820, the Post Office had produced a surplus of one million dollars. *See* FULLER, *supra* note 4, at 50.

46. *See* REPORT OF THE POSTMASTER GENERAL, 1843, 28th Cong., 1st Sess. 7–8 (1843).

47. Respecting modern Postal Service concerns about Treasury financing, see *infra* note 111 and accompanying text. In 1843, these concerns about loss of autonomy and control on the part of postal officials were stated as follows: "The department should sustain itself by its own income . . . . If this principle should be abandoned, and the Post Office made to lean upon the Treasury for support, I should fear that the constant vigilance so necessary for its useful administration would be abandoned by those charged with its affairs." REPORT OF THE POSTMASTER GENERAL, 1843, *supra* note 46, at 7-8.

cotton in particular) also needed market information (as from New York to New Orleans) more quickly. When the Post Office failed to respond to these needs, private firms did. These firms provided faster delivery by messenger services known as "express mail" companies.

These express mail services successfully avoided the monopoly. Earlier, the Post Office had believed that its private competition mainly consisted of transportation firms, such as coach and steamboat firms, that also undertook to carry mail. Therefore, in 1825 the statute establishing the monopoly was amended to preclude competition by the owners or operators of these transportation firms.[48] But as amended, the postal act might be read as precluding the competition of *only* those transportation firms. The private express companies saw this loophole. Consequently, they carried mail by messengers who were merely ticketed passengers (and of no affiliation with transportation firms) on coaches and trains. The Post Office asked the courts to enjoin this practice. The courts, however, viewed the monopoly suspiciously, read the postal act in the same manner as the private express companies, and refused to enjoin these companies in their postal operations.[49]

As had commercial interests, citizens in friendly correspondence also commenced to abandon the Post Office in favor of private firms, and in 1841 postage sales decreased.[50] In part, high postal rates may have caused this decrease. As historian Wayne Fuller illustrated the high rates, the postage on a letter from New York City to Troy, New York, was eighteen cents; the freight on a barrel of flour was twelve cents.[51] Also, the decrease in postal business may be attributed to a public perception of an inequity in the system.

Postal costs were significantly less than postage paid on the short, high-volume urban routes in the East.[52] Profits from these

---

48. An Act to Reduce into One the Several Acts Regulating the Post Office, § 19, 4 Stat. 107 (1825); An Act amendatory of the Act Regulating the Post Office, 4 Stat. 238 (1827).

49. *See* United States *v.* Adams, 24 F. Cas. 761 (S.D.N.Y. 1843) (No. 14,421); United States *v.* Kimball, 26 F. Cas. 782 (N.D.N.Y 1844) (No. 15,531); United States *v.* Pomeroy, 27 F. Cas. 588 (N.D.N.Y. 1844).

50. The Post Office largely attributed this decrease in revenues to the competition of private express companies. In his report of 1843, the postmaster general explained that the principal cause for the decreased revenues was "the operation of numerous private posts, under the name of expresses, which have sprung into existence within the past few years." REPORT OF THE POSTMASTER GENERAL, *supra* note 46, at 600.

51. FULLER, *supra* note 4, at 61.

52. The modern Postal Service has acknowledged that "in high-delivery-density-urban areas . . . the margin between postal costs and postage

routes became a cross subsidy for the expansion of postal service into the West, for rural service, and for service to special postal clients such as newspapers. Eastern customers, therefore, felt that much of the cost of the postal system was unfairly taxed to them, and so they enthusiastically commenced to evade the monopoly.[53]

In the 1840s, then, the elimination of the postal monopoly was a matter of considerable debate. A private firm, the Wells and Company messenger firm, offered to take charge of all Post Office operations and to offer a uniform postage of five cents (as compared with the current postage of eighteen cents). Later in that decade, a commentator said that if the Post Office were to continue, "[it] must be enabled *to recommend itself to the public mind*. It must secure to itself a virtual monopoly, by the greater security, expedition, punctuality, AND CHEAPNESS, with which it does its work, than can be reached by any private enterprise."[54] Altogether, in the 1840s the situation resembled that of England two centuries past under Cromwell, when private firms had offered to "maugre all oppositions and abuses of the monopolizer."

The Post Office response was in part bombastic: it spoke of the private express as "plunderers of the public revenues."[55] In another part, the Post Office tried to justify the monopoly. First, it argued that postal service was in the "public interest" in the same manner as, say, the military. As there was a government monopoly respecting the military, so must there be a similar monopoly respecting postal service.

The flaw in this public interest argument is that while postal service is indeed in the "public interest," same as the military, the Post Office is unlike the military in that postal service can be priced and charged to its beneficiaries while military service cannot. In terms of public choice, this flaw is to conflate the public interest and "public goods." Many items, such as groceries and medicine, serve the public interest, but these items can be and are delivered by private firms. Only certain items, like national defense, are public goods that the private sector can neither price nor deliver according to price.[56]

---

rates is greatest . . . ." STATUTES RESTRICTING THE PRIVATE CARRIAGE OF MAIL AND THEIR ADMINISTRATION, REPORT BY THE BOARD OF GOVERNORS TO THE PRESIDENT AND CONGRESS COMMITTEE PRINT, HOUSE COMMITTEE ON POST OFFICE AND CIVIL SERVICE, H.R. DOC. NO. 622–9, 93d Cong., 1st Sess. 123 (1973) [hereinafter STATUTES RESTRICTING THE PRIVATE CARRIAGE OF MAIL].

53. FULLER, *supra* note 4, at 62.

54. JOSHUA LEAVITT, CHEAP POSTAGE 13 (Freeman and Bolles 1848) (emphasis in original), *quoted in* HALDI, *supra* note 6, at 10.

55. REPORT OF THE POSTMASTER GENERAL, *supra* note 46, at 5.

56. In 1970, this distinction was precisely noted in the "Kappel Report" on the Post Office: "All Government services must be paid for one way or anoth-

Obviously, letters resemble groceries more than they resemble the national defense. Thus, the Post Office was confused about public goods. But private firms were not. They understood that postal service was in the public interest. But they further understood, and laid claim to, their superior ability to serve this interest.

The second justification for the monopoly was the now famous "cream-skimming" argument, which the Post Office then expressed as follows:

> These private expresses will only be found to operate upon the great and profitable thoroughfares between great commercial points, whilst the extremes are left to depend upon the operations of the United States mail, crippled and broken down for the want of means.[57]

This cream-skimming argument was weak at a few points. First, the fact that cream was being skimmed was, from the viewpoint of the skimmees, the very inequity in the system.

Second, there was little if any empirical support for the assumption that private firms would not operate "at the extremes." In fact, then and certainly later, there was evidence to the contrary.[58] The most famous piece of evidence is the Pony Express, which was commenced over a remote Western frontier as a private service and only later, after its initial success, taken over by the Post Office.

Third, the cream-skimming justification could be, and was, turned around to form the basis of a constitutional attack on the postal monopoly. As mentioned earlier, the Constitutional Convention in Philadelphia considered the proposal to enlarge the Constitution's "acts for raising a revenue" to include "a postage on all letters

er; most can be paid for only though taxes. Unlike national defense or public health, however, postal services can be and always have been sold to users." THE PRESIDENT'S COMMISSION ON POSTAL ORGANIZATION, TOWARDS POSTAL EXCELLENCE 22 (Government Printing Office 1968) [hereinafter KAPPEL REPORT].

57. REPORT OF THE POSTMASTER GENERAL, *supra* note 46, at 6.

58. According to Carl Scheele:

> Private express lines were a principal feature of western communications during the early period of settling the Far West. While the Government provided mail service on "principal routes," the express companies offered supplemental and rival service . . . . Such express services were offered by both individuals or small organizations as well as the large national companies such as the Adams, American, Nations, and Wells Fargo concerns.

SCHEELE, *supra* note 3, at 83.

and packages passing through the general post-Office, to be applied to such federal purposes as they shall deem proper & expedient."[59] This proposal, however, was rejected. Instead, the means of raising general revenues, as listed in Article I, section 8, became "taxes, duties, imposts, and excises"—and not postage.[60] Now, as cream was produced from urban Eastern routes for the benefit of Western routes, was not revenue being raised in the East and transferred West to maintain public works there? It would be hard to say no, especially considering our Revolutionary War position that the revenue-raising feature of the British monopoly, which transferred money from the colonies and to England, was in effect a tax. Therefore, the argument in 1840 was that the Post Office's monopoly actually produced general revenues and was therefore unconstitutional.[61] "If they [the people] wish to have their letter transported for less than it really costs," it was said, "let the deficiency be paid out of the general treasury."[62]

---

59. 1 FARRAND, *supra* note 29, at 243.

60. The argument here, as stated in the 1840s, was that Article One's "enumeration" of the means of raising general revenues "confines the government to them." And that "we think it clear neither of the indefinite terms, taxes, duties, imposts, and excises, can include post-office charges." *The Post Office Monopoly*, THE MONTHLY LAW REPORTER 1849, at 385, 396.

61. *See id.* at 385.

62. During this 1840s debate, the courts seem to have viewed the constitutionality of the postal monopoly as an open question. *E.g.*, United States *v.* Pomeroy, 27 F Cas. 588, 590 (N.D.N.Y. 1844) (No. 16,605) (Noting, but not deciding, "the far more important question . . . whether the constitution confers upon congress the power to restrain a private citizen from carrying letters in competition with the mail of the United States"). By 1910, however, the constitutionality of the postal monopoly was taken to be settled. In Williams *v.* Wells Fargo & Co., 177 F. 352, 356 (8th Cir. 1910), the court stated that "[w]hile at one time questioned, there remains no doubt that, under the constitutionality authority granted, Congress may, as it has done, reserve to the postal department of the government a monopoly. . . ."

In reaching this conclusion of constitutionality, the courts do not appear to have given full-dress treatment to the arguments for or against the monopoly. Instead, the courts felt that the weight of history determined the outcome. In the *Wells Fargo* case, the court relied on the history of the postal monopoly in England and in North America. 177 F. at 358. In United States *v.* Kochersperger, 26 F. Cas. 803 (E.D. Pa. 1860) (No. 15,541), the court noted that "[n]o government has ever organized a system of posts without securing to itself, to some extent, a monopoly of the carriage of letters and mailable packets." Otherwise, the courts simply deferred to the power of Congress to itself determine the scope of its postal power. In this regard, the leading decision is *In re* Orlando Jackson, 96 U.S. 727 (1878), where the Supreme Court, while addressing whether Congress had the power to exclude lottery tickets from the mail, generously defined Congress's postal power.

The congressional reaction to all this—the deficits, the success of private firms, the attacks on the monopoly, the public demand for lower rates—was the Postal Acts of 1845 and 1851.[63] This reaction was not especially circumspect. The act of 1851 reduced postage but simultaneously precluded the Post Office from closing offices or routes because of a deficit and also required the Post Office "to establish new post offices and place the mail service on any new mail routes established . . . in the same manner as if this act had not been passed."[64] This last provision was no doubt in response to what some congressmen had considered the "imperious rule" of the Post Office: the Post Office would not open post roads as ordered by Congress until the postal system produced the necessary revenues.[65] Still, someone had to pay, and someone in addition to the usual skimmees; with the new reduced rates, that much cream was not available. The money, of course, would have to come from Congress, and in the years ahead Congress habitually subsidized postal operations with appropriations from the Treasury. Thus, the idea of the Post Office as a self-sufficient operation was abandoned, at least until 1970.[66]

Additionally, the act of 1845 retained the postal monopoly and bolstered it yet again, this time by eliminating the loophole through which the private express companies had passed. Without a limitation on the manner of delivery, as had previously been the case, the act made unlawful the regular delivery of letters by "private express" firms in competition with the Post Office. In this form, the monopoly has continued to the present time.[67]

63. An Act to Reduce the Rates of Postage, to Limit the Use and Correct the Abuse of Franking Privileges, and for the Prevention of Frauds on the Revenues of the Post Office Department, 5 Stat. 732 (1845); An Act to Reduce and Modify the Rates of Postage in the United States, and for other Purposes, 9 Stat. 587 (1851).

64. An Act to Reduce and Modify the Rates of Postage in the United States, and for other Purposes, 9 Stat. 587, 590 (1851).

65. FULLER, *supra* note 4, at 56. The practice of Congress was freely to establish such routes as its constituents might ask; for instance, Congress commissioned a route in East Tennessee "from Newmarket, in Jefferson County, by Blaine's Crossroads, Lea's Springs, Powder Spring Gap, and Joseph Beelor's to Tazewell, in Claiborne County." *Id.*

66. From the 1840s, "when deficit financing became a way of life for the Post Office," until 1970, postal expenditures exceeded postal revenues "[d]uring all but 17 years." KAPPEL REPORT, *supra* note 56, at 22.

67. Today, the letter monopoly is established as follows:

Whoever establishes any private express for the conveyance of letters or packets, or in any manner causes or provides for the conveyance of the same by regular trips or at stated periods over

Postal Missions and Methods

Respecting its missions and methods, we should keep in mind that whatever it did, the Post Office has for much of its history done so grandly: "In the nineteenth century, the domestic federal government was, for the most part, the Post Office and [it] was the major federal organization for the distribution of economic and political benefits."[68]

Postal Missions. The general mission of the Post Office is to distribute written communications. But this mission has had several included missions. A brief, but not necessarily exclusive, listing of these included missions is provided below.

Dissemination of intelligence. When the Constitution was ratified, the very project that was the United States compelled an immediate postal mission. This mission was the dissemination of "intelligence." To the framers, intelligence was a term of art, meaning information about government and politics. The Post Office, as George Washington informed Congress, was an "instrumentality in diffusing a knowledge of the laws and proceedings of the Government."[69] In relation to consensual government, intelligence was intended to provide a better-informed consent and to reduce distrust of the new government. Newspapers carried by the Post Office throughout the nation (either free or at a reduced rate) were a principal means of this dissemination of intelligence.[70]

> any post route which is or may be established law, or from any city, town, or place, between which the mail is regularly carried, shall be fined not more than $500 dollars or imprisoned not more than 6 months, or both.

18 U.S.C. § 1696(a).

68. SELLING THE REORGANIZATION OF THE POST OFFICE 2 (Case Study, John F. Kennedy School of Government, Harvard University, 1984) [hereinafter SELLING THE REORGANIZATION].

69. George Washington, Third Annual Address (October 25, 1791), *in* 1 A COMPILATION OF THE MESSAGES AND PAPERS OF THE PRESIDENTS, 1789-1897, at 107 (James D. Richardson ed., United States Government Printing Office 1898), quoted in RICH, *supra* note 43, at 68.

70. In 1791, in a House debate on the Postal Act, the postal function of disseminating political information, by newspapers and other means, was explained as follows:

> The establishment of the Post Office is agreed to be for no other purpose than the conveyance of information into every part of the Union . . . . That information has proved highly serviceable to the present Government; for wherever

Diffusion of knowledge. As the print media grew in this country, it grew as a source of the literary, cultural, and scientific attainments of the American people. Promoting these attainments came to be viewed as a postal mission. As well as newspapers, books and magazines were primary sources of cultural and scientific knowledge. But while newspapers were subsidized from the outset, books and magazines were not. For sixty years, books were at best a blind spot in postal laws (these laws did not refer to books). When books were not a blind spot, they were disfavored or banned from the mails. Their bulk was one reason; their content (fiction) seemed to be another.

In 1814, Postmaster General Meigs forbade the mailing of books, later explaining that "the mails were . . . overcrowded with novels and the lighter kind of books for amusement."[71] In 1851, though, an act of Congress specifically admitted books to the mails, and the next year, an additional act provided specially reduced rates for books.[72]

Unlike books, magazines were from the start generally mailable, but at higher rates than newspapers. In 1825, however, Congress reduced magazine rates.[73] Fuller reports that Congress was moved to take this action because of the increased interest of Americans for magazines.[74] The next twenty-five years were a "seedtime" for these publications, when their number rose from less than a hundred to about six hundred.[75]

Commerce. The first comprehensive postal act of the United States, the act of 1782 under the Articles of Confederation, explicitly

> the newspaper had extended, or even the correspondence of the members, no opposition has been made to the laws; whereas, the contrary was experienced in those parts which the information had not penetrated; and even there the opposition ceased, as soon as the principles on which the laws had been passed, were made known to the people.

3 ANNALS OF CONG. 254 (1791).

71. Ironically, postal policy had inspired the "lighter" kind of books. Literally and figuratively (as entertainment), the books were light. They were printed in a newspaper format and mailed as newspapers in order to gain newspaper rates. As such, these books were the first paperbacks. For the publishers, these paperbacks were a profitable enterprise. The American public, on its part, acquired a new taste for novels and for this cheaper price of books. FULLER, *supra* note 4, at 124.

72. An Act to Reduce or Modify the Rates of Postage in the United States, and for Other Purposes, 9 Stat. 587 (1851); 10 Stat. 39 (1852).

73. An Act to Reduce into One the Several Acts Regulating the Post Office, 4 Stat. 79 (1825).

74. FULLER, *supra* note 4, at 125.

75. *Id.* at 123.

cited commerce as a mission. This act recited that "the communication of intelligence with regularity and dispatch from one part of these United States to the other is essentially requisite to the safety as well as the commercial interest thereof."[76] The "commercial interest" has continued as an obvious mission of the Postal Service. Today, about 80 percent of first-class mail consists of business correspondence.

Personal correspondence. This mission, as winsomely described in a congressional report, was that of "affording to friends, residing in different portions of the Union, the sweets of frequent friendly interchanges of sentiment and good feeling so desirable; and thus, by free and familiar intercourse, drawing still closer the bond of union."[77]

A bond of union. Montesquieu's observation that democracy was viable only within a small territory, greatly worried the Framers.[78] This worry inspired Madison's *Federalist* No. 10, which addresses and supports the viability of a large republic.[79] Binding this large republic was viewed as a primary mission of the Post Office. The post roads, therefore, were not simply arteries for the diffusion of "intelligence," knowledge, commerce, and "friendly interchanges of sentiment." These roads were also seen as sinews that bound the nation.[80]

Censorship. Unlike the missions described earlier, censorship has been more problematic. Given that newspapers, books, and magazines greatly affected and reflected the moral and political tone of the country, it was inevitable that Congress would be urged to use its postal power to preserve the right sort of moral and political tone. In the second half of the nineteenth century, Congress commenced to do so.

Cheap second-class postal rates subsidized the distribution of pornographic materials, and there had been a surge in the distribution of these materials. Also, mail advertising was offering a newer mode of contraception: Charles Goodyear's newly perfected rubber products. Before 1863, the Post Office had at times assumed the power to "exclud[e] from the mails obscene and scandalous printed material."[81] In 1863, Congress explicitly gave the Post Office this pow-

76. An Ordinance for Regulating the Post Office of the United States of America, 7 J. OF CONG. 383 (1800 ed.).

77. FULLER, *supra* note 4, at 81.

78. THE FEDERALIST NO. 9, at 52–56 (Alexander Hamilton) (Jacob Cooke ed., 1961).

79. THE FEDERALIST NO. 10 (James Madison) (Jacob Cooke ed., 1961).

80. *See, e.g., supra* note 70.

81. DOROTHY G. FOWLER, UNMAILABLE 56 (University of Georgia Press 1977).

er in an act that provided that "no obscene book, pamphlet, picture, print, or other publication of a vulgar and indecent character, shall be admitted into the mails of the United States."[82] Materials pertaining to contraception were made unmailable in 1873.[83]

Post Office censorship also includes political censorship. The first efforts at such censorship were, however, defeated. In 1835, the rise of antislavery sentiments alarmed the Executive Branch. According to the report of the Postmaster General, "Ferocious bands were in the possession of ample funds and a powerful press, and for the first time that instrument had been seized upon to be wielded against the peace of the South."[84] Thereafter, President Andrew Jackson asked Congress to refuse "transmission through the mails of certain publications of dangerous tendency."[85] But Congress refused to do so on the grounds that the postal power did not extend that far.

The Senate committee assigned Jackson's proposal explained that the First Amendment "withdraws from Congress all right of interference with the press, in any shape or form whatsoever."[86] The committee, therefore, was "constrained to adopt the conclusion that Congress has not the power to pass such a law . . . ."[87] On these grounds, Congress rejected the bill. The Post Office itself, however, soon closed the mail. In the years before the Civil War, southern post-

82. Act of Mar. 13, 1863, § 16, 13 Stat. 507.

83. An Act for the Suppression of Trade in, and Circulation of, Obscene Literature and Articles of Immoral Use, 17 Stat. 598 (1873).

84. 12 CONG. DEB. 3795–96 (1836). In 1835, the Postmaster General reported to Congress:

> A large number of individuals have established an association in the Northern and Eastern States, and raised a large amount of money for the purposes of effecting the immediate abolition of slavery. One of the means resorted to has been the printing of a large mass of newspapers, pamphlets, tracts, and almanacs containing exaggerated, and in some instances false, accounts . . . . These they attempted to disseminate throughout the slave-holding states by the agency of the public mails. *Id.*

85. *Id.* at 36. In his message to Congress, President Jackson had stated: "I must also invite your attention to the painful excitement produced in the South by attempts to circulate through the mails inflammatory appeals addressed to the passion of slaves, . . . calculated to stimulate them to insurrection, and to produce all the horrors of servile war." *Id.* at 1723. Jackson then proposed "a law as will prohibit . . . the circulation in the southern States, through the mail, of incendiary publications intended to instigate the slaves to insurrection." *Id.* at 1724.

86. *Id.* at 72.

87. *Id.*

masters would not deliver antislavery publications—newspapers included—and sympathetic postmasters general abided this practice. This postal action abetted the diverging intellectual environments that led to war.[88]

Early in this century, attitudes in Congress changed, and that body enacted legislation that closed the mail to "seditious" publications. The Espionage Act of 1917 provided that "[e]very letter, writing, . . . newspaper, pamphlet, book or other publication . . . containing any matter advocating or urging treason, insurrection, or forcible resistance to any law of the United States is hereby declared to be nonmailable."[89] The Post Office applied this provision according to a bad-tendency test. Under this test, speech critical of public laws was said to have the tendency to promote resistance to the laws. Accordingly, publications such as socialist newspapers were denied second-class mail privileges because of their opposition to American involvement in World War I.[90] During the cold war, this same bad-tendency theory of censorship was used amid a general purge of "un-American activities."[91]

Today, the mail is still subject to moral and political censorship. More stringent applications of the First Amendment, however, have restricted the scope of this censorship. The "obscene" publications that can be barred from the mail are more tightly defined.[92] Similarly, the bad-tendency test respecting political materials has been replaced with the "clear and present danger" doctrine that is more protective of speech.[93] Furthermore, courts no longer allow the Post Office simply to assume a power of censorship. Congress must precisely authorize such censorship, if it is done at all.[94]

Postal Methods. Outside the censorship area, the missions of the Post

88. *See* CLEMENT EATON, FREEDOM OF THOUGHT IN THE OLD SOUTH 196–215 (Duke University Press 1940); FOWLER, *supra* note 78, at 21–41.

89. 40 Stat. 217 (1917).

90. *See* FOWLER, *supra* note 81, at 114–15.

91. *Id.* at 144.

92. *See* Miller *v.* California, 413 U.S. 15 (1973).

93. *See* Brandenburg *v.* Ohio, 395 U.S. 444 (1969).

94. *See* Hannegan *v.* Esquire, 327 U.S. 147 (1945). Also, using the Post Office to inculcate morality has been criticized, most notably by Justice Harlan of the Supreme Court, on federalism grounds. In Roth *v.* United States, 354 U.S. 476 (1957), Justice Harlan concurred in upholding a state law against certain obscene materials, but dissented respecting the federal postal law that made similarly obscene materials unmailable. He explained:

> [T]he interests which obscenity statutes purportedly protect
> are primarily entrusted to the care . . . of the States. Con-

Office as described above have not been questioned. In a sentence, the Postal Reorganization Act of 1970 catches and continues most of these missions. The act provides that "[t]he Postal Service shall have as its basic function the obligation to bind the nation together through personal, educational, literary and business communications of the people."[95] But while the postal missions have not been generally questioned, the methods used in service of these missions have.

The methods subject to question have been several and various. But most of them can be placed together in two large categories. One category is political methods, in the sense of congressional management of postal affairs. The Post Office was too important to the country, and to the constituents of legislators, for Congress to take much of a hands-off attitude. Early on, Congress reserved to itself the power to set postal rates, to determine postal routes, to hire postmasters, and eventually to set the pay and conditions of work for the whole postal work force. Another political control was the subsidization of postal operations by direct congressional appropriations. Postal officials viewed these congressional controls (operational controls and subsidies) with chagrin. Indeed, before and during the reorganization of 1970, they would claim that this "politicization" of postal operations accounted for the Post Office's many ills.

In another category, postal methods have been questioned on grounds of equity and economic efficiency. The various missions served by the Post Office have their costs. Who is to bear them? The Post Office differs from most government agencies in that its services can be priced and charged to the beneficiaries. Many of these beneficiaries, however, are special clients, such as newspapers, publishers, or advertisers. These "special mailers" have the incentive (the focused benefits of special postal rates) and the organization sufficient to lobby as special interests. Another large postal client, of course, is the general public. For this client, the benefits and burdens (postage) are more diffuse. Organization is difficult because of communication and free-rider problems. Quite likely, then, the general public will bear all their costs and then some, while postal service to special mailers will be subsidized. This, of course, is exactly how the postal power has been deployed and how postal services have been arranged.

gress has no substantive power over sexual morality. Such powers as the Federal Government has in this field are but incidental to other powers, here the postal power, and are not of the same nature as those possessed by the states.

Id. at 504–05. As Harlan explained, a "blanket ban" by the federal government was less dangerous to speech than action among the individual states where there was room for a beneficial heterodoxy. *See id.* at 505.

95. 39 U.S.C. § 101.

The monopoly in first-class mail that the Post Office came into, and thereafter vigorously defended, allows the Post Office to pass postal costs to the general public without fear of losing this clientele to private firms. Therefore, the Post Office has used this monopoly to cause the general public to pay the full costs of its mail, and then some, to subsidize the service provided special mailers. As the courts have noted, the first-class monopoly has been operated to "'confer[ ] pecuniary advantages of great consequence' upon certain classes of mail, always at the expense of first class."[96] In contrast, special mailers are not restricted by a postal monopoly and have enjoyed subsidies.

Postal subsidies for special mailers have been arranged in two ways. One way is overtly to provide special rates, as by the frank, through which public officials use the mail without charge, or as by the below-cost rates assigned second-class mail. Another method of subsidization is through the accounting and allocation of postal costs. A special mailer, such as advertisers, may be charged its direct costs. But by conventions of Post Office accounting, direct costs have been only a fraction of total postal costs. These other costs are indirect costs (or "institutional costs") that have usually amounted to half of total postal costs. The Post Office's practice has been to allocate these indirect costs to first-class mail, and thus to the general public. Consequently, special mailers (who use second-class and third-class mail) avoid the full costs of postal service.

The Reorganization of 1970

In 1970, the history of postal operations included large deficits, troubled labor relations, dissatisfaction with service, and the inequity of using first-class mail to subsidize special mailers. Reform had languished, however, possibly because of World War I, the Great Depression, and World War II. But in 1970, the time for reform had come, partly because the Post Office, at least in its higher management, wanted a particular form of reorganization and had lobbied hard for it and partly because events—a notorious breakdown of postal service in Chicago and then the illegal postal strike of 1970 that precipitated a national emergency—focused attention on postal problems.[97]

The time may have been ripe for the greatest overhaul of postal

96. National Ass'n of Greeting Card Publishers v. United States Postal Serv., 569 F.2d 570, 587 (D.C. Cir. 1976) (quoting Lewis Publishing Co. v. Morgan, 299 U.S. 288, 303–04 (1913)).

97. In Chicago, the world's largest post office (thirteen stories and sixty acres of work space) had simply broken down. For weeks the mail was not

operations in our history, but there were problems. One of which was a certain irrationality that has occasionally distorted our political processes. This irrationality starts with the push of special interests with various and contradictory demands. To be sure, the aspiration in our Constitution is to provide a legislative structure that forces a certain rationality, in the form of a compromise (in the direction of the general public interest) of these competing demands.[98]

The modern administrative state, however, has rearranged constitutional structure so to sometimes defeat this aspiration of beneficial legislative compromise. Rather than Congress itself working out the differences among competing interests, the alternative that the administrative state offers is for legislators to avoid the political costs by delegating the compromises to an agency. This passing of the buck may be done in two ways. One way is through legislation that is so general that it resolves nothing and provides no direction to the agency. Such legislation will simply instruct the agency to work "in the public interest."

Another way of passing the legislative buck is to enact statutory directives that on their face seem detailed and precise, but on closer inspection simply represent a wish list of various and conflicting demands of special interests. In these instances, Congress has neither resolved the differences among these interests nor moved toward the public interest. Instead, Congress has simply recorded the various special interest demands in a statutory form, and passed them on, as a list of "diverse objectives," to an agency.[99]

In several ways, the Postal Reorganization Act of 1970 does

---

delivered and there was a backlog of over 10 million pieces. Inefficient management, methods, and equipment were the problems in Chicago.

98. THE FEDERALIST NO. 10, *supra* note 79.

99. In Panama Refining Co. *v.* Ryan, 293 U.S. 388 (1935), the Supreme Court explained how a statute consisting merely of "diverse objectives broadly stated" amounts to a failure by Congress to meet the primary legislative function that the Constitution has invested in it. In *Panama Refining*, Congress had delegated an authority to regulate the transportation and sale of oil. In reviewing the delegation, the Court explained that its task was to ensure that Congress, rather than the agency to which it had delegated power, had done the primary legislative work of establishing national policy. In the delegation in question, Congress had, to be sure, included a number of directives and goals, such as to "induce" labor-management unity, to increase productivity, to reduce unemployment, to eliminate unfair competitive practices, and so on. To the Court, these "diverse objectives broadly stated" simply showed that Congress had established no policy at all, but had instead merely listed and passed on to an agency the conflicting goals of various special-interest groups. *See id.* at 418.

establish postal policy. The act clearly eliminates patronage and clearly commits the terms of employment of the postal work force to collective bargaining.[100] But in other parts, the act is more nearly a recital of various and diverse objectives. For instance, the act denotes the purpose of ending the inequity in postal rates; however, the act also provides that "institutional costs," which are usually counted as one-half of total postal costs by the Postal Service, may be charged to first-class mail.[101] The act acclaims greater productivity through automation but then requires that automation be subject to, and controlled by, collective bargaining.[102] The act speaks against special interest groups but then establishes a Postal Service Advisory Commission that must consist of these groups.[103] The Postal Reorganization Act of 1970, therefore, inclines not toward rationality but toward the "crisis in rationality" that comes about when "the state is unable to reconcile the numerous specific demands of competing economic groups with a more systematic interest in the rational administration of certain necessary functions."[104]

The Players. As postal officials accurately noted, the average citizen would not be particularly influential in effecting the reorganization he wanted.[105] The groups that would be influential were the postal managers themselves, the postal unions, and the special mailers. These groups and their agendas are discussed below.

   Postal managers. This group planned and led the political bat-

---

Later, in National Television, Inc. v. United States, 415 U.S. 336, 342 (1974), the Court endorsed the principle that "Congress is not permitted to . . . transfer to others the essential legislative function with which it is . . . vested." Because the delegation in question (the Independent Offices Appropriations Act) had left the agency free to pick among competing interests "in the manner of a legislative body," the delegation was to that extent unconstitutional.

100. 39 U.S.C. § 1002 (eliminating patronage); 39 U.S.C. § 1206 (providing for collective bargaining).

101. 39 U.S.C. § 3622(b). How this section allocates postal costs to various clients is discussed at notes 164–165, *infra*.

102. 39 U.S.C. § 2010.

103. Four members of the Advisory Council are from labor, four from "major mail users," and three are "representatives of the public at large." 39 U.S.C. § 206.

104. Charles G. Benda, State Organization and Policy Information: The Reorganization of the Post Office Department 67 (Harvard University, Program on Information Resource Policy 1978).

105. As previously noted, for the general public the benefits and burdens (postage) of postal service are quite diffuse. Among the general public, organization is difficult because of communication costs and free-rider problems.

tle.[106] In 1967, the Postmaster General, Lawrence O'Brien, called for a drastic change in Post Office organization. Rather than "props for the tottering structure," he called for rebuilding it.[107] Thereafter, top postal management asked for a special commission of "distinguished citizens" with "broad managerial expertise" to study postal reform.[108] President Johnson appointed such a commission, which was led by Frederick Kappel, formerly the chief executive officer of AT&T, and which otherwise consisted of members largely drawn from the business community. Not surprisingly, the Kappel Commission found:

> The Post Office's principal failure is one of management. . . . The organization of the Post Office as an ordinary cabinet department guarantees that the nominal managers of the Post Office do not have the authority to run the postal service. The important management decisions of the Post Office are beyond their control and therefore cannot be made on the basis of business judgment.[109]

The "important management decisions" (about revenues, rates, and labor) had long been out of the hands of postal officials and in the hands of Congress.[110] Labor (the postal unions) and special postal clients (publishers, direct mail advertisers, and so forth) had estab-

---

Accordingly, Bill Dunlop, who headed the Post Office's marketing program for reorganization, explained the difficulty in marshaling public support:

> The average Joe was for reorganization because it was reform. And we did try to generate grass-roots support through our ads. We asked people to join CCPR [the Citizens Committee for Postal Reform] or send a donation. But the response rate was poor . . . so there was no getting around the fact that we weren't a true citizens' movement.

SELLING THE REORGANIZATION, *supra* note 68, at 34.

106. *See, e.g.*, Pt. 2, *Postal Modernization Hearings*, *supra* note 2, at 231–32. *See generally* BENDA, *supra* note 104; SELLING THE REORGANIZATION, *supra* note 68. The postal managers undertook what they referred to as a "massive selling job." An internal memorandum to Postmaster General Blount explained: "It should be accepted that a massive selling job will be required for any plan that will result in Congress relinquishing control over the bulk of postal operations." *Id.* at 9. The selling was organized by a marketing specialist who produced a master marketing plan. *See id.* at 11–15.

107. BENDA, *supra* note 104, at 20.

108. *Id.* at 51–52.

109. KAPPEL REPORT, *supra* note 56, at 33.

110. The extent to which control of the Post Office was seen as out of the hands of postal managers, and in the hands of Congress, was shown in this

lished special relations with Congress. These groups, therefore, could bypass postal managers and instead bargain with Congress. This legislative bargaining not only was a loss of management control but also was seen as producing both special benefits for special interests and undue costs for the Post Office. For instance, Congress had consistently granted union requests for pay raises "in a process totally independent of productivity, work rules or most other matters normally discussed during wage negotiations."[111]

Postal managers expressed, and the Kappel Commission adopted, the view that the Post Office could be rehabilitated if it was under the postal managers' control rather than congressional control. The commission rather extravagantly predicted that "at least 20% of postal costs—well over a billion dollars—would be saved if the Post

---

dialogue between Rep. Steed, chairman of the House Postal Appropriations Subcommittee, and Postmaster General O'Brien:

> REP. STEED: [W]ould this be a fair summary: that at the present time, as the manager of the Post Office Department, you have no control over your workload, you have no control over the rates of revenue, you have no control over the pay rates of the employees that you employ, you have very little control over the conditions of the service of these employees, you have virtually no control . . . of your physical facilities . . . ?

> POSTMASTER GENERAL O'BRIEN: Mr. Chairman, I would have to generally agree with your premise, . . . that it is a staggering list of "no control" . . . .

UNITED STATES POSTAL SERVICE, HISTORY OF THE UNITED STATES POSTAL SERVICE: 1775-1993, at 16 (United States Postal Service 1993).

Congress had consistently approved pay increases, and done so without regard to management concerns such as productivity. Also, Congress had micromanaged some postal services. For instance, in 1969 legislation respecting terms of employment "was amended at the behest of the employee unions to specify a Monday-through-Friday regular work week (assigned by seniority) and special split-shift limitations. This had sudden and serious cost and scheduling implications for the Post Office." KAPPEL REPORT, *supra* note 56, at 40.

111. KAPPEL REPORT, *supra* note 56, at 40. Or, for instance, a special in-county rate set by Congress for newspaper delivery allowed the delivery of "a five pound Sunday newspaper in the city of publication for a penny." *Id.* at 39. Congress had never developed the capacity to manage the Post Office, so the undue influence of special interests is not surprising. "In 1968, Congress did not have one person on all of its staff who studied postal rates full-time. Instead every few years a handful of congressmen listened to thousands of pages of testimony from powerful second class, non-profits, and third class mailers—all of whom brought in their own accountants to demonstrate that they were paying more than the Post Office's cost of handling the mail." SELL-

Office management was free to plan and finance postal operations."[112] The items that management wanted to control were postal rates, labor relations, and financing.[113]

Postal officials wanted to control rates because they felt that Congress set rates too low (because of special interest bargaining) and adjusted the rates too late (because of delays inherent in the legislative process). Respecting finances, postal officials hoped to rely on postal revenues and bonds rather than congressional appropriations. In management's view, the problems of "treasury financing" were threefold: (1) it led to a "detailed congressional and executive involvement with all postal matters" that made internal management difficult; (2) it made capital planning (and improvements such as automation and modern facilities) difficult; and (3) it removed incentives for efficient operations.[114]

These various arguments against legislative control and in favor of Post Office control were expressed in a rhetoric of "business practices." This talk was extended, perhaps reflexively, to include the form of restructuring favored by postal managers. A board of governors was to have general control of the Post Office. This board (rather than the U.S. president) was to appoint the postmaster general (the CEO).[115] But in the business world, there are matters of substance beyond these matters of form. In real business, decisions are calibrated both according to competition and according to information provided by customers free to choose other, more responsive suppliers. Terms and conditions of labor are calibrated according to the productivity of competitors. Inefficient allocations of resources are subject to bankruptcy. The Post Office, even after reorganization as planned by the postal managers, remained a government program not subject to these disciplines. Therefore, for the Post Office, "business practices" did not correspond to the practices of a private firm.

Instead, "business practices" were terms of art in the 1970 reorganization. These words referred simply to an allocation to the Post Office, as opposed to Congress, of major portions of a service that otherwise continued as a government operation. In controlling this operation, postal managers might indeed be more knowledgeable

ING THE REORGANIZATION, *supra* note 68, at 4.

112. KAPPEL REPORT, *supra* note 56, at 24.

113. Also, postal managers wanted to end the system of selecting postmasters by means of patronage. *See id.* at 40–41.

114. *See id.* at 142. Respecting capital planning, a complaint was that "the Post Office must stand in line with far more urgent national needs in order to obtain capital; . . . all postal funds, including revenues from the users, must pass through the appropriations process." *Id.* at 35.

115. *See id.* at 55.

and more responsive than Congress. But again, this better control is the traditional argument for administrative agencies and administrative control, as opposed to congressional control, of a government program. It is not particularly an argument respecting business practices.

The work force. In 1970, the Post Office had nearly 716,000 employees, about a quarter of the (civilian) federal employment.[116] Most of these employees (88 percent) were union members. But partly because of disparities of work (as between carriers, clerks, messengers, and maintenance) and location (urban and rural), the work force in 1970 was split among eleven unions that had not always got along.[117] Nonetheless, postal employees and their unions had a great deal of power. The work force was spread throughout each of the nation's congressional districts. Also, postal employees had a long history and experience in organization and political action, and their unions were active, high-spending lobbyists.[118] Postal employees were, therefore, a force to be reckoned with in the reorganization of 1970.

For much of the nineteenth century, though, the postal work force was of a different quality. Then, it largely consisted of postmasters. In 1850, for instance, about 90 percent of the postal workers were postmasters who had gained their position through patronage.[119] These postmasters generally had some standing in the community and some other position, such as publisher of the local newspaper or proprietor of a general store, that related to postmastership. Each postmaster usually had a small staff of two or three clerks whom he hired and for whom he determined pay and working conditions.

Toward the end of the nineteenth century, though, Post Office employment began to change in the direction of clerical and blue-collar employees who worked under more industrial conditions. The change commenced in 1863 with the beginning of urban free delivery that required city post offices with a large work force. Mail volume increased, while the collecting and sorting of mail continued to be

---

116. The work force was composed of 308,000 clerks, 195,000 city carriers, 49,000 rural carriers, 48,000 mail handlers, 22,000 maintenance workers, 11,000 motor vehicle workers, and 6,000 special-delivery messengers. Also, managerial and support employees were about 76,000 in number. *See id.* at 100.

117. *See id.* at 112. *See generally* JOHN WALSH & GARTH MANGUM, THE LABOR STRUGGLE IN THE POST OFFICE: FROM SELECTIVE LOBBYING TO COLLECTIVE BARGAINING 43–93 (M.E. Sharpe, Inc. 1992).

118. SELLING THE REORGANIZATION, *supra* note 68, at 5.

119. *See* BENDA, *supra* note 104, at 37 (citing Bureau of the Census figures).

done by hand. The strain increased and the workday lengthened: "Postal workers no longer wore tall beaver hats to work and could no longer afford silver-topped canes. They worked 'longer hours in overcrowded, ill ventilated and poorly lit workrooms.'"[120]

The year that urban free delivery began, New York postal workers formed a "social and mutual benefit" association.[121] Other such associations followed, and soon these associations were active in Congress. In the 1880s, these associations gained legislation that classified postal jobs, set pay levels, and provided an eight-hour day with overtime pay. This political activity increased and continued. In 1904, for instance, postal workers were credited with preventing the reelection of the chairman of the House Ways and Means Committee.[122] In large part, the political activities of postal workers were directed toward higher pay. To this end, they strove to separate their pay from postal revenues. For instance, in 1927 they backed a bill that declared that "compensation of postal employees shall be adequate and just and, together with working conditions, shall be based upon American standards, without regard to postal revenues."[123]

Postal managers resisted the associational and political activities of the postal work force. These officials felt that employee appeals to Congress unduly impaired their authority, and in 1895, the postmaster general ordered that employee petitions to Congress had to be sent through his office.[124] In 1903, President Roosevelt followed with an executive order to that effect.[125]

In 1912, however, Congress passed the Lloyd-LaFollette Act, which ended the gag-order practice.[126] This act also more generally improved conditions of government employment. It established the right of civil-service employees to organize collectively (so long as they did not strike) and provided that they receive notification of

---

120. WALSH & MANGUM, *supra* note 117, at 46 (quoting KARL BAARSLAG, HISTORY OF THE NATIONAL FEDERATION OF POST OFFICE CLERKS (Allied Printing 1945)).

121. KAPPEL REPORT, *supra* note 56, at 114.

122. *See* BENDA, *supra* note 104, at 60.

123. 68 CONG. REC. 2741–42 (1927). This bill was not passed. Under the Postal Reorganization Act of 1970, however, the postal unions finally separated their pay from postal revenues. Under reorganization, the measure of compensation is not postal revenues. Instead, postal workers are to be paid according to wages prevailing outside the Postal Service, in comparable parts of the private sector. 39 U.S.C. § 1003.

124. *See* WALSH & MANGUM, *supra* note 117, at 74.

125. *See id.* at 75.

126. 37 Stat. 360 (1912).

charges and a hearing before they were discharged.[127] The Post Office blistered the act. In his annual report, Postmaster General Burleson stated,

> [T]he conduct of these [employee] organizations at this time is incompatible with the principles of civil service and the good administration of the Postal Service. They are fast becoming a menace to public welfare and should no longer be tolerated or condoned. It is earnestly recommended that the [Lloyd-LaFollette Act] be repealed.[128]

Later, the hostility of postal managers to these employee activities softened, and in 1921, the postmaster general announced measures to "humanize" the service. These measures included employee councils and improved working conditions.[129]

After World War II, the friction between the postal work force and postal managers increased again. The political activity of the postal unions continued, so that "[i]n the twenty-five years preceding 1970, postal employees received 18 pay increases."[130] In the face of this political activity, postal managers again worried about their lack of control. As previously noted, these officials complained that their authority—to contain costs by controlling pay,[131] to require reasonable levels of performance (productivity lagged far behind pay), and to commence automation—was limited. The employees' political clout had created working conditions that were not amenable to efficient operations. Automation and mechanization were sorely lacking. Training was deficient to nonexistent. There were few incentives for merit. Not only were promotions not especially linked to merit, but also there were virtually no promotions: eight out of ten workers retired from the Post Office at the same level they had entered.

In a dramatic illustration of the labor problems in the Post Office, the illegal strike of 1970 forced President Nixon to declare a national emergency and activate both the military reserve and the National Guard to deliver mail. But whatever injury the postal strike caused the public, the strike benefited the postal workers. After the strike began, postal unions and the Executive Branch commenced high-level negotiations. President Nixon forwarded Congress a memorandum of agreement produced by these negotiations, and

---

127. *See id.* at 414.

128. 1917 POSTMASTER GEN. ANN. REP. 2.

129. *See* BENDA, *supra* note 104, at 63.

130. *Id.* at 68.

131. As a component of total postal costs, labor costs increased from 70 percent in the early 1940s to 80 percent in the late 1960s. *See id.* at 68.

thereafter, the memorandum became part of the Postal Reorganization Act of 1970.[132] (Indeed, that act's full title is the Postal Reorganization and Pay Adjustment Act of 1970.) The concessions rolled into the act included a 14 percent pay increase and a compression (to eight years) of the time for advancement through pay grades.[133] The memorandum of agreement also provided for collective bargaining and binding arbitration, and these features became part of the act.[134]

Special mailers. From the start, clients with special deals were a part of Post Office operations. Politicians had the frank. Newspapers got free mail services by virtue of "exchange privileges" and otherwise enjoyed reduced rates. "Exchange privileges" referred to the practice whereby newspaper publishers exchanged copies of their papers postage free. The privilege was a means of transmitting news and information among newspaper publishers, who in turn passed this information to their readers. The origins of the privilege probably lie in the fact that the early postmasters in North America themselves had the frank and were publishers. With the advent of wire services, though, the exchange privileges were not so useful and came to an end. Apart from, and more important than, exchange privileges was the fact that the general distribution of newspapers to general customers was subsidized by special rates. The first postal act under the Constitution (the act of 1792) set newspaper rates at one cent per copy for distances less than 100 miles, as compared with six cents for a one-page letter sent less than 30 miles.

These benefits that newspapers enjoyed were, of course, justified in terms of appropriate postal missions such as disseminating

132. Pt. 2., *Postal Modernization Hearings, supra* note 2, at 1083–85.

133. As agreed to by the Executive Branch and the postal unions, the 14 percent pay raise was in two steps. In the first step, the agreement provided for a governmentwide pay increase of 6 percent, which was enacted as the Federal Employees Salary Act of 1970, Public Law 91–231, § 2(a)(1), 84 Stat. 195 (1970). The second step was an additional 8 percent pay increase for postal workers, which was included in the Postal Reorganization and Pay Adjustment Act, Pub. L. No. 91–375, § 9, 84 Stat. 719, 784 (1970).

The pay raise was probably not solely the result of the strike. The unions had sought it before the strike, and the White House understood that at some point it would use the pay raise to settle union opposition to postal reorganization. White House assistant John Erlichman explained: "Nixon felt strongly about postal reform and he felt strongly that the pay raise issue gave him leverage. He knew that sooner or later he would have to give in to the unions and he wanted postal reform in return." SELLING THE REORGANIZATION, *supra* note 68, at 31.

134. 39 U.S.C. §§ 1201–09.

political intelligence and general knowledge. Newspapers, though, were influential interest groups. For instance, newspaper publishers were credited with writing the legislation in 1879 that established the present classification system for the mails and that reserved special rates for the newspapers' medium of second-class mail.[135] As previously discussed, books and magazines eventually got special rates, and their publishers joined the ranks of special clients.

In the 1920s, another group of special mailers came forward. In 1925, the Direct Mail Advertising Association, consisting of advertisers that used third-class mail, was formed. Perhaps because these advertisers (sometimes referred to as "junk mailers") could not (as publishers could) claim special rates because of appropriate postal missions, the agenda of this group had a different focus. They lobbied for bulk rates, and in 1925 Congress provided those rates. Direct advertisers also lobbied to reduce the postal costs (some part of which they might bear) associated with free or reduced rates to various other postal clients. The advertisers argued that revenues generated by the Post Office should not underwrite these special rates; instead, legislative appropriations should cover such rates.[136] Eventually, these direct mailers succeeded; the Postal Policy Act of 1958 declared that "public service items . . . should be assumed directly by the Federal Government and paid directly out of the general fund of the Treasury . . . ."[137] And as we shall see, the Postal Reorganization Act of 1970 continued this practice.[138]

As postal deficits grew in the twentieth century,[139] postal managers commenced to oppose special mailers, especially in relation to the subsidies those mailers received. The Kappel Commission referred to these subsidies as "irrational and often inequitable."[140] Because postal managers generally opposed "treasury financing," they also opposed the efforts of special mailers to have postal deficits covered by congressional appropriations. Moreover, the interests of second-class mailers, who as quality mailers received the best rates, differed from those of third-class "junk" mailers. So, in the years just before the 1970 act, the conflict among postal managers and special mailers, and

---

135. *See* BENDA, *supra* note 104, at 92.

136. The agenda was "that postage rates on paid mail matter shall be determined by the cost of the service given such mail matter, exclusive of all free services and public welfare projects which have been or shall hereafter be adopted in connection with the Postal Service." 68 CONG. REC. 2741–42 (1927).

137. 72 Stat. 136 (1958).

138. See *infra* text accompanying note 156.

139. After World War II, the postal deficit grew from less than $200 million to over $1.5 billion in 1970. 1970 POSTMASTER GEN. ANN. REP. 146-49.

140. KAPPEL REPORT, *supra* note 56, at 22.

among special mailers themselves, focused attention on these mailers and their special deals. But as we shall further see, the attention paid these deals seems to have come to naught.

The Postal Reorganization and Salary Adjustment Act of 1970. In 1969, President Nixon advised Congress: "Total reform of the nation's postal system is absolutely necessary . . . . The ills . . . cannot be cured by partial reform."[141] Reorganization under the act was indeed significant, consisting mainly of a reallocation of control. Control was relinquished by the Congress and reassigned to the Postal Service, to a new Postal Rate Commission, to a process of collective bargaining, and to the courts. Still, because of the pull of 200 years of history, the specific and powerful influence of special interest groups, and the only diffuse representation of the public interest, the "total reform" of which President Nixon spoke was not as thorough as it could have been.

The "business-practices" format. In many respects, the 1970 act conformed to the agenda of the postal managers. Much as the Kappel Commission had recommended, the Postal Service was removed from the president's cabinet and placed under an eleven-member Board of Governors. Nine members of this board are "outside directors" selected by the president.[142] The other two members are "inside directors," namely the postmaster general and the deputy postmaster general. The board has (or shares) a primary operational control respecting capital improvement, rates, and the pay and performance of employees.[143] Also, the board selects the postmaster general.[144] Otherwise, the act relieved the Postal Service of a number of obligations imposed on other government agencies. With some few exceptions, "no federal law dealing with public or Federal contracts, property, works, officers, employees, budgets, or funds . . . shall apply to the exercise of the powers of the Postal Service."[145] This omnibus exclusion from laws ordinarily applicable to federal agencies includes the Administrative Procedure Act.[146]

With this new organization, postal officials would, they said, be

141. Special Message to the Congress on Postal Reform (May 27, 1969), *in* Pub. Papers 406, 406 (1969).

142. 39 U.S.C. § 202(a).

143. *Id.* at §§ 401–04.

144. *Id.* at § 202(c).

145. *Id.* at § 410.

146. However, rate-making decisions are subject to the standards of judicial review provided by section 706 of the Administrative Procedure Act. 5 U.S.C. § 706.

able to run the Postal Service according to business methods, thus improving service while saving a billion dollars a year. But when the act was debated in Congress, individual legislators were not so sanguine. Their doubts, however, seemed not well focused. To some, the "business-practices" format appeared inconsistent with the public service function of the Postal Service. As grandly expressed by Representative Wright,

> The Post Office has one purpose in being, and one purpose only—service to the people of the United States . . . . Today, the advocates of change are trying to reverse this most basic, fundamental and time honored concept.[147]

An error in this sentiment is that while postal service does indeed benefit the public, it is not a public good such as to require the government to provide it. Another error is that the new Postal Service was not fully converted to business practices. As we said, in real business, management decisions are calibrated according to competition and according to information provided by customers free to choose other and more responsive suppliers; terms and conditions of labor are calibrated according to the productivity of competitors; and efficient allocations of resources are aided by the bankruptcy of inefficient allocators.

These true business methods were not a feature of the new Postal Service. Thus, on further thought, the question that bothered legislators was that they were being asked to relinquish control of the Post Office, but to whom and to what? To an outfit disciplined by business practices? Was this really the case? These worries were vaguely expressed like this: "We have serious doubts at least, about the managerial board of directors that works so well for General Motors . . . being capable of administering the public interests . . . ."[148]

These legislators, it seems reasonable to think, doubted that the new Postal Service was subject to business controls, and they wanted an effective control. Their idea of a good control was that of a Postal Service run by one person who was in turn responsive to the president. As Senator McGee explained, "[A] Postmaster General who has the complete responsibility and is directly responsible to the president, is an understandable, necessary price that we have . . . to pay to preserve the public interest in a national postal monopoly."[149] The McGee-Fong bill, therefore, substituted presidential responsibility for

---

147. BENDA, *supra* note 104, at 117.

148. Pt. 2, *Postal Modernization Hearings, supra* note 2, at 1405.

149. *Id.* at 1410.

that of "a board of directors that meets . . . in a moonlighting opera-tion."[150]

This McGee-Fong proposal did not clear Congress. (It was raised again, and again unsuccessfully, amid a $1 billion bailout for the Postal Service in 1976.) Also, the sense of that proposal has most recently been the subject of constitutional litigation. In *Silver v. United States Postal Service*, an individual was convicted of mail fraud.[151] In defense, he alleged that the Postal Service's power was flawed because the effective control of the service was in the hands of the postmaster general, who had not been appointed by the president as the Constitution's Appointment Clause requires.[152] The three-judge panel split on this issue.

Two judges were of the opinion that control did lie in the Board of Governors and that its members were appointed consistently with the Appointments Clause. The dissent, however, was of the opinion that the board had only a formal control. Functionally, the postmaster general had control, and thus he ought to be subject to presidential appointment. The dissent's general position was that "a closer exami-nation shows that the Governors by themselves . . . do not function as a `Head of Department' within the management scheme of the Postal Service."[153] But again, this was a dissent. The court's majority acceded to the formal line of authority that the act establishes.

Self-sufficiency. As proposed by the postal managers (who had long opposed "treasury financing") and as agreed to by the postal unions (who in turn got their pay separated from revenues), the 1970 act provides for a "self-sufficient" Postal Service. The act states that "postal rates and fees shall provide sufficient revenues" to cover postal costs. Capital expenditures are to be financed by bonds rather than congressional appropriations.[154] The act's only permanent

150. *Id.* at 1403. While the president appoints the Board of Governors, this board is not a part of his cabinet. Therefore, the president is *not* free to remove board members—as he would a postmaster general who is a cabinet member—simply because he disagrees with their performance or policies. *See* Humprey's Executor *v.* United States, 295 U.S. 602 (1935).

151. 951 F.2d 1033 (9th Cir. 1991).

152. U.S. CONST. art. II, § 2, cl. 2.

153. 951 F.2d at 1044. Nine of eleven members of the Board of Governors are appointed by the president; the other two members are the postmaster general and the deputy postmaster general. Thus, the nine members subject to presidential appointment were not completely in formal control of the Postal Service.

154. These bonds are tax exempt. They are not, however, backed by the full faith and credit of the United States. 39 U.S.C. § 2005(4)(5).

appropriation covers the revenues forgone where the Postal Service provides services, such as free delivery to blind people or reduced rates for educational publications, required of it by Congress.[155]

Rate making. The postal managers proposed that rate making be transferred from Congress and to them, with Congress—for a sixty-day period after a rate was set—retaining a veto. The Direct Mailers Association objected to this proposal. They were opposed to a discretionary rate-making power in the Postal Service and favored a check on that discretion. Given the delays and the lack of expertise in Congress, the sixty-day legislative veto did not seem much of a check to them. Therefore, these mailers submitted a counterproposal: (1) a rate commission, separate from the Postal Service, to pass on rates (this instead of a legislative veto); (2) procedural controls consisting of administrative-type hearings (open hearings on the record and free of ex parte contacts) for rate making; (3) substantive controls consisting of statutory guidelines for calculating rates; and (4) judicial review to ensure that the substantive and procedural controls were followed.[156] These various provisions, as the U.S. Court of Appeals for the District of Columbia would come to say, had a general aim of ensuring equity in postage rates.

The inequity in postal rates arose from the cross subsidies that ran from first-class mail (where the monopoly is) to special mailers. As said by the courts, these cross subsidies have "'conferred pecuniary advantages of great consequence' upon certain classes of mail, always at the expense of first class."[157] In 1955, the Post Office adopted a rate-making formula in which this cross subsidy was spelled out:

> Second-class mail should produce revenues sufficient to recover 50 percent of costs assigned to it . . . ; third-class mail should recover 75 percent of such costs; and . . . the difference should be reallocated to first-class mail and domestic airmail in recognition of their higher service and value factors.[158]

In this formula, the "value factor" mostly refers to the fact that among

---

155. *Id.* at § 2401(c). The act did, however, provide for a number of transitional appropriations. *Id.* at §§ 2004, 2401.

156. *See Postal Modernization Hearings, supra* note 2, at 560–65.

157. *See* National Ass'n of Greeting Card Publishers *v.* United States Postal Serv., 569 F.2d 570, 588 (D.C. Cir. 1976) [hereinafter *National Ass'n of Greeting Card Publishers I*] (citations omitted).

158. Post Office Dep't Cost Ascertainment Report for FY 1955, *quoted in National Ass'n of Greeting Card Publishers I*, 569 F.2d at 587 n.61.

patrons of first-class mail, there is not much price elasticity of demand. Undoubtedly, the reason for this inelasticity is that the postal monopoly extends only to first-class mail. In other words, if postage is too high, special mailers (not subject to the monopoly) can turn to private firms. The general public, however, has to deal with the Postal Service, and therein is the higher "value factor" in that mail.[159]

This practice of charging higher rates within the postal monopoly has always been objected to and resisted. Before the Revolutionary War, the colonists claimed that these rates were an unconsented to tax. Today, these rates are simply said to be unfair. The burden of cross subsidies, however, falls largely on a group—the general public—that has only a diffuse representation in Congress. In 1970, however, one special mailer, the bulk-rate mailer, had come to pay more than its share of postal costs. The postage on bulk-rate mail amounted to 200 percent of the postal costs attributed to it, while second-class mail paid only about half its costs.[160] So, for this and other reasons, direct mailers opposed the discretionary authority of postal managers to allocate rates among various classes of mail. Hence, they counterproposed administrative, statutory, and judicial controls to curtail this discretion.[161]

Consistent with this proposal, Congress eliminated the legislative veto provision, established a rate commission to pass on rate hikes, allowed for administrative hearings and procedures for rates, furnished statutory guidelines, and provided for judicial review.[162] But there is considerable diversity and slippage in the substantive rate-making guidelines that Congress provided, enough to create a "crisis in rationality" of the sort previously described.

The act's substantive guidelines, as established by section

159. Put more technically, the Postal Service has market power over first-class mail because the statutory monopoly makes the price elasticity of supply essentially zero. *See* William E. Landes & Richard A. Posner, *Market Power in Antitrust Cases*, 94 HARV. L. REV. 937 (1981).

160. *Postal Modernization Hearings, supra* note 2, at 1419.

161. *Id.* at 561–65.

162. The process by which the Postal Rate Commission operates in relation to the Postal Service to set postage rates is complex. The Postal Service Board of Governors initiates rate proceedings by requesting a rate change. A new rate is determined by the Postal Rate Commission, and then submitted back to the Board of Governors as a recommendation. The board may then approve, reject, modify, or allow under protest the recommended rate. 39 U.S.C. § 3625(a). A useful description of the process by which rates are set, and how judicial review of that process is obtained, is found in *National Ass'n of Greeting Card Publishers I*, 569 F.2d at 588.

3622(b), require that rates be set according to:

> (1) the establishment and maintenance of a fair and equitable schedule;
> (2) the value of the mail service actually provided . . . to both the sender and the recipient, including but not limited to the collection, mode of transportation, and priority of delivery;
> (3) the requirement that each class of mail or type of mail service bear the direct and indirect postal costs attributable to that class or type plus that portion of all other costs of the Postal Service reasonably assignable to such class or type;
> (4) the effect of rate increases upon the general public, business mail users, and enterprises in the private sector of the economy engaged in the delivery of mail matter other than letters;
> (5) the available alternative means of sending and receiving letters and other mail matter at reasonable costs;
> (6) the degree of preparation of mail for delivery . . . performed by the mailer . . . ;
> (7) simplicity of structure [for the system];
> (8) the educational, cultural, scientific, and informational value to the recipient of mail matter; and
> (9) such other factors as the Commission deems appropriate.[163]

Calculation of postage rates is not simple. The identification and attribution of postal costs are difficult. Otherwise, postal history has established certain practices and words and phrases peculiar to postal rate making. In light of these practices and these semantics, it is apparent that the enumerated standards of section 3622(b) are at odds. The first standard, subsection (1) of section 3622(b), speaks of fairness and equity, which in postal history refers to the inequity and unfairness in charging the general public with more than its share of postal costs. Consistent with this direction of fairness and equity, subsection (3) "requires" that each class of mail bear all the costs attributable to it. But then subsection (8) states that the educational value of materials should be taken into account, a statement that seems to refer to the historical practice of subsidizing second-class mail. More important, subsection (2) provides that the "value of service" may be taken into account in determining rates, presumably referring to the

---

163. 39 U.S.C. § 3622(b).

old practice of calculating first-class rates according to an elasticity of demand formula. That practice, of course, had set the table for cross subsidies.

The act's rate-making guidelines turn out to be, to say the least, less than precise. An institution that no doubt understood this, and that at the same time saw its own special role as that of infusing rationality into these sorts of schemes, was the U.S. Court of Appeals for the District of Columbia Circuit.[164] In 1976, the Postal Service had in three rate hikes raised first-class postage from three to thirteen cents. In *National Association of Greeting Card Publishers v. United States Postal Service*, the D.C. Circuit reviewed the third rate hike and in doing so tried to make sense of the act's rate-making guidelines.[165] The court first looked for a *Grundnorm* in the act and found one: fairness. This mandate of fairness, the court found, precluded cross subsidies. In this regard, the court first noted the historic practice of cross subsidies and the unfairness therein: "Discrimination in postal rate making in favor of certain preferred classes of mail and to the great disadvantage of first class mail has long been a part of our postal system."[166] Then, the court found that the 1970 act was intended to end this practice. In this regard, the court looked to legislative history that showed "a central and express aim of both Houses of Congress to . . . get 'politics out of the Post Office.'"[167] Lobbying for cross subsidies had been a primary source of these politics. Thus, the court found further evidence that, in the Reorganization Act of 1970, Congress meant to end those subsidies.

The court then applied this general view of the act to the case before it. The Rate Commission had allocated about half the total postal costs on a "cost-of-service" basis. The remaining 50 percent, however, was allocated on a "value-of-service" basis. Value of service was calculated according to an "inverse elasticity rule" that assigned the remaining costs to first-class mail.[168] Petitioners had argued against this inverse elasticity rule by explaining that it "preserv[ed]

164. That court stated: "The ratemaking process under the Act has reflected a constructive interaction between the Postal Service and this court that has, to a large extent, developed and sharpened the governing concepts." National Ass'n of Greeting Card Publishers v. United States Postal Serv., 607 F.2d 392, 396 (D.C. Cir. 1978) [hereinafter *National Ass'n of Greeting Card Publishers II*].

165. *National Ass'n of Greeting Card Publishers I*, 569 F.2d 570 (D.C. Cir. 1976).

166. *Id.* at 587.

167. *Id.* at 588.

168. The looseness in this operation was later described, in *Greeting Card II*, as follows: "The remaining 51 percent was 'reasonably assigned' by two USPS employees using . . . a vague formula that consisted essentially of

historical rate differentials and otherwise unduly and unreasonably discriminate[d] against first-class mail."[169] In view of the act's emphasis on fairness, the court accepted this argument as correct.

The court squared this result with the terms of section 3622(b) by reading subsection (3) respecting cost of service as the one "concrete" part of section 3622(b).[170] The court noted that section 3622(b)(3) provided that cost of service was a "requirement" and made no such provision respecting any other factor.[171]

The court was now prepared to say how the Postal Rate Commission had erred. It had erred in the second step of its rate-making process when it had allocated half of the total postal costs to first-class mail according to a value-of-service ("what the traffic will bear") standard. That standard could not be used, the court reasoned, because of section of 3622(b)(3)'s "requirement" that cost-of-service accounting be carried as far as possible. The court directed the Postal Service and the Postal Rate Commission to drop its value-of-service approach and to use instead indirect cost accounting to allocate fully postal costs according to cost-of-service factors.[172]

Three years later, the Postal Service and the Rate Commission (now in its fourth rate-making proceeding) had not conformed to the above decision. Consequently, in *National Association of Greeting Card*

---

value-of-service considerations." 607 F.2d at 400.

169. *National Ass'n of Greeting Card Publishers I*, 569 F.2d at 584. Value of service as determined by an inverse relation to elasticity of demand ("Ramsey pricing") is not an unconventional means of setting rates in order to cover fixed costs. *See National Ass'n of Greeting Card Publishers II*, 607 F.2d at 402–03; BREYER, *supra* note 11, at 52–55. Nevertheless, the Postal Service context is unconventional because of its statutory monopoly, the cross subsidies running from it, and the "dominant objective in Congress" of eliminating those subsidies. *National Ass'n of Greeting Card Publishers II*, 607 F.2d at 404. For an economic criticism of the inverse elasticity rule in postal operations, see William B. Tye, *Postal Service: Economics Made Simple*, 3 POL'Y ANALYSIS & MGMT. 63 (1983).

170. *National Ass'n of Greeting Card Publishers I*, 569 F.2d at 580.

171. *Id.* at 585.

172. The single "key" that the Postal Service had used to measure cost of service was volume variability. The court noted that there were other keys, such as "weight, volume and number of pieces of mail" and so forth that the Postal Service might also use. *Id.* at 583. The court also understood that there would be a small residuum of institutional costs that could not be "reasonably" allocated as indirect costs. These costs, the court found, might be allocated by other than cost-of-service principles. In this regard, the court stated that "[t]he residuum of costs is subject to discretionary allocation in accord with the noncost factors set forth in the Act." *Id.* at 589.

Publishers II,[173] the Court of Appeals strongly restated *National Association of Greeting Card Publishers I.* In this restatement, the court emphasized that the 1970 act left no room for an "unstructured . . . discretion in the USPS staff to allocate more than half the costs of the Service"[174] and reemphasized that the "dominant objective of Congress . . . was the prevention of discrimination among classes of mail."[175] And just so, a rationality was infused into the Reorganization Act of 1970.

The Supreme Court overturned that rationality. In 1980, an appeal was filed from the fifth rate proceeding. This time the appeal was filed by second-class mailers, *Newsweek* and *Time* magazines, and joined by the Postal Rate Commission (and in part by the Postal Service). Also, this appeal was filed not in the District of Columbia but in New York with the U.S. Court of Appeals for the Second Circuit.[176] The whole object of this appeal was to upset the D.C. Circuit's interpretation of the 1970 act. And the Second Circuit did. It found that "the D.C. Circuit erred . . . in holding that Section 3622(b) requires the PRC [Postal Rate Commission] to attribute and assign costs to the maximum extent possible using cost-of-service principles."[177] This ruling was appealed to the Supreme Court, and that Court, to resolve the split among the circuits, agreed to hear the case.[178] In the Supreme Court, the issue, as that Court described it, was "the extent to which the Act requires the responsible federal agencies to base postal rates on cost-of-service principles."[179]

The Court's opinion, by Justice Blackmun, addressed this issue from a standpoint of deference to postal officials. The Court explained that "the Rate Commission applies the factors listed in § 3622(b). Its interpretation of that statute is entitled to due deference."[180] Then, the Court found that the D.C. Circuit had erred in reading the act as removing politics from rate making by committing rate making to strict legal controls. All that the act did, according to the Court, was

---

173. *National Ass'n of Greeting Card Publishers II*, 607 F.2d 392 (D.C. Cir. 1978).

174. *Id.* at 399.

175. *Id.* at 403.

176. Newsweek, Inc. *v.* United States Postal Serv., 663 F.2d 810 (2d Cir. 1981). The Second Circuit refused to transfer the case to the D.C. Circuit, explaining that *"Newsweek* and *Time* have properly run—and won—the race to the courthouse." *Id.* at 1192.

177. *Id.* at 1200.

178. National Ass'n of Greeting Card Publishers *v.* United States Postal Serv., 462 U.S. 810 (1983).

179. *Id.* at 812.

180. *Id.* at 821.

change the venue for politics. In this regard, Justice Blackmun wrote for the Court:

> Congress did not eliminate the ratesetter's discretion; it simply removed the ratesetting function from the political arena, by removing postal funding from the budgetary process . . . and by removing the Postal Service's principal officers from the President's direct control. . . . In addition, Congress recognized that the increasing economic, accounting, and engineering complexity of ratemaking issues had caused Members of Congress, "lacking the time, training, and staff support for thorough analysis" to place too much reliance on lobbyists . . . . Consequently, it attempted to remove undue price discrimination and political influence by placing ratesetting in the hands of a Rate Commission, composed of "professional economists, trained rate analysts, and the like" . . . and subject only to Congress's "broad policy guidelines." Congress sought to insure that the Postal Service would be managed "in a businesslike way."[181]

This is a restatement of the traditional, and largely discredited, rationale for administrative agencies. This rationale is to take social decisions out of Congress and transfer those decisions to forums dominated by experts, who will presumably make social policy according to disinterested and scientific, as opposed to political, judgments. Certainly, this talk is not about managing the Postal Service "in a businesslike way." Be that as it may, the opinion declared a broad discretion on the part of postal officials that the courts should respect.

Thereafter, the opinion dissected section 3622(b) and its ratemaking guidelines and agreed with the "Rate Commission's consistent position that Congress did not dictate a specific method [cost-of-service]"[182] for calculating rates. Instead, the commission in its discretion could assign direct costs on a cost-of-service basis and then assign the remaining costs "on the basis of the other eight factors set forth by § 3622(b)"[183] (apparently leaving the Postal Service free to assign, as it has in the past, about half its total costs according to an inverse elasticity rule and value-of-service principles).[184] And so the

---

181. *Id.* at 822 (citations omitted).
182. *Id.* at 834.
183. *Id.* at 826.
184. The inverse elasticity rule is not a "benchmark requirement" but

D.C. Circuit's attempt to synthesize the rate-making guidelines according to principles of fairness and cost-of-service principles was ended.

But, in one respect, the Supreme Court was probably right. The act has no coherent set of controls. Therefore, a large amount of discretion was in fact delegated, and perhaps the courts cannot change those facts.

The work force. In 1970, the postal unions entered the legislative process with a special tail wind. Their illegal strike in 1970 had gained them a memorandum of agreement with the Executive Branch that contained important concessions. President Nixon forwarded the agreement to Congress.[185] There, as legislators explained with a not-rocking-the-boat metaphor, this agreement and its concessions were taken to be a fully accomplished and binding fact.[186] As previously noted, part of the agreement was a one-time buyout consisting of a 14 percent pay raise. Eight percent was provided by an across-the-board pay raise for federal employees. Six percent was a pay raise for postal employees only, and this amount was written into the 1970 act.[187] Also, the agreement and then the act compressed the time of advancement through pay grades to eight years, provided for collective bargaining and binding arbitration, and provided that postal wages would be set according to wages prevailing in comparable sectors in private industry.[188]

Respecting wages, postal workers secured their long-standing aspiration of separating their pay from postal revenues.[189] Absent from the act, however, are features that link pay to productivity. Present in the act are features that ensure that the Postal Service will remain labor intensive. There is, for instance, the provision that makes automation subject to collective bargaining.[190]

rather a principle that the Postal Rate Commission may use if it wishes. *See* Direct Marketing Ass'n *v.* American Newspaper Publishers Ass'n, 778 F.2d 96, 103–04 (2d Cir. 1985).

185. Pt. 2, *Postal Modernization Hearings, supra* note 2, at 1077–85.

186. *Id.* at 961–62.

187. *See supra* note 123.

188. Respecting conditions of employment under the act, see 39 U.S.C. §§ 1001–11; respecting collective bargaining and arbitration, see 39 U.S.C. §§ 1201–09.

189. *See supra* text accompanying note 123.

190. The act provides: "The Postal Service shall promote modern and efficient operations and should refrain from expending any funds, engaging in any practice, or entering into any agreement or contract, *other than an agreement or contract under chapter 12 of this title*, which restricts the use of new

Today, the postal work force is probably stronger and better organized than ever. The force numbers over 700,000. Union representation is more consolidated. Instead of eleven unions, as was the case before 1970, there are now four: the American Postal Workers Union, the National Association of Letter Carriers, the National Association of Post Office Mail Handlers, and the Rural Letter Carriers Association. The American Postal Workers Union and the National Association of Letter Carriers represent about 80 percent of postal workers.[191]

Effective postal reform would probably run counter to the labor-intensive system of the Postal Service and the postal monopoly that supports the system. Thus, postal workers now appear to be one of the most conservative and resistant of special interest groups. To illustrate, in 1977, about one-third of all postal employees would retire within a decade. This fact prompted this testimony, by a strategic-planning official of the Postal Service, before the National Commission on the Postal Service: "Unfortunately, this is a limited opportunity [for reform]. If the Commission and Congress concur in a short-term remedy that simply patches up the system, the hundreds of thousands employed to replace these retirees can be expected to have sufficient political clout to prevent major changes for twenty or thirty years to come."[192]

The Monopoly. The statutory monopoly for first-class mail underwrites the Postal Service. After the Supreme Court decision in *National Association of Greeting Card Publishers*, first-class mail continues to bear its own costs as well as the "institutional costs" that are about 50 percent of total postal costs. Thus, those most injured by the monopoly are the public at large, the general letter-writers and general business clients. This group, though, had no focused input into the 1970 act. The interest groups that were influential naturally support the monopoly. The postal managers need the monopoly because it is the mainstay of their organization and their positions. They want to be self-sufficient, and without the monopoly they would not be. Special mailers feed on the cross subsidies that the monopoly supports. The

---

equipment or devices which may reduce the cost or improve the quality of postal services . . . ." 39 U.S.C. § 2010 (emphasis added). Chapter 12 agreements are collective bargaining agreements.

191. WALSH & MANGUM, *supra* note 117, at 69–70.

192. *Quoted in* Peter J. Donnici, Larry L. Hillblom, L. Patrick Lupo & Mary Beth Collins, *The Recent Expansion of the Postal Monopoly to Include the Transmission of Commercial Information: Can It Be Justified?*, 11 U.S.F. L. REV. 243, 300–01 (1977).

postal unions have become especially energetic supporters, a fact which is not surprising considering that a quarter of the salaries of the postal work force of over 700,000 seem to be monopoly rents.

The Kappel Commission advocated broad reform but nonetheless recommended that the postal monopoly be retained. Accordingly, the 1970 act retained the monopoly in the form held since 1845.[193] In time-honored fashion, though, the act did provide that a blue-ribbon panel should study the monopoly. That panel was formed and headed by Frederick Kappel of the Kappel Commission that had recommended keeping the monopoly. The panel recommended that the monopoly stay in place, the reason being the historical one of avoiding cream skimmers.[194]

The one change that the postal monopoly panel did recommend was for the Postal Service to assume a rule-making authority and issue rules better defining the monopoly.[195] The Postal Service did assume that authority. In 1974, it enacted a set of rules that extend the monopoly into new areas of electronic and commercial communications if the Postal Service chooses to venture there.[196] So far it has not.[197]

Another development has the been the emergence of the postal unions as energetic defenders of the monopoly. In a series of cases, these unions have maintained a hard line of litigation, challenging all efforts—by firms or by the Board of Governors—to avoid or relax the monopoly. In this litigation posture, an interesting question is how these unions have "standing."

The postal monopoly is justified in that it enables mail delivery to those members of the public for whom the cost of service would

---

193. *See* 18 U.S.C. § 1696(a), *quoted at supra* note 67.

194. STATUTES RESTRICTING THE PRIVATE CARRIAGE OF MAIL, *supra* note 52, at 4–7.

195. *See id.* at 13-14. Whether the Postal Service can assume that authority, absent a directive from Congress would seem to be an issue in administrative law. *See* ALFRED C. AMAN, JR. & WILLIAM T. MAYTON, ADMINISTRATIVE LAW 90–98 (West Publishing Co. 1993).

196. 39 C.F.R. § 310.1 (1993). For a discussion of these new rules, see Donnici, Hillblom, Lupo & Collins, *supra* note 192.

197. It seems unlikely that the Postal Service will ever use this authority— to extend its monopoly to include electronic communications—that it has claimed. Probably, whatever legitimacy that the monopoly for written messages has is based wholly on Anglo-American history. There is no such history respecting electronic matters, and no doubt a Postal Service move to extend its monopoly into this area would be too startling and would upset too many established practices to be feasible.

otherwise be too high.[198] The monopoly is not and cannot be justified—either logically or politically—on the ground that it benefits postal workers. But in *National Association of Letter Carriers v. Independent Postal System*, it was.[199] In that case, a company maintained that a service it proposed to offer, of transferring business greetings at Christmas, did not constitute the delivery of letters. The National Association of Letter Carriers sought to enjoin those deliveries. In court, standing was in issue. The union claimed that it had standing because the private delivery service would cause its members to suffer "significant loss of work time, overtime, employment opportunities, future pension and insurance benefits."[200] The court found that this loss of benefits by competition from the private sector was an injury sufficient to create standing, especially since in the court's view employee interests were in the "zone of interests" protected by the monopoly statute.[201] This decision may or may not represent an appropriate application of standing. But it did legitimate the authority of a resourceful interest group to guard the monopoly through litigation, an authority that has been vigorously deployed.[202]

Conclusion

The Postal Service is not, as the reorganization of 1970 would have it, a business organization. The service is not subject to the incentives and controls of the free market, as are business firms. Essentially, the Postal Service is an administrative agency, to which the 1970 reorganization transferred a number of primary functions formerly performed by Congress. (To be sure, the service is an unusual agency: the business it regulates is itself, and thus it is itself one of its special interest problems.) In theory, this fuller transition of the postal power to administrative power is not necessarily an altogether bad transition. But the premises under which the transition was made were incorrect. Among these premises was the belief that postal problems would be solved by transferring their resolution to experts (the postal managers) who would be controlled *not* by politics but by a disinterested and professionally informed judgment. If administrative law

---

198. STATUTES RESTRICTING THE PRIVATE CARRIAGE OF MAIL, *supra* note 52, at 119–83.

199. 470 F.2d 265 (10th Cir. 1972).

200. *Id.* at 270.

201. *Id.* at 270-71.

202. *See, e.g.*, American Postal Workers Union *v.* React Postal Services, Inc., 771 F.2d 1375 (10th Cir. 1985); Associated Third Class Mail Users *v.* United States Postal Serv., 440 F. Supp. 1211 (D.C. Cir. 1977).

teaches us anything, it is that the avoidance of political pressure is a vain hope. The politics is simply transferred to a new forum in the agency.

A set of legal controls is one means of blunting politically informed agency decisions. To an extent, the act purports to allow for meaningful judicial review. But as we have seen in the case of the crucial rate-making function, this attempt largely fails. The act's provisions are not sufficiently coherent to offer clear guidelines for courts; instead, the provisions run toward the "diverse objectives broadly stated" mode that offers no control at all.

More rational solutions to postal problems should be studied and offered. Trimming the monopoly (and therefore inclining the service toward market controls) or the possibility of better statutory controls are subjects that can be usefully studied. We must understand, however, that the continuing vitality of the forces that have shaped postal history will make the implementation of any solutions exceptionally difficult. Perhaps only windows of opportunity—as when the system breaks down or when electronic technology completely sidesteps the postal monopoly—will allow for effective reform.

Commentary by Richard J. Pierce, Jr.

William Mayton's comprehensive history of the Postal Service will prove to be a gold mine for all participants in the postal reform debate. I have only one quarrel with his treatment of the subject. His adulation of the D.C. Circuit for attempting unsuccessfully to provide a solution to the historical problems in the form of cost-of-service regulation is misplaced. Cost-of-service regulation never has, and never will, improve the efficiency of any market. It is invariably a source of inefficiency. Nor does it provide means of eliminating or reducing cross subsidies. Rather, it is invariably a source of cross subsidies attributable to the need to engage in inherently arbitrary allocation of common costs.

When asked to contribute to this volume, I felt anxiety because of my dearth of knowledge of the postal market. He saw my ignorance as a potential advantage: it would free me to look at the issues broadly based on my experiences with regulatory reform in other contexts. I now believe he was right. As I read Mayton's excellent history, I was struck by the many close parallels with the histories of the industries I know well: transportation, natural gas, and electricity.[1]

1. *See* RICHARD J. PIERCE, JR., ECONOMIC REGULATION: CASES AND MATERIALS (Anderson Publishing Co. 1994).

Politicians first create a monopoly and then defend that monopoly against myriad recurrent competitive threats. As Thomas Jefferson long ago recognized, politicians act in this manner in pursuit of a single goal: to create monopoly rents that they then can distribute to favored constituents and constituencies as a form of patronage. The identity of the favored groups and the mechanisms for distribution of the monopoly rents have changed over time through a process that might be called dynamic capture, but the basic political goal remains the same at all times: reward those who reward you. This game has produced the same results in the postal context as in the contexts that I know well: inefficiency, high prices, and low service quality.

Fortunately, I think that the time will soon be ripe for implementing real postal reform. Two developments over the past fifteen years have transformed public perceptions of central planning and government-operated or regulated monopolies. First, the collapse of the Soviet empire demonstrated the extraordinary hubris inherent in the belief of many that central planners can produce results superior to those attainable through decentralized market forces. Second, each of the many transitions from reliance on pervasive regulation of a government-created monopoly to a legal regime that relies primarily on market forces, both in the United States and in other countries, has produced billions of dollars in annual consumer gains. Each of those successes has reinforced the negative public perception of the institution of regulated monopoly and provided new impetus for additional reforms.

Powerful evidence of this transformation in public perception is available from two sources. First, regulatory reform movements are gaining momentum all over the world. Europe and Japan are following the U.S. lead in reforming their natural gas markets, while the United States and many other countries are following the lead of Great Britain and New Zealand in reforming their electricity markets. Second, the median position of U.S. politicians on issues of this type has changed dramatically. As one of my colleagues recently documented, President Nixon's agenda in this area was well to the left of the agendas of most liberal Democrats today.

I suspect, however, that we are still a few years short of the time when conditions will render real postal reform politically viable. Any meaningful regulatory reform will have effects that include elimination of monopoly rents and bloated costs. The current beneficiaries of the status quo (primarily postal employees) attained that favored position because of their political muscle. They will use that same muscle to resist any meaningful reform. The proponents of reform can overcome that potent source of resistance only in ideal conditions.

111

I expect two changes in conditions to enhance the political prospects for postal reform in the next few years. First, the continuing reform of the U.S. electricity industry will yield large price reductions to most consumers, an average reduction of about 20 percent. That will enhance the credibility of proponents of postal reform and detract from the credibility of defenders of the status quo. Second, the revolution in telecommunications technology will produce forms of competition that will overwhelm the defenders of the postal monopoly. The resulting fiscal crisis in the Postal Service will disarm the proponents of the status quo and compel some form of revolutionary reform.

If my prediction is right, the proponents of postal reform have a few years that they can put to good use in devising a reconstituted postal system. I lack the detailed understanding of the postal market required to make a significant contribution to such an effort at present. It seems likely, however, that provision of postal service is a "network" industry, broadly analogous to natural gas, electricity, and telecommunications, in the sense that some functions involve large indivisibilities. As such, it probably is not a good candidate for a pure laissez faire legal regime. Some individual or group must perform the difficult task of devising a legal regime that relies primarily on market forces but that retains narrow government roles of some types. The active participants in the telecommunications reform debate may be the best candidates to perform this service to the public. Twenty years from now, the telecommunication and postal markets are likely to be a single market.

Discussion

QUESTION: The telecommunications industry is shifting from monopoly toward open competition. There is more competition in the customer-premise equipment market, the long-distance market, and now even the local market. The telecommunications industry also has universal service subsidy mechanisms for high-cost areas and low-income customers. Do you think that the telecommunications industry should be used as a model when evaluating the next step in the evolution of the postal industry? And, if so, do you think that the recent developments in telecommunications might be the window of opportunity that you mentioned?

RICHARD J. PIERCE, JR., Columbia University: Yes to both questions. Although the transition in telecommunications is far from complete, it can still be a useful model. Telecommunications is also a network industry, and as such it is a source of potentially useful information and analysis that can be carried over into the postal reform debate. The same can also be said of the natural gas and electricity industries.

WILLIAM TY MAYTON, Emory University School of Law: Various people have tried many times to include telegraph and telephone under the authority of the Post Office. And during World War I, the Post Office did assume a regulatory authority respecting electronic communications. This regulation was not so well received by industry, and after the war the Post Office gave it up. Therefore, the Post Office has thought that these two kinds of communications—written and electronic—are sufficiently similar to fall under "postal" regulation. But in the beginning, communication was written, and historically the Post Office attended to that. Consequently, a reason we do not, today, have Post Office regulation of telecommunications is apparently historical—electronic communication was not a part of the original postal power.

QUESTION: It is my impression that in most other countries the telephone company is part of the postal service. This has been one of the biggest obstacles to overcome in the deregulation of telecommunications, because the postal service, which has government clout behind it, fights deregulation vigorously. Are there any countries that have really freed up the postal service and made it a totally private, competitive industry?

PROFESSOR PIERCE: Sweden has repealed its private express statutes. Holland has also, and they are now in the very early stages of a privatization initiative—although the details are not at all clear yet. The Argentines are also selling their postal service to entrepreneurs.

5

Agency Costs and Governance in the United States Postal Service

R. Richard Geddes

When the owners of a firm are distinct from its managers, "agency costs" arise. Utility-maximizing managers will, absent institutional constraints, allocate firm resources to maximize their own utility rather than firm value. Agency costs refer to the costs of controlling managers as well as to the loss of firm value. The problem is most severe in large, diffusely held corporations, whether public or privately owned, because no single owner has the incentive to monitor management intensively. Ever since Adolph Berle and Gardiner Means pointed out their celebrated "separation of ownership and control," there has been considerable interest among economists in solutions to the agency problem.[1] Economists have since pointed out numerous ways in which market forces inside and outside the privately owned corporation operate to encourage managers to act in owners' interests.[2]

There is a consensus in the literature that aspects of private property rights help focus the efforts of managers in private firms through a number of control mechanisms. There is less consensus about how managerial control mechanisms operate in government-

I am grateful to the Institute for Humane Studies at George Mason University for financial assistance, and to Douglas Adie, Douglas Ashton, Jim Dorn, George Hall, Leonard Merewitz, David Sappington, Roger Sherman, Gregory Sidak, and many others for helpful comments and suggestions. All remaining errors are my own.

1. *See* ADOLPH BERLE & GARDINER MEANS, THE MODERN CORPORATION AND PRIVATE PROPERTY (MacMillan 1932).

2. *See* Eugene F. Fama & Michael C. Jensen, *Separation of Ownership and Control*, 26 J.L. & ECON. 301 (1983); Eugene Fama & Michael C. Jensen, *Agency Problems and Residual Claims*, 26 J.L. & ECON. 327 (1983).

owned enterprises. If important managerial control mechanisms are market based, however, and markets require defined and enforced property rights to operate, then many control mechanisms will be attenuated in public firms. Hence, public firm behavior will be less aligned with owner welfare. This chapter examines these issues through comparison of the governance structure of the United States Postal Service with that of a private corporation. This is a constructive comparison because changes in the organization of postal services brought about by the Postal Reorganization Act of 1970 were intended to help solve corporate control problems. "Corporatization" of postal services invites such a comparison.

The weaknesses of the managerial structure of the old U.S. Post Office as a department of the federal government became clear in the 1960s. Mail volume was increasing rapidly while the Post Office continued to use antiquated equipment. Performance grew worse until, in October 1966, Chicago's immense post office became paralyzed by a backlog of mail exceeding 10 million pieces.[3] The facility was in chaos for three weeks, and mail delivery across the nation was disrupted. Public attention quickly focused on postal reform. The President's Commission on Postal Organization viewed the problem as caused by the lack of independence of managers in operating the organization.[4] In response, the Postal Reorganization Act changed the internal structure of the Post Office, creating a new, independent entity—the United States Postal Service. In addition to liberating the Postal Service from Congress, the goal of reorganization was to adopt the managerial techniques and internal control structures of the modern corporation and apply them to government-owned postal services.

In this chapter, I examine the Postal Reorganization Act from a property-rights perspective and compare Postal Service managerial controls with those of a private corporation. Although it is rarely recognized, the citizens of the United States own the Postal Service. At some time and in some form, they have paid for the assets of the Postal Service.[5] U.S. citizens are thus akin to equity holders in large, private corporations. What rights do these owners retain as purchasers of those assets? I will show how the bundle of rights granted

3. *See* JOHN TIERNEY, POSTAL REORGANIZATION: MANAGING THE PUBLIC'S BUSINESS 9 (1981).

4. PRESIDENT'S COMMISSION ON POSTAL ORGANIZATION, REPORT OF THE COMMISSION, TOWARDS POSTAL EXCELLENCE 33 (Government Printing Office 1968) [hereinafter PRESIDENT'S COMMISSION].

5. To the extent assets were funded out of general revenues before the act, they were paid for through direct taxes. The Postal Service had a positive equity position of $1.7 billion at the start of operations in July 1971, which

to owners changed after the act and how these changes affected the mechanisms available to the owners of the Postal Service in controlling the agency problem. The analysis reveals that the act created only ineffectual methods for owners to control managers. Since ownership remained in government hands, no new external managerial control mechanisms were created. Therefore, agency problems are likely to be just as severe as they were before the act.

In the first part of this chapter, I review managerial control mechanisms in large, privately owned corporations and discuss how these mechanisms are a consequence of property rights inherent in private ownership. In the second part, I show how these control mechanisms differ in government-owned firms. In the last part, I apply this analysis to the United States Postal Service.

Property Rights and Agency Costs in Privately Owned Firms

A firm, whether public or private, is a legal entity comprising a set of contracts between resource owners who are cooperating within the framework of the firm.[6] These contracts specify, among other things, the rights and responsibilities of resource owners regarding such matters as the division of labor, the sources of capital, and the ownership of residual earnings of the firm. The legal owners of the firm are typically those who have property rights in firm-specific physical assets.

The phrase "property rights" refers not to a single right, but to a set or "bundle" of rights granted to owners of an institution. The specifics of the bundle of rights constituting ownership determine the nature of the institution—that is, whether it will be a sole proprietorship, a partnership, a corporation, a nonprofit, or some other structure. In an important way, the bundle of rights defining the institution determines the mechanisms available to owners in controlling agency costs.[7] Generally, ownership of any asset is constituted by a bundle of rights and can be said to consist of three elements: (1) the right to use the asset; (2) the right to appropriate the returns on the

---

represented the value of citizen-owners' investment. The Postal Service also received an "equity infusion" of $1 billion from taxpayers through a 1976 law. *See* Postal Reorganization Act Amendments of 1976, Pub. L. No. 94–421, § 2(d), 90 Stat. 1303 (1976); Postal Reorganization Act, Pub. L. No. 91–375, §2002, 84 Stat. 842, 865–55 (1970); S. Rep. No. 966, 94th Cong., 2d Sess. 2 (1976), *reprinted* in 1976 U.S.C.C.A.N. 2400, 2401.

6. Michael C. Jensen, *Organizational Theory and Methodology*, 50 ACCT. REV. 326 (1983). *See also* FRANK H. EASTERBROOK & DANIEL R. FISCHEL, THE ECO-NOMIC STRUCTURE OF CORPORATE LAW 1–39 (Harvard University Press 1991).

7. Fama & Jensen, *Separation of Ownership and Control, supra* note 2.

asset; and (3) the right to change its form, substance, and location.[8] Within the context of a firm, the first element translates into an exclusive ownership right, or "exclusivity." The second translates into the right to the net cash flows of the firm—that is, the right to be a "residual claimant." The third element implies that the owner has the right to transfer ownership of the share to another party, or "transferability," as well as specific "control rights" over how the firm is run.

In contrast, ownership rights in a government corporation like the Postal Service are *public* property rights. These rights are demonstrably different from private property rights when analyzed in the context of the three elements identified above. We see that

• The public property right is not exclusive—that is, there is common ownership based on citizenship.

• The firm's owners are not given direct ownership rights to the residual cash flows of the firm—that is, they are not "residual claimants" of the firm.

• The ownership right is not transferable.

The owners of the public firm thus have rights associated with ownership only in the sense that they can transfer them by changing citizenship, obtain residual cash flows through tax reductions or rebates (and bear residual losses through deficits or tax increases), and affect resource allocation decisions (investment and financing) through a voting-to-bureaucracy mechanism. Since there are fewer rights associated with ownership in government corporations, ownership rights are attenuated relative to private ownership.[9]

The details of private property rights arrangements adjust to the trade-off between agency costs and capital raising, specialization of management, and other benefits. Different sets of private property rights, and thus different institutional arrangements, are optimal depending upon the type of investments that the firm must fund.[10] For example, small amounts of relatively low-risk investment can be undertaken by a sole proprietorship in which the owner provides all necessary capital. Agency costs are eliminated in this form since the owner is also the manager, but it disallows capital-intensive production as well as specialization of managerial and risk-bearing activities.

8. Erik Furubotn & Rudolf Richter, *The New Institutional Economics: An Assessment, in* THE NEW INSTITUTIONAL ECONOMICS 1 (Erik Furubotn & Rudolf Richter eds., Texas A&M Press 1991).

9. *See* Louis DeAlessi, *The Economics of Property Rights: A Review of the Evidence,* 2 RES. L. & ECON. 1 (1980).

10. Eugene Fama & Michael Jensen, *Organizational Forms and Investment Decisions,* 14 J. FIN. ECON. 101 (1985).

Alternatively, partnership may be the optimal arrangement for a professional association in which assets are mainly in the form of human capital and where mutual monitoring is important.

In the case of activities requiring large amounts of risky capital (for example, steel mills or auto factories), the property rights arrangements must allow capital to be raised at low cost. This is accomplished by spreading the risk of investment over many investors, which is achieved by making rights fully alienable and requiring owners to have little other role in the organization. This "open corporation" form of organization creates benefits by raising low-cost capital and allowing specialization, but is costly due to the resources necessary to control agency costs. The open corporate form of ownership refers specifically to firms with shares that are fully alienable and can thus be distinguished from "closed" or "closely held" corporations in which some or all shares are not transferable. Since any large-scale postal delivery operation, public or private, is likely to require large amounts of risk capital, it is most appropriate to examine postal operations within the context of the open corporate form, in which rights are fully transferable.

Thus, different organizational forms have different rights structures and have alternative mechanisms for economizing on agency costs. Specific rights granted to owners of private open corporations encourage solutions to agency problems, which are now reviewed. These can be categorized into those external and those internal to the firm.

External Control Mechanisms. The transferability aspect of private ownership rights is critical for several control mechanisms in modern corporations. When combined with rights to residual cash flows, it provides not only the ability but also the incentive to control managers effectively. Transferability and residual claimancy form the basis for markets in ownership rights, from which stem several control mechanisms: the stock market, debt ratings, ownership concentration, and the market for takeovers.

The stock market. Transferability of ownership rights creates a market in those rights, which continuously prices or values the right. Stock prices provide valuable but inexpensive signals regarding the effectiveness of current management in maximizing owners' wealth, since they rapidly reflect the expected effect of managerial decisions on current and future net cash flows. Owners do not need to be experts in analyzing the efficacy of managerial decisions to discern probable effects on future cash flows; they need only observe a firm's stock price. Large abnormal changes in share values lead to abnormal gains or losses for shareholders, who thus have an incentive to hold managers accountable for such abnormal returns. The stock-price mechanism exerts considerable pressure, both externally and internally, on management to contain agency costs and operate in the interest of owners.[11]

Debt ratings. Most organizations that issue tradable stock also issue debt. Capital structures comprising either all equity or all debt are rarely observed. Because the issuance of publicly traded debt helps lower contracting costs through specialized evaluation of default risk,[12] it is often associated with transferable ownership interests.

Banks that issue credit to private companies specialize in the evaluation of default risk. The granting, denial, and interest rate on a credit line provide signals to owners regarding the riskiness of investment decisions. Banks frequently review the efficacy of their credit decisions, thus updating the signal. Firms often pay for, and subsequently advertise, bank confirmation of a credit line that they do not use, indicating the value of this signal.[13]

Perhaps more important, large corporations frequently purchase ratings of publicly held debt from rating agencies (such as Moody's, Dunn and Bradstreet, and Standard and Poor's) that have a powerful incentive to maintain the integrity of their ratings. These ratings play a role similar to bank debt in the monitoring of investment risk and are readily available to both bond- and stockholders. This specialized evaluation of default risk on debt lowers agency costs, since owners can observe ratings on debt issues to infer the riskiness of managerial investment decisions, rather than engage in costly and specialized evaluation themselves.

Debt ratings by banks and others provide a check on cavalier

---

11. Numerous empirical studies support the proposition that stock markets help solve agency problems. Managerial removals are correlated with negative abnormal stock returns. Also, managerial pay packages are often structured so as to correlate managerial wealth with stockholder wealth, as reflected by returns. *See, e.g.,* Anne T. Coughlan & Ronald M. Schmidt, *Executive Compensation, Management Turnover, and Firm Performance,* 7 J. ACCT. & ECON. 43 (1985); Jerold B. Warner, Robb L. Watts & Karen H. Wruck, *Stock Prices and Top Management Changes,* 20 J. FIN. ECON. 461 (1988); Michael Weisbach, *Outside Directors and CEO Turnover,* 29 J. FIN. ECON. 431 (1988).

12. *See generally* Eugene Fama, *Contract Costs and Financing Decisions,* 63 J. BUS. S71 (supp. 1990).

13. *Id.* at S87.

investment decisions by managers, constraining them to undertake only those projects within an acceptable risk category. Like the signaling value to owners of abnormal stock returns, abnormal variations in bond prices provide owners with market assessments of the risk of the firm's debt.

Additionally, debt can help solve agency problems associated with "free cash flows." Free cash flows are defined as cash flows in excess of those necessary to fund all projects with a positive discounted net present value. A firm with large free cash flows faces more severe agency problems since excess cash flowing into the firm may prompt managers to undertake investment activity that depresses the equity value of the firm.[14] It is preferable to motivate managers to disgorge the cash. The issuance of debt serves as a more effective tool for forcing bond managers to pay out free cash flows in the future than would promises of dividend increases. Overall, both private and publicly held debt helps lower the cost of managerial monitoring by owners.

Ownership concentration. The concentration of ownership in a firm with tradable residual claims is endogenously determined by the benefits and costs of that concentration. If ownership shares are diffusely held, then no single owner has the incentive to monitor managers intensively. As ownership becomes more concentrated, however, the benefits and costs of monitoring are borne by single owners having a greater incentive to monitor.[15] The limiting case is total ownership concentration—that is, a sole proprietorship, in which monitoring costs are zero and the problem of agency costs is solved.

Because ownership in private firms becomes more concentrated as the benefits from concentration increase, we expect the intensity of managerial monitoring to increase as well. Concentration thus varies in ways that are consistent with maximization of firm value. By allowing ownership concentration to increase with the benefits of more intensive monitoring, the transferability of ownership rights provides an additional monitoring device. If shareholders expect a

14. *See* Michael C. Jensen, *Agency Costs of Free Cash Flow, Corporate Finance, and Takeovers*, 76 AM. ECON. REV. PAPERS & PROC. 323 (1986).

15. *See* Harold Demsetz & Kenneth Lehn, *The Structure of Corporate Ownership: Causes and Consequences*, 93 J. POL. ECON. 1155 (1985). Demsetz and Lehn refer to the wealth gain from increased monitoring through increased concentration as the "control potential" from concentration. *Id.* at 1156. They find, for example, that the control potential increases with the riskiness of the firm's environment and decreases with regulatory intensity. *Id.* at 1160.

wealth gain from greater monitoring, they can alter concentration accordingly. This is not possible in government-owned firms.

The market for takeovers. The transferability of ownership rights implies that management teams compete for control of firm assets through the purchase of rights on the market. Competing management teams can circumvent entrenched boards and managers to gain control of a firm's decision process by gaining control of the voting rights that attach to the firm's common stock. This change in control can occur through tender offers or proxy contests.

Takeovers are a costly but effective way of allowing competition among managers for the control of assets, thus ensuring that assets are employed in their highest-valued use.[16] This competition implies that poor management teams will be replaced when the cost of their inefficiency exceeds the transactions costs of a takeover. The market for corporate control disciplines managers to use the firm's assets effectively. Empirical evidence supports the hypothesis that takeovers operate to maximize shareholder wealth.[17]

Internal Control Mechanisms. Other mechanisms for controlling agency costs are internal to the firm. Their effectiveness is, however, related to the transferability of ownership shares. I briefly discuss two internal control mechanisms: managerial pay packages and managerial turnover.

Managerial pay packages. Corporate contractual arrangements allow the board of directors to determine the pay of senior management. Pay packages typically include salary, bonuses, stock options, and restricted stock and are designed to align the senior manager's compensation with the wealth of the firm's owners.

Empirical evidence clearly shows that managerial pay varies with returns to stock ownership.[18] If owners are dissatisfied with managerial performance, they can reduce managerial wealth directly by selling their shares, which will reduce the share price by imparting

16. *See* Henry Manne, *Mergers and the Market for Corporate Control*, 73 J. POL. ECON. 110 (1965).

17. Gregg Jarrell, James Brickley & Jeffrey Netter, *The Market for Corporate Control: The Evidence Since 1980*, 2 J. ECON. PERSPECTIVES 49 (1988); Michael Jensen & Richard Ruback, *The Market for Corporate Control: The Scientific Evidence*, 11 J. FIN. ECON. 5 (1983).

18. *See, e.g.*, Coughlan & Schmidt, *supra* note 11; Kevin J. Murphy, *Corporate Performance and Managerial Remuneration: An Empirical Analysis*, 7 J. ACCT. & ECON. 11 (1985).

FIGURE 5-1
THE PRIVATELY OWNED CORPORATION

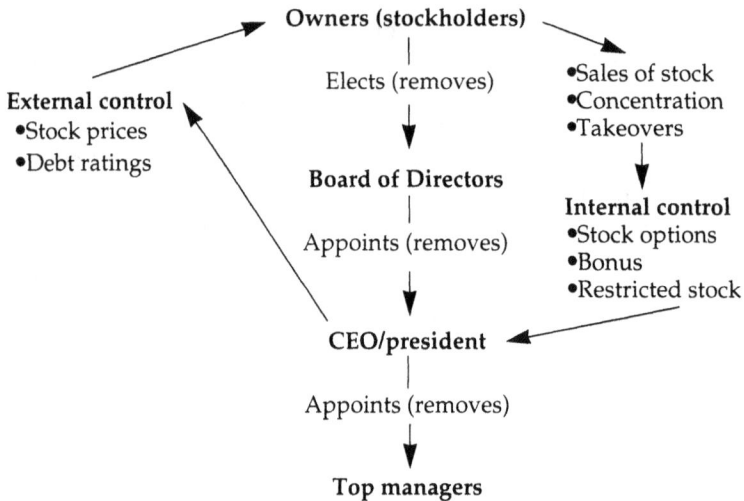

```
                    ┌──────► Owners (stockholders) ──────┐
                    │                │                    ▼
                    │         Elects (removes)       •Sales of stock
   External control │                │               •Concentration
   •Stock prices    ▲                ▼               •Takeovers
   •Debt ratings    │         Board of Directors          │
                    │                │                     ▼
                    │         Appoints (removes)     Internal control
                    │                │               •Stock options
                    │                ▼               •Bonus
                    │          CEO/president ◄──────  •Restricted stock
                    └───────         │
                             Appoints (removes)
                                     │
                                     ▼
                               Top managers
```

new, negative information to the market.

This control mechanism stems directly from the transferability aspect of ownership shares. As long as the firm has an effective incentive-pay package in place, its owners need not rely solely on the board to affect managerial wealth. Managerial pay tied to owner wealth is thus an important control device.

Managerial turnover. The firing or retention of senior managers by the board depending upon changes in owner wealth is an obvious way to reduce agency problems. The threat of firing during periods of poor firm performance encourages managers to act in the interests of owners. In private firms, the board can use both accounting returns and stock returns as measures of owner wealth in its decision to retain or fire management. Empirical evidence is consistent with the proposition that CEO removals are correlated with owner wealth.[19]

A Synthesis of Control Mechanisms. Figure 5–1 provides a visual

19. Warner, Watts & Wruck, *supra* note 11, find that managerial removals are correlated with a firm's stock returns, but only if performance is extremely good or bad. Like signals from the product market, managerial turnover may occur too late to warn shareholders of risks associated with their ownership stake.

summary of the mechanisms by which the owners of a privately owned corporation can control their managers. The election of the board by owners is an important right, but it may not be the central control device. Figure 5–1 emphasizes the role played by external control devices that result from tradable residual claims. CEO performance affects stockholders by changing their wealth and imparting to them new information; both effects manifest themselves in stock prices and debt ratings. As long as the corporation has incentive-pay plans in place, its owners can respond by directly affecting CEO wealth through stock sales, takeovers, and changing ownership concentration—all of which are a direct consequence of tradable residual claims.

For our analysis, it is crucial that sales of stock create a direct link between CEO wealth and the decisions of the corporation's owners. An ineffective board can be circumvented, as owners can independently sell stock, which in turn affects CEO wealth through the internal governance mechanisms of options, bonuses, and so forth. Sales of stock lower stock prices, thus decreasing the value of CEO-held options and restricted stock.

The control mechanism of hostile takeovers operates as perhaps the least subtle method of external control. Once the board has appointed a CEO and established an efficient compensation policy (that is, one that links CEO wealth to measures of owner wealth), its only critical role is the removal of underperforming managers. If the market for corporate control operates smoothly, owners will be able to replace top managers through takeovers, even in the face of intransigent boards.[20] Changes in the concentration of ownership help facilitate managerial monitoring since ownership can become more highly concentrated when returns to more intensive monitoring are higher. If ownership concentration remains diffuse, as in large state-owned enterprises, owners could not accumulate sufficient ownership shares to compensate them for costly monitoring activities.

In general, the rights embedded in private ownership of the modern corporation allow powerful managerial incentive and control mechanisms to evolve and operate. Although the control rights expressly granted to firm owners are important, the transferability and residual claimancy rights inherent in private property are critical for effective corporate governance. As the property rights structure of

20. Problems can result when state case law prohibits the market for corporate control from operating properly. For example, Delaware's recent decision in the *Time Warner* case effectively prohibited owners from accepting an attractive tender offer from a hostile suitor. Paramount Communications, Inc. *v.* Time Inc., 571 A.2d 1140 (Del. 1990).

an organization changes, we expect managerial control mechanisms to change also. We now consider the extent to which these mechanisms are available in a government firm such as the Postal Service.

Property Rights and Agency Costs in Government-owned Firms

The bundle of rights associated with public ownership, or ownership by citizens of the assets of government firms, differs substantially from that of private ownership. These differences affect the type of mechanisms available to owners in controlling agency costs. The attenuation of rights inherent in public ownership has as its corollary a reduction in available control mechanisms. This section will examine general issues regarding corporate control in government-owned firms. The changes in both internal and external governance mechanisms will be discussed.

External Control Mechanisms. Since government-owned firms do not, by definition, have ownership shares that are tradable, the effectiveness of *external* control mechanisms is reduced—that is, nontransferability raises the cost of external control to prohibitively high levels. Ownership rights are not priced or valued in a market specializing in transfer of those rights. Control costs are increased because the effect of managerial decisions on cash flows, and hence firm value, is not discernible through price signals. If an owner wishes to predict the effect of a decision on firm value, the owner must invest time, effort, and skill in forming the forecast, rather than observing the reaction of the firm's stock price or bond rating to the decision. Thus, managerial decisions are more likely to go unscrutinized.

Lack of pricing of property rights also implies that the benefits to owners of monitoring are reduced: owners cannot directly benefit from more effective monitoring through a higher share price. Capitalization of the future consequences of current monitoring through a higher current price of the right is inhibited because the right is not traded on a market. Owners have less incentive to monitor and the equilibrium level of monitoring of public managers will be low relative to private managers.

Government-owned corporations do not issue debt that is bonded by the firm's net cash flows. Instead, the debt is guaranteed by the tax revenues of the relevant jurisdiction. The capital market does not provide discipline through debt assessment for any financing activity conducted by government managers unless these decisions materially affect the ability of the jurisdiction to extract tax revenue. Thus, ratings assigned to government-issued debt are more likely to reflect the willingness of the jurisdiction to tax citizens to repay bondholders than the riskiness of managerial investment decisions per se. Debt ratings of government firms provide relatively poor information to firm owners on the prudence of managerial decisions, thus raising the cost of managerial monitoring.

Hostile takeovers of government-owned firms are not possible because tradable residual claims do not exist. Owners are not able to buy shares on a market with the intention of replacing entrenched managers. Thus, lack of transferability implies that it is more costly for competing management teams hoping to gain control of the decision process to do so: the disciplining effect of tender offers, mergers, and proxy fights is nil.[21] Ownership concentration cannot change in response to greater benefits of monitoring, since ownership concentration is fixed in the government firm. Notably, ownership concentration in the government firm is typically fixed at an extremely diffuse level. That is, since there is proportional ownership among all citizens in the jurisdiction, the value of each ownership share is likely to be very low. The returns from more intensive monitoring will be very low even if they could be perfectly appropriated by owners. Thus, the diffuse ownership structures necessitated by government ownership exacerbate the agency problem.

Internal Control Mechanisms. Public ownership implies that control rights are retained through the voting mechanism, which allows public owners to affect agency costs. In a manner analogous to the election of a board of directors, owners can elect representatives who are committed to controlling agency costs in government firms. These representatives can pressure managers to operate the firm efficiently.

There are several reasons to believe that internal control mechanisms will be less effective in public firms, however. First, representatives are elected to represent owners on a variety of issues. They are therefore less likely to represent accurately the intensity of owners' concerns about agency costs than are board members of a private firm, whose primary focus is overseeing the decision process of that firm. Second, members of the board of a private corporation are often experts in overseeing a firm's decision process and can be chosen for their specialized human capital. Since elected representatives are con-

---

21. Investor-owned utilities can and do purchase nearby municipally owned utilities in the equivalent of a hostile takeover. However, because ownership cannot be obtained in blocks, but rather is an all-or-nothing proposition subject to the outcome of the municipal political process, takeover costs are likely to be very high.

cerned with a variety of issues, they are less likely to have firm-specific information or to be experts in overseeing a firm's decision-making process than are elected members of the board of directors of a private firm. For these reasons, we expect boards of public firms to be less effective in controlling agency costs than boards of private corporations. Nothing in the public-property structure of government firms prevents the internal control mechanisms of incentive pay or managerial turnover from operating per se. Managerial wealth (and managerial turnover) can be tied to accounting measures of owner wealth through incentive pay packages.[22] Although accounting measures may be poor measures of economic profit and hence owner wealth,[23] the public-property-rights structure of government firms makes other measures unavailable. It is not possible to tie incentive pay packages and managerial turnover to abnormal stock returns in a government firm, as ownership shares do not trade. Moreover, since managerial incentive mechanisms cannot be linked to the prices of tradable residual claims, there can be no direct feedback mechanism by which owners express their preferences concerning governance of the firm by altering managerial wealth. Dissatisfied owners cannot directly reduce managerial wealth.

Relative to private firms, government firms therefore have fewer mechanisms at their disposal to control agency costs. These firms must rely more heavily on attenuated internal control mechanisms to contain agency costs. Consequently, government-owned firms will be less effective than private firms at monitoring managers.

Property Rights, Agency Costs, and the Postal Reorganization Act

Corporate Governance in the Post Office. Article I, section 8, of the Constitution states: "The Congress shall have Power . . . To establish Post Offices and post Roads."[24] This provision has been interpreted as granting power to the federal government to provide postal services and to have monopoly power over letter mail. Before 1971, these services were provided by the Post Office as a cabinet-level department of the federal government. The president appointed the postmaster general, with the advice and consent of the Senate, and the postmas-

---

22. While accounting information may provide a measure of "implied owner wealth" in government firms, without the right to the residual, it is doubtful that owners would ever benefit from increases in these measures.

23. *See, e.g.,* Franklin M. Fisher & J.J. McGowan, *On the Misuse of Accounting Rates of Return to Infer Monopoly Profits,* 73 Am. Econ. Rev. 82 (1983).

24. U.S. Const. art. I, § 8, cl. 7.

FIGURE 5–2
THE POST OFFICE DEPARTMENT

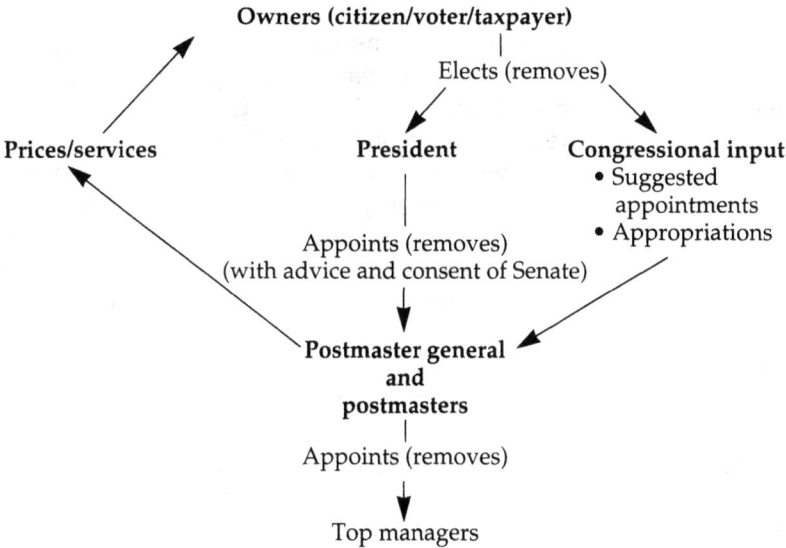

Owners (citizen/voter/taxpayer)

Elects (removes)

Prices/services   President   Congressional input
                                            • Suggested
                                              appointments
                         Appoints (removes) • Appropriations
              (with advice and consent of Senate)

Postmaster general
and
postmasters

Appoints (removes)

Top managers

---

ter general appointed postmasters. Congressional input into appointment of postmasters was significant and came in the form of recommendations to the president, which were generally accepted. Predictably, Congress frequently made these recommendations to maximize political benefits.[25] In addition, Congress exercised control over the Post Office through annual appropriations and was often accused of providing inadequate funds.

The postmaster general was equivalent to the chief executive officer of the Post Office, with postmasters acting as lower-level managers. These managers were acting as agents of citizen-owners of the Post Office in the allocation of its assets. Citizen-owners of the Post Office were granted internal control rights over their managerial agents in that they could elect the president, who would appoint the postmaster general, as well as members of Congress, who would influence the appointments of postmasters through the advice and consent function, if not also through more informal political means. Citizen-owners did not have transferability rights of ownership: they could not sell their "shares" in the Post Office to other parties. Nor

---

25. Congressmen sometimes viewed postmaster appointments as a political burden, however. *See* TIERNEY, *supra* note 3.

did owners have residual claims; they could not directly contract for the difference between revenues and payments to factors of production. Governance of the Post Office as a cabinet-level department is summarized in figure 5–2.

Unlike private owners, citizen-owners of the Post Office had only prices and service levels as signals of managerial performance. That is, if prices increased rapidly or if service quality declined, then owners would receive information on CEO performance.

Price and service levels even in a perfectly functioning market, however, are likely to provide only garbled information on CEO performance given the number of variables determining these quantities. Two factors confounded the use of prices and quality in the product market to infer managerial performance in the Post Office. First, price information was filtered through a complex rate-setting mechanism, increasing the informational distortions. Second, the Post Office had (and the Postal Service has) a legal monopoly on first-class mail. This distortion in the product market surely garbles price signals relative to those in a competitive market, as price can be expected to diverge routinely from marginal cost. Similarly, quality signals may be distorted by the lack of competition.

Thus, observed prices and service quality in the market for postal products provided very poor information on CEO performance. Owners could not sell shares when negative signals were observed. Rather, they could resort only to the tenuous mechanism of trying to influence appointments of postmasters general and local postmasters through presidential and congressional elections. Due to a lack of transferability and residual claimancy, there was no feedback mechanism to affect the wealth of either the postmaster general or the postmasters, since there was no direct link between managerial pay and owner action. Election feedback occurs only with a substantial lag, requiring new elections for new appointments.

Thus, the only penalty available for poor performance by any postmaster general was firing, which could be ordered only by the president. The cost in political capital of firing a cabinet-level appointee is likely to be so high that the president would not resort to this control mechanism until performance had become extremely bad in the sense of being both conspicuous to voters and damaging to the president. There is no case of a president removing the postmaster general.

As figure 5–2 shows, the direct links between owners' welfare and senior manager wealth were weak in the Post Office. A level of severe agency problems existed between owners and their congressional representatives, as well as between Congress and management.

Effective external mechanisms were absent. Even if owners had access to accurate, instantaneous information about managerial performance, it was not possible for them to influence managerial incentives. Since managerial income was not based on owner welfare, managers replaced the maximization of owner welfare with other goals, particularly political ones.

Agency costs were severe in the Post Office in terms of managerial inefficiency and resource misallocation. Anecdotal evidence from the period supports this prediction.[26] Improper use of firm resources manifested itself in many ways, including the failure to use the proper mixture of resources and the failure to adopt new technologies in the face of increasing demand. As mentioned above, this became increasingly apparent by the end of the 1960s.

Corporate Governance under the Postal Reorganization Act. As the failure of governance mechanisms in the Post Office became increasingly clear, calls for change intensified. The main problem was believed to be management's lack of independence from the political process. In its report, the President's Commission on Postal Organization stated:

> The organization of the Post Office as an ordinary Cabinet department guarantees that *the nominal managers of the postal service do not have the authority to run the postal service.* The important management decisions of the Post Office are beyond their control and therefore cannot be made on the basis of business judgement.[27]

Given these concerns, how did reorganization seek to improve managerial performance?

Pursuant to the Postal Reorganization Act of 1970,[28] the Post Office ceased operating as a department of the federal government on July 1, 1971, and began operating as a "public corporation." Since congressional control was seen as the main cause of the political manipulation of the Post Office, a goal of the act was to grant postal managers more autonomy and flexibility in rate setting and management techniques, as well as to establish budgetary independence. In effect, the act "corporatized" the organization.[29] Congress hoped to

---

26. *See* Douglas K. Adie, Monopoly Mail: Privatizing the U.S. Postal Service (1989); Tierney, *supra* note 3.

27. President's Commission, *supra* note 4, at 33 (emphasis in original).

28. Pub. L. No. 91-375, 84 Stat. 719 (1970) (codified at 39 U.S.C. § 101 *et seq.*).

29. *See* Tierney, *supra* note 3, at 1.

achieve this goal by vesting the Postal Service with characteristics of both governmental bodies and privately owned corporations. The main changes effected by the act were as follows:[30]

1. A new governance structure was adopted. An eleven-member Board of Governors was created. Nine governors are appointed by the president, with advice and consent of the Senate. These nine then appoint the postmaster general, and these ten then appoint the deputy postmaster general.

2. The independent Postal Rate Commission, whose commissioners are also appointed by the president with the advice and consent of the Senate, was established to recommend postal rates and classifications to the Board of Governors. The commission can review rate increase proposals, but it lacks subpoena power. It cannot reject rate proposals; it can merely recommend rates to the Board of Governors. A recommended change in a rate proposal is sent to the Board for reconsideration, and the board can modify the proposal in any way it wants, as long as the vote to do so is unanimous.

3. An independent personnel system was established, with provisions for direct collective bargaining.

4. Provisions for a general "public service" subsidy were created, whereby the Postal Service was to receive subsidies until 1979, at which time it was expected to become self-financing. Thus, a budgetary constraint was imposed.

5. Rates for each class of mail were required to cover the costs "reasonably assignable" to that class.

6. The Postal Service was authorized to borrow money and issue public bonds to finance postal buildings and mechanization.

Although all aspects of the reorganization relate in some way to firm governance, we will focus on two major changes: establishment of a Board of Governors and of the Postal Rate Commission. These changes will be analyzed in terms of their effects on both internal and external control mechanisms.

Internal control mechanisms. Through the establishment of the Board of Governors and the Postal Rate Commission, managers were made less accountable to Congress directly, thus diminishing the cor-

30. *Id.* at 23.

poration's susceptibility to political manipulation. The commission and the board were interposed between the managers of the Postal Service and the directly elected agents of its owners, Congress and the president. The Postal Rate Commission is confronted with the difficult task of regulating the Postal Service, but given very little power to carry it out. It is intended to play a role similar to a state public utility commission, in that it should regulate rate levels and structure in accordance with "the public interest." Tools to achieve these ends are, however, limited. As mentioned, it can make only a "recommended decision" to the Board of Governors, which can be overruled. It does not have subpoena power nor the power to affect directly the Postal Service's costs since it cannot directly control expenditures.

Moreover, since the Postal Service does not have transferable equity shares, the commission has no power to affect the market value of its equity. An essential control device used by state public utility commissions is to affect the market value of equity via their decisions regarding rates, cost disallowances, and other variables, which affect managers for the reasons discussed above. While the commission can certainly affect revenues through recommended decisions, this is a less direct mechanism for controlling managerial incentives than decreasing the market value of equity.

The changes in the management structure regarding the board can be analyzed from an agency-cost perspective. In a private firm, the board of directors is directly elected by firm owners. Power over compensation plans, monitoring of top managers, and ratification of new projects is delegated to the board.[31] Owners, however, typically retain control rights over such decisions as board membership, audits, takeovers, and new stock issues. Board members have the incentive to act in owners' interests, since the value of their reputation (and hence human capital) as expert decision makers declines if they are removed or otherwise perceived as ineffective.

The board created by the act is a powerful entity more independent than private boards. It can veto the recommendations of its regulator, as well as appoint top managers.[32] Provided it is unanimous, the board can set its own rates with very little oversight.[33]

31. *See* Fama & Jensen, *Separation of Ownership and Control, supra* note 2.

32. This includes recommendations on rates as well as other concerns. For example, in 1980 the board unanimously rejected the PRC's recommendation concerning E-COM and returned it for "clarifications and modifications." U.S. Postal Service, Board of Governors, Notice Rejecting the Recommended Decision of the Postal Rate Commission Dkt. No. MC78-3, at 1–4 (Feb. 22, 1980). For a discussion of these issues, see TIERNEY, *supra* note 3, at 164.

33. *See* ADIE, *supra* note 26, at 131.

The act undoubtedly achieved the objective of giving the management of the Postal Service greater autonomy. Owners, however, were not given any additional control rights over the board and may have less internal control than before the act. Since they cannot directly vote board members out, owners are unable to remove board members who are not effectively controlling the firm's decision process. Consequently, there is little risk to board members who perform ineffectively. Owners can only elect a president in the tenuous hope that, amid all his other responsibilities, he will monitor the board so as to serve the interests of owners. Presidential appointment of board members thus has two additional levels of agency problems relative to the private firm: one between the owners and the president and a second between the president and the board. There is no reason to assume that the new, powerful board would behave in the interests of owners, as it was given no incentive to do so. Although board members do have the incentive to develop reputations as experts in corporate control to enhance the value of their human capital, that incentive is negligible in the Postal Service because few measures of owner wealth, and hence firm performance, are available.

A legal battle fought in the final days of the Bush administration proved how few internal control rights owners are provided by the act.[34] A federal court ruled that the president, acting on behalf of voters, *does not have* the power of removal over board members, because removal power would violate the independence of the Postal Service. In early January 1993, President Bush sent letters to members of the Board of Governors threatening to remove them if they did not abandon their legal challenge to a two-cent discount for bar-coded, machine processed first-class mail, which was supported by the Postal Rate Commission.[35] On January 7, Judge Louis Oberdorfer of the U.S. District Court in Washington temporarily barred the president from carrying out the threat.[36] The judge suggested that the Postal Service was an independent agency, outside the control of the executive. On January 8, President Bush defied the injunction and attempted to replace one member of the board.[37] On January 16, a fed-

---

34. This topic is addressed in more detail in Neal Devins, *Tempest in an Envelope*, 41 UCLA L. Rev. 1035 (1994).

35. *Bush Reportedly Threatens Postal Board over Rate Rise*, N.Y. Times, Jan. 5, 1993, at A11.

36. *Bush Temporarily Prevented from Dismissing Postmaster*, N.Y. Times, Jan. 8, 1993, at A13; Mackie v. Bush, 809 F. Supp. 144 (D.D.C. 1993).

37. *Bush Defies Judge and Names New Member to Postal Board*, N.Y. Times, Jan. 9, 1993, at I10.

eral court ruled that the president may not dismiss members of the Board of Governors.[38] As a result, it is now apparent that the citizens of the United States do not have any legal rights of removal of their agents on the Board of Governors, through any elected representative. The board, which is supposed to act in their interests, is completely out of their control. This certainly compounds agency problems in the Postal Service to a level beyond that in any private corporation. Private firm owners can directly proxy vote board members off the board in large private corporations.

Thus, the creation of the Board of Governors achieved managerial autonomy only by placing the board completely out of the control of the people who matter most: the owners of the Postal Service. In doing so, it did not help solve agency problems but instead made them worse. Congress should have added control rights to owners to help direct the board's incentives at the same time it was created. But Congress did not. Presumably, the commission was created to help address the inadequate incentives facing the board. From an internal governance perspective, however, the commission is weak. It has no power to review board decisions regarding managerial appointments, removals, incentive structures, ratification of projects—or even rates, provided the board is unanimous.

In short, Congress inadequately designed the internal governance structures for the Postal Service when it enacted the Postal Reorganization Act of 1970. This inadequacy of internal governance is especially damaging when owners lack outside control through transferability and rights to residual cash flows, since no alternatives are available.

External control mechanisms. The first external control problem is the *lack of transferability of equity and debt.* Because the Postal Service is government owned, its citizen-owners by definition do not have the right to sell their shares or the right to the firm's residual cash flows. The agency problems in government-owned firms mentioned earlier therefore apply to the Postal Service. Stock prices are not available to reveal information regarding the expected effect of current managerial decisions on future cash flows. Thus, it is not possible to tie managerial incentives to this measure of owner welfare.

In addition, bond ratings do little to reflect the capital market's assessments of managerial decisions. Although the Postal Service has sometimes gone to the private market to borrow, it often goes to the Treasury. Postal Service debt is not legally backed by the federal

---

38. *Court Blocks Dismissal of Postal Governors,* N.Y. TIMES, Jan. 17, 1993, at I22.

government. Nevertheless, many private lenders may expect that the federal government would not allow a default of its debt. Such expectations are well founded. For example, the *Annual Report of the Postmaster General, Fiscal Year 1981*, states, "Such (debt) obligations shall not be obligations of the U.S. Government unless the Secretary of the Treasury, upon request of the Postal Service, determines that it would be in the public interest to pledge the full faith and credit of the Government of the United States."[39] Therefore, it appears that de facto federal government backing exists.

Such expectations distort the informational value of ratings for the Postal Service's investment decisions per se. Since borrowing from the Treasury does not allow for a market-based debt rating, this debt is also useless for managerial monitoring. Neither privately placed nor publicly traded debt issued by the Postal Service can be of much value to those who wish to monitor Postal Service managers.

Fortunately, the Postal Reorganization Act placed borrowing limits on the Postal Service. The current limit is $2 billion in any one year for capital purposes and $1 billion for operating purposes. Total debt outstanding cannot exceed $15 billion.[40] The debt of the Postal Service is not identified with any one project.

Owners of the Postal Service therefore do not have access to inexpensive market assessments of the prudence of managerial decisions. The lack of transferability of rights implies that the capital markets do not discipline managers for any corporate financing activity, suggesting that the deployment of capital in Postal Service projects is inherently inefficient relative to private firms.

The second external control problem is the *attenuation of residual claims*. It is virtually impossible for the owners of the Postal Service to appropriate the residual from its operations. The residual must pass through many political channels before reaching the owners. No direct dividends, share buybacks, or share-price increases are possible. For owners to receive any residual earnings from either increased revenues or lower costs, the earnings must first be transferred back to the elected body, through direct payments or lower subsidies for the Postal Service, and then to owners through lower taxes or lower budget deficits. The probability that owners will receive any residual earnings is negligible, which decreases the benefit to them of monitoring managers.

Because property rights to the residual cash flow of the Postal

---

39. 1981 U.S. POSTAL SERV., ANNUAL REPORT OF THE POSTMASTER GENERAL 20.

40. *See* Quarterly Financial Report Program, Pub. L. 101–227, § 3(a), 103 Stat. 1943, 1944 (1989), codified at 39 U.S.C. § 2005(a).

TABLE 5–1
INDEX OF RELATIVE INSTITUTIONAL (OVERHEAD) BURDENS

	1984 Rates	1987 Rates	USPS Proposed 1990 Rates	1990 Actual Rates
First-class letters	1.14	1.20	1.35	1.24
Third-class bulk reg.	0.89	0.84	0.79	0.93

SOURCE: U.S. Postal Rate Commission, *Opinion and Recommended Decision,* Postal Rate and Fee Changes, 1990, Dkt. No. R90-1, at ii. Dates refer to year of rate proposal.

Service are undefined, it is likely that any residual will be expropriated by politically influential groups. This expropriation could take the form of higher factor prices (for management, labor, and materials), depending upon the relative influence of the suppliers of these inputs. A firm facing competition in product markets cannot allow expropriation of the residual by paying higher prices to suppliers, since this will force the firm out of business. Or the expropriation could take the form of less-than-compensatory prices being charged for certain services, which would transfer the residual to well-organized groups of customers. Numerous studies support the hypothesis that the real residual earnings of the Postal Service, which are probably significant because of its monopoly power, are expropriated by politically powerful groups, such as organized labor, rather than owners.[41] There is also evidence that the smaller, more concentrated, highly organized groups of customers are paying less of the cost of mail delivery than are more diffuse groups,[42] as table 5–1 illustrates.

First-class mail (55 percent) and third-class mail (38 percent) account for the bulk of the Postal Service mail stream. The "institutional burdens" refer to the amount of "noninstitutional" or nonallocatable costs that the particular class of mail is carrying relative to the average. For example, in 1984, first-class mail had an institutional burden of 1.14, which means it was covering 114 percent of

41. *See, e.g.,* Douglas K. Adie, *How Have Postal Workers Fared since the 1970 Act?, in* PERSPECTIVES ON POSTAL SERVICE ISSUES 74 (Roger Sherman ed., American Enterprise Institute 1980).

42. This is the result predicted by the economic theory of regulation. *See* George J. Stigler, *The Theory of Economic Regulation,* 2 BELL J. ECON. & MGMT. SCI. 1 (1971).

the average burden. First-class mail users are highly diffuse and not well organized. In contrast, third-class, bulk-rate regular mail is used mainly by business mailers to distribute advertising materials and the like. Its users are likely to be less diffuse and more highly organized. In 1984, first-class mailers carried a much larger share of the burden than third-class, 114 percent relative to 89 percent, for a ratio of 1.28. The ratio of burdens increased to 1.43 in the 1987 rate proposal. The rates *proposed* by the Postal Service in 1990 would have exacerbated a trend of first-class customers paying more and third-class customers paying less of the institutional burden by increasing the ratio to 1.71. This suggests that Postal Service management wishes to provide politically influential groups with benefits. The recommended decision of the Postal Rate Commission in 1990, which was not over- turned by the governors, lowered the actual ratio of burdens to 1.33. These outcomes are consistent with expropriation of the residual by politically influential groups.

The third external control problem concerns the *weak control over the Board of Governors*. In a privately owned corporation, owners often need not be concerned about the identity of board members. The time costs to discovering details of the qualifications of each potential member are high. It is rational for owners not to attempt to compile such information, given the alternative external control mechanisms available. These mechanisms allow shareholders to pay less attention to the board, observe more immediate indicators of CEO perfor- mance, and take actions that directly affect CEO wealth. In other words, private firms substitute external control mechanisms for the direct control of managers through boards. The existence of this sub- stitute lowers the benefits of monitoring through a board of directors.

In organizations like the Postal Service, which lack external con- trol mechanisms because of the attenuation of transferability and residual claims, the ability to monitor managers through the board becomes relatively more important in controlling agency costs. It is therefore critical that owners of government firms have direct control over the board. The Postal Reorganization Act, however, gave owners only weak, indirect control over the Board of Governors through the president. This roundabout arrangement raised the cost of monitoring managers through the board in a setting where the benefits were high because of a lack of substitute control mechanisms. Congress thus compounded the agency problem already existing in the Post Office.

A fourth problem of external control is *lack of ownership concen- tration*. Ownership is likely to be very diffuse in any government- owned firm. Consequently, owners cannot accumulate shares in response to greater benefits of monitoring managers, nor can owners

FIGURE 5-3
GOVERNMENTAL STRUCTURE OF THE UNITED STATES POSTAL SERVICE

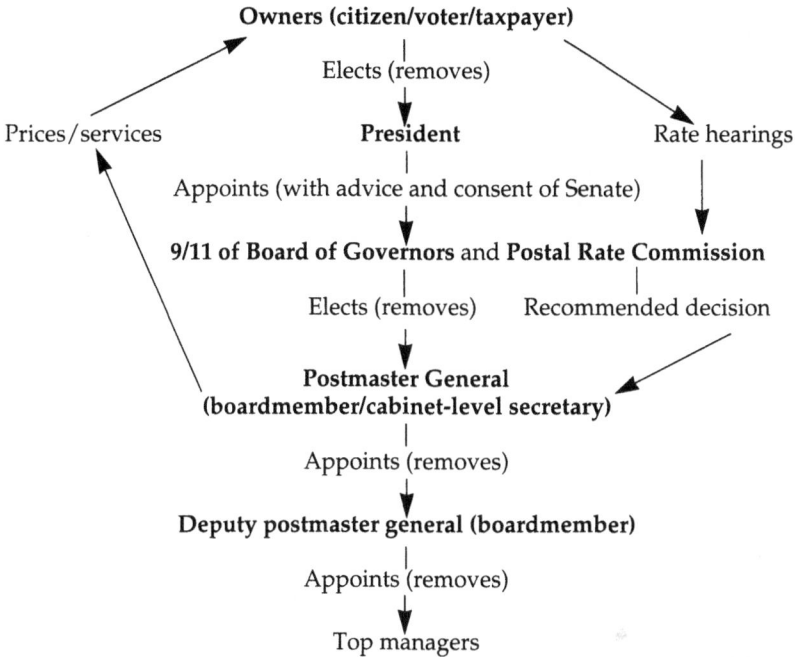

Owners (citizen/voter/taxpayer)

Elects (removes)

Prices/services   **President**   Rate hearings

Appoints (with advice and consent of Senate)

9/11 of Board of Governors and **Postal Rate Commission**

Elects (removes)   Recommended decision

Postmaster General
(boardmember/cabinet-level secretary)

Appoints (removes)

Deputy postmaster general (boardmember)

Appoints (removes)

Top managers

disaggregate their shares in response to lower benefits.

Because the Postal Service is owned by all American citizens collectively, the number of potential monitors of management is very large, but their ownership is very diluted.[43] Consequently, free riding or "shirking" by owners is likely to occur. The populist ownership of the Postal Service per se raises agency costs by diminishing monitoring incentives. Of course, owners are unable to capture any gains from monitoring.

The governance structure of the Postal Service is summarized in figure 5–3. Note that the postmaster general's salary is limited to cabinet-level salaries, thus prohibiting the use of effective incentive-pay devices. Comparing figures 5–2 and 5–3, we see that no additional external monitoring mechanisms were created by the act relative to

43. For example, in 1993 the value of all Postal Service assets was $47,281 million. Given a U.S. population of 250 million, this is an approximate value per person of postal assets of only $187. This ignores the liabilities of the Postal Service, which currently exceed its assets.

the Post Office. The internal governance structure of the organization was made more complex, but nothing ensured that the organization would be more inclined to operate efficiently. Indeed, the firm may be *more* politicized than before the act, but with different political interests exercising power through the rate hearings and board mechanisms.

In summary, owners have no more property rights after postal reorganization than they did before. Congress and the president, however, have less power to act on behalf of firm owners. The act created an institutional structure that mimics a private corporation but that creates no strong incentive for managers to operate in the interests of owners. Instead, postal reorganization uses the investments of owners, the citizens of the United States, to provide politically powerful groups with the returns from those investments.

Conclusion

The central governance issue in the Postal Service, as in any firm, is how to encourage managers to operate the firm to optimize owner welfare. In the case of the Postal Service, owners are taxpayers who have paid for the invested capital of the corporation. If managers do not operate in the interest of owners, agency costs are incurred. It is important to consider why managers have the incentive to contain costs and manage efficiently in any organization. If managers and owners are the same individuals, as in sole proprietorships and partnerships, they benefit directly from better management. If they are separate groups, which is efficient because it allows specialization in management and ownership functions, managers must be given incentives to operate in the interests of owners.

Managers in private corporations have a fiduciary responsibility to maximize the value of the owners' investment, but many powerful incentive devices are created by markets to align managerial and owner incentives further. Rights retained by owners under private ownership, most notably transferability and residual claimancy, allow numerous, effective managerial control mechanisms both inside and outside the firm's managerial structure to operate, thus lowering agency costs. By definition, owners of government firms do not have these rights.

The Postal Reorganization Act was analyzed from a property rights perspective, with particular attention paid to governance mechanisms and resulting agency costs. From this perspective, the Postal Reorganization Act was a failure. There was no "incentive alignment" in the act. While managers have more autonomy, there is no reason to expect that they are more likely to act in the interests of the owners than before the act. The act did not create any additional mechanisms that allow owners to receive timely, accurate information on managerial performance; nor did it allow owners to affect managerial well-being any more directly than in the Post Office. In both cases, owners' behavior has little impact on managerial incentives.

It is often asserted that government firms have different (or "better") goals than private firms, and therefore the attenuation of owners' rights is justified to obtain the central control necessary to achieve these goals. In the case of the Postal Service, "universal service at reasonable cost" is often the goal mentioned to justify government ownership. It is difficult to understand how government ownership helps achieve this goal, however, since the above analysis implies that agency costs, which are real resource costs, will be paid by customers in monopolized markets via higher prices as well as by firm owners. For universality of letter mail, one who does not pay the relatively high price for delivery does not obtain the service, and government ownership appears to increase this price.

The Reorganization Act can be understood as an attempt to create the trappings of the governance structures of private corporations, which have evolved out of decades of market operation, without actually vesting any additional rights in owners. Since effective governance mechanisms are *derived from* rights retained by owners, this effort was doomed to failure.

There are, however, improvements that can be made in the regulatory process. The situation can be improved by granting more control rights to the Postal Rate Commission. For example, the ability of the Board of Governors to overrule the commission should be abolished. This would eliminate any "chilling effect" on the commission of an overriding vote by the governors. Second, the Postal Rate Commission should have the ability to subpoena any documents it wants from the Postal Service. Third, the Postal Rate Commission should have more control over the costs of the Postal Service, particularly wage costs, which form the bulk of the Postal Service's costs. Such control would provide at least some check on the rapid growth of labor costs. In addition, the president should be given the power to remove board members.

Even with such regulatory changes, however, substantial agency costs are likely to persist. Nothing short of granting owners well-defined and guaranteed rights of transferability, exclusivity, and residual claimancy will greatly affect agency costs and managerial control. There are no methods by which the structure of state-owned enterprises can be modified to solve adequately incentive and governance problems when there is a separation of ownership and control without actually granting owners these new rights, which would require privatizing the firm. If there were, central planners in formerly Communist states undoubtedly would have discovered them long ago.

Commentary by David E. M. Sappington

Professor Geddes's chapter makes and ably supports an important observation: the Postal Reorganization Act of 1970 did not create the strongest incentives for cost-minimizing, value-maximizing performance by the Postal Service. The thesis of the chapter is that the act did not activate the control mechanisms that have generally proved effective under private ownership—most notably, property rights to residual cash flows and transferability of these rights. Therefore, the act did not do all it could to foster the incentives for efficient operation that are often observed in privately owned firms.

This main point of the chapter is developed by fashioning fairly stark contrasts between public and private ownership. The author implicitly presumes capital markets to be nearly perfect, which serves to downplay the control problems that can arise even in private corporations. In particular, the self-interested free-riding by shareholders that can limit the efficacy of monitoring and takeovers is afforded little attention. The chapter also abstracts from conflicts among owners of private firms that can limit the discipline owners impose on managers. Conflicts commonly arise over such issues as socially responsible investment, diversification, and managerial compensation. The chapter also tends to downplay the role that reputation and career concerns can play in motivating public sector managers to labor diligently. Although bottom-line performance may be somewhat more difficult to measure in public enterprises, I suspect that alternative prospective employers can acquire useful information about the relevant dimensions of the performance of individual Postal Service managers. Thus, the black-and-white contrasts between control structures in public and private firms are, in practice, more likely to be different shades of gray. The approach taken in the chapter, however, is probably a reasonable approximation for expository purposes, as it enables the author to drive home his main point more clearly.

While the absence of transferable claims to the residual cash flows of the Postal Service is indisputable, it seems to this novice observer that there may be other institutions that provide managerial discipline in the Postal Service, some of which were introduced by the

Postal Reform Act of 1970. As Professor Geddes points out, the act imposed a total budget constraint for the Postal Service and limited the extent of cross subsidies among postal services. These measures would seem to provide meaningful incentives for cost control and to make the performance of individual managers more transparent. Given the widely diffused ownership of the Postal Service, it is conceivable that a meaningful budget constraint might provide nearly the effective discipline that transferable rights to profits would provide.

The growth and development of competitive suppliers of postal services would also seem to impose meaningful discipline on Postal Service managers. Carriers like Federal Express now offer services that substitute for similar service provided by the Postal Service. The competition that these carriers provide can force the Postal Service either to supply high-quality service at reasonable prices or to forfeit the profits attainable from large segments of their operations. The development of the "information superhighway" will also bring pressure to bear on the Postal Service. Electronic mail and services like automatic bill paying are making inroads on what traditionally have been services supplied almost exclusively by the Postal Service. Privately owned postal centers can also help to discipline the performance of traditional post offices. All of these new and developing sources of competitive pressure, coupled with meaningful budget constraints, would seem to supply useful discipline within the confines of public ownership of the postal system.

There is no doubt, however, that Professor Geddes's main point is valid. The existing postal governance structure provides weaker discipline than does the governance structure of the typical private corporation. The question that remains, therefore, is why most postal services continue to be provided directly by the government rather than by private firms. The answer may be the same as in many regulated industries—parties that gain from government intervention and control are reluctant to have the control removed, even when government control is no longer best for society as a whole. Initially, when the mail was the primary form of long-distance communication in the United States, the mail service was viewed as vital to the nation's infrastructure and security. Reasonable arguments for subsidized government provision of mail service at that time could be made. More recently, other reliable means of communication have emerged, and even certain segments of mail service are being provided at reasonable cost by private suppliers. But, as Professor Geddes points out, some well-organized, politically powerful parties—organized labor, in particular—appear to have benefited substantially from government ownership of the Postal Service. Any attempt now to end government ownership would likely come at great political risk. The losses from such a change would be borne by a (relatively) small, concentrated, politically powerful group, while the per capita gains would be small and would accrue to a widely dispersed, unorganized group of constituents—the perfect recipe for political disaster.

But organized labor is not the only group that may benefit from government ownership of the Postal Service. Government ownership permits the pursuit of goals that differ from the goals of a profit-maximizing private firm. Equity and fairness are among the goals a government may pursue. In particular, mail delivery to rural customers may be provided on exactly the same terms as mail delivery to urban customers, even though the former group is more costly to serve. Thus, isolated, rural customers may oppose private ownership of the Postal Service. Many citizens have also grown accustomed to the mail delivery to their doorstep that the government provides six days each week. These customers may object to private ownership of the Postal Service, fearing that a profit-maximizing firm would quickly implement less frequent delivery to clustered mailboxes. And government ownership enables consumers to register their preferences via voting, rather than by purchasing goods and services in the marketplace—a preferred method of representation for some.

Given that immediate, complete private ownership of the United States Postal Service seems unlikely, it remains for us to determine how the best possible performance can be motivated under government ownership. Professor Geddes provides the bad news that the government structure created by the 1970 Postal Reorganization Act does a poor job of enabling owners to control the activities of managers. Is any good news available regarding alternative means of securing desired performance? The selective, partial competition described earlier appears useful in this respect. The threat of losing profitable customers to competitors, coupled with demanding budget constraints and limits on cross subsidies, can provide useful discipline.

But additional steps might be taken to improve the performance of the Postal Service. The compensation of top managers might be tied to key measures of productivity and service quality. Simple summary statistics of the Postal Service's performance might also be published regularly. Statistics that compared the performance of the Postal Service with private mail carriers might be informative. Experiments with additional privatization of components of the postal delivery system might also be undertaken. In addition, certain mail services might be phased out gradually in lieu of further increases in postal rates.

Even if changes of this sort are implemented, however, the reality remains that government ownership of the Postal Service will likely result in higher costs of mail delivery. Bureaucratic procedures and rules hinder the efficient operation of government enterprises. The short-run challenge is to minimize the losses from government ownership of the Postal Service. The long-run challenge is to determine whether private or government ownership best serves society, and if private ownership is superior, to find a politically acceptable means of transferring control from government to private hands.

Discussion

MICHAEL A. CREW, Rutgers University: Is the United Parcel Service a publicly traded corporation?

ANSWER: No, it is a management-owned corporation. The majority of UPS stock is held by present and retired managers and the estates of deceased managers.

QUESTION: Do you know what percentage management owns?

ANSWER: Current management, which consists of over 30,000 managers, holds 70 percent.

QUESTION: What about the ownership structures of Federal Express and RPS Roadway?

ANSWER: Federal Express is a publicly traded company. RPS Roadway is a subsidiary of Roadway Services. Roadway Services is traded on the NASDAQ. RPS is widely held but not publicly traded.

QUESTION: Are there any equity interests in RPS that are publicly traded?

ANSWER: No. The RPS Board of Directors determines the price of the stock every quarter. The price is based on consultations with the company's banks and consultants.

QUESTION: As an economist with the Postal Service for a number of years, I conducted a survey on the attitudes of Americans toward opening the postal industry to more competition and transferring ownership of the Postal Service to stockholders. The respondents to my survey were very supportive of the idea of distributing a substantial ownership stake to postal employees. Based on my survey, there seems to be support for giving postal employees as much as a 50 percent ownership interest in a privately held postal service. If my figures are still correct, would it affect your conclusions regarding the transfer of the Postal Service to a more concentrated ownership structure? More broadly, do you believe the transfer of ownership to postal employees, and possibly institutional investors, is something worthwhile?

R. RICHARD GEDDES, Fordham University: My analysis suggests that privatizing the Postal Service would be beneficial. In terms of ownership rights, that means the new owners (postal employees or otherwise) would become the residual claimants of the firm. Presumably, they would have a legal right to the net cash flows of the firm, and these rights would be transferable. That is, the owners could sell their interests in a secondary market. In effect, the Postal Service would be an open corporation. Your comment, however, seems to assume that the rights would not be fully transferable. If that is true, then I am unsure about how the proposal would work.

As for your second question, diffuse ownership reduces the incentives for individual owners to monitor a firm intensively. But there are ways of alleviating this problem. For instance, mutual funds and pension funds act as a conduit for the transfer of monitoring responsibilities from a diverse group of individuals to a smaller number of expert managers with the incentive to monitor. Ownership by such institutional investors would arguably exert a positive influence.

QUESTION: If the employee-owner of a privatized postal service is to benefit when the value of the organization increases, a mechanism must be created to value the equity interests that he holds. In addition, the Postal Service must show a profit with some regularity for equity interests to increase in value. Profitability, however, is precluded by the break-even constraints imposed by the Postal Reorganization Act of 1970. This statutory obstacle inhibits the Postal Service's responsiveness to prospective ownership schemes. Are you recommending some substantial statutory changes?

PROFESSOR GEDDES: I am not recommending a change. Instead, I am suggesting that privatizing the Postal Service is not enough. We cannot simply stick the postal workers of the United States with a 50 percent stake in a new, privately held corporation with $5 billion in

144

negative net equity. If you think the American postal workers have low morale now, just wait until they find out that they have a stake in a negative asset and responsibility for a large portion of the debt that they did not have when they were only employees. If we give postal employees ownership, it must be ownership in something viable.

COMMENT: Presumably, one would allow the equity owners of a private monopoly a just and reasonable rate of return. If this is true, then we are simply adopting public utility regulation and accepting all the advantages and disadvantages that come with it. And regardless of the disadvantages of public utility regulation, it is preferable to the current situation. The role of the Postal Rate Commission is also relevant. The commission is a highly imperfect control mechanism, even when compared with public utility regulation, because public utility regulation allows for some kind of equity interests and the ordinary control mechanisms that public utility commissions exercise are absent. Allowing an equity interest to be established in the Postal Service and converting the Postal Rate Commission into an organization that sets the rate of returns established for the equity interest would be superior to the present situation.

If, however, we were to move toward a more fully competitive market, compared with a market in which a lesser form of competition applies, then I think Professor Pierce is correct: all the evidence shows that a fully competitive market is superior to public utility regulation. A book by John D. Donahue called *The Privatization Decision*[1] notes that twenty years of empirical evidence on the issue of private ownership of public-type services and competition reveal that private ownership is important but competition is even more important.

COMMENT: Professor Geddes, how would your model be affected if instead of considering taxpayers as the owners of the Postal Service, we considered rate payers to be the owners? I believe that we would have a concentration of large mailers and associations of large mailers, with the potential to influence strongly the management of the Postal Service. Furthermore, in our discussion of control, nobody has mentioned the role of the customer. Stock prices reflect how successful a business is. If a private, monopoly business does not provide what customers want, then they will leave and the firm's stock price will drop. The monopoly situation is different. Customers cannot affect the operations of a monopoly. Whether they like the product or service is not important. Because of the break-even requirement in the

---

1. John D. Donahue, THE PRIVATIZATION DECISION (Basic Books 1989).

Postal Reorganization Act of 1970, there is always the risk of a bailout. Maybe the owners are the ratepayers now.

PROFESSOR GEDDES: It does not matter whether the taxpayers or the rate payers are the owners. The point is that the ownership share in the firm currently is not transferable. Even if the owners are viewed as the rate payers, they still have no claim to the net cash flows of the firm and thus no incentive to monitor Postal Service activities on a large scale.

COMMENT: If the Postal Service is run well, postal rates will not rise. If it is run badly, postal rates will rise. Thus, rate payers and taxpayers have a real vested interest.

PROFESSOR GEDDES: I agree. And I also think that interest is exercised powerfully. Under the current regime, decisions are politically driven. To be sure, some market forces are operating. But the Postal Rate Commission is a political forum. Economic theory suggests that highly organized interest groups can get preferential postal rates at the expense of the less organized. We would expect advertisers who use the mail extensively to be interested in lower rates and to be adept at using the political process to get them.

Unless you guarantee transferability, exclusivity, and residual claimancy to whatever group is ultimately defined as the owners, however, my analysis predicts that rates will be determined according to political rather than economic criteria. The firm will effect cross subsidies from the politically weak to the politically strong. Far from breaking even, the firm will suffer losses. We simply will not get performance out of the firm, regardless of how ownership is defined. Even if we defined the owners to be only persons living in Alaska, this result would not change.

QUESTION: What do you think of plans to have incentive compensation for senior managers in the Postal Service?

PROFESSOR GEDDES: There are some problems with the performance measures. Many of them, though, can be manipulated internally. In fact, in the absence of market forces and rated debt instruments, I am not sure what the performance measures mean.

For example, the Postal Service once performed a number of test mailings to see how quickly it delivered pieces. The test mailings ultimately failed, however, when the test items were found to be easily identifiable by postal workers. Postal workers simply identified which mailings were being tested and expedited them.

A second example of the problems associated with internal performance measures is the Italian postal service's attempt to link compensation to the number of pieces of mail handled by each employee. To influence the measurements, Italian postal workers simply made sure that each piece of mail was handled by at least six or seven people. Consequently, service slowed dramatically.

Profit measures are also a poor proxy for performance and economic profits. Economists generally think that net income is a poor measure of economic profit, even for unregulated, competitive, privately owned firms. Even executive compensation is often not based purely on accounting numbers because CEOs can easily manipulate them through depreciation schedules and so forth. Although the mechanisms may differ slightly, the same manipulation of accounting measures of performance could occur in the Postal Service.

Stock market measures, though, are not easily manipulated. That is why they are so important as potential performance measures, and that is why my analysis emphasizes the need for external measures such as stock markets. In terms of compensation at the Postal Service, at least one-half of all incentives should be in the form of stock returns or something related to equity value—as gauged by the market, not accountants.

COMMENT: Mailers exercise their viewpoint powerfully, but they do it formally by statistical and legal means rather than informally through political channels. Also, the owners of the Postal Service receive information by way of the media. Newspapers know that almost everyone who reads them is an owner of the Postal Service. Egregious examples of poor management end up in the press. This theme has been dominant in the defense industry. But the impact is hard to measure.

PROFESSOR GEDDES: The point about the big mailers' using statistical and legal methods is important because the rate-making process is a virtual showcase for these methods. My point, however, is that the big mailers will be more successful in a political forum than in more market-dominated forums where consumers are diffuse. Although consumers do have the Office of the Consumer Advocate to work on their behalf, it is not as well funded as the big mailers. Perhaps the rate-making process can be improved. But politically powerful groups will probably capture most of the benefits.

It is also true that the press and other watchdog groups can disseminate useful information. The diffusion of ownership, however, is extremely severe in the case of the Postal Service. Its assets are small on a per capita basis. I used 1993 data for the book value of the assets and calculated the value, ignoring the liability side. But we know that the assets are really net negative. It is not worth a given consumer's time to overcome informational and monitoring problems to increase the value of the Postal Service. Ownership is simply too diffuse.

COMMENT: The value of the assets of the Postal Service as counted on its books is the depreciated value of original purchases. The figure is not close to the market value of the assets.

PROFESSOR GEDDES: Right, it is not a market-based measurement and thus not entirely accurate. But, the value does not include the liabilities side of the balance sheet either.

J. GREGORY SIDAK, American Enterprise Institute: Are there any current estimates of the value of the assets?

ANSWER: I have heard estimates of $10–20 billion.

WILLIAM TY MAYTON, Emory University School of Law: The letter mailers are too diffuse to have any clout. Therefore, a system of administrative legal controls would give these mailers some protection in the rate-making process. I think this was an aspiration of the Postal Reorganization Act of 1970. My impression, however, is that the standards in the act and the practices of the Rate Commission are not sufficiently laid out. Due to an absence of real legal standards, the system of administrative controls remains essentially political. More specifically, the established practice is absolutely discretionary. I guess you could call it rate making based on a record with facts. But what are the facts based on?

COMMENT: I think the commission's procedures are rather identifiable and the adversarial process of an open and public hearing provides a good opportunity for the contention and debate of evidence. I do not see it as a political entity.

PROFESSOR MAYTON: If, for example, the commission has the authority to allocate 50 percent of institutional costs according to an inverse elasticity rule, the commission will have a large degree of latitude and will invariably use it to the detriment of first-class mailers.

COMMENT: Maybe that latitude will be used in a way that Congress specified concerning educational and scientific value, the value to the mailer, and what the commission calls the "nine criteria." The commissioners do have some direction from Congress.

PROFESSOR MAYTON: That is what the split between the D.C. Circuit and the Supreme Court was about. The D.C. Circuit said that a real legal standard was needed, but the Supreme Court disagreed.

COMMENT: While the nine criteria in the 1970 act are very flexible, a lawyer can predict with reasonable certainty how the Postal Rate Commission will resolve a particular issue through the body of evidence that has been built over time. I do not know that outcomes are any more unpredictable before the Postal Rate Commission than they are before other rate regulators. There is always some discretion in how a regulator may resolve a particular issue. But this is a common problem in rate regulation generally and not unique to the Postal Service and the Postal Rate Commission.

6

Pricing, Entry, Service Quality, and Innovation under a Commercialized Postal Service

Michael A. Crew and Paul R. Kleindorfer

Postal services, like other traditional network industries such as telecommunications, gas, and electricity, are facing significant competition and technological change. In postal services, competition in message transport services from electronic media can be expected to grow, as will the number of efficient competitors that can compete with the postal administration in performing some of the steps in the traditional postal value chain. For example, consolidators, presort bureaus, and communication-intensive companies that are large enough to sort and drop-ship their mail into the downstream, local delivery network of the national postal service.

The issue of how postal services and postal regulators should react to the influx of competition is an open but vital question. Increasingly, governments and consumers have answered this question with a policy favoring competition. Consequently, there has been a strong trend toward the commercialization of postal administrations, which is evident in increased technological innovation, increased attention to service quality, and the introduction of new services to compete more effectively. Two basic questions have emerged in this process of commercialization:

  • What forms of regulation are appropriate to ensure that essential postal services, such as local delivery, continue to be provided by the Postal Service at reasonable rates and service quality and to encourage "efficient entry" by competitors into various elements of

We would like to thank Robert Cohen, Stephen Sharfman, and J. Gregory Sidak for helpful advice and comments on an earlier draft.

the postal value chain?

• What ownership and governance structures are appropriate to encourage the proper balance between commercialization and profit-orientation of the Postal Service and its traditional public mission of providing universal service?

The economic and regulatory foundations of these questions and their likely evolution within the postal industry will be the subject of this chapter. We see increasing competition and technological change driving this evolution inexorably toward commercial operation of postal services. In step with this evolution, we propose a new framework for regulatory governance of the Postal Service. This framework embodies price-caps for monopoly services, incentives for new product introduction and service quality, and openness to competitive entry.

In the first section, we review the experience of commercialization of postal service in various countries, including the United States. In the next section, we explore regulatory issues in a commercialized postal service, including the pricing of postal services offered to competitors. In the third part, we discuss issues of residual claimants and ownership issues. We conclude with some questions for research and policy.

The Commercialization of Postal Services

By *commercialization*, we mean the process of transforming an organization into one that maximizes its economic profits, possibly subject to constraints to provide universal service, to avoid the exercise of monopoly power, and to protect the public welfare from environmental or health risks and other forms of public restrictions on the private pursuit of profit. To be a commercial enterprise in this sense requires something more than just a stated objective of maximizing profit. The organization must also exhibit both the internal and the external incentive structures, the measurement and accounting architectures, and actual behavior demonstrating its strategic intent to accomplish this objective. In what ways have postal services, worldwide, begun to move in the direction of commercialization?

Postal service is big business. Consider the United States. The United States Postal Service handles 37.5 percent of the world's mail,[1] with a work force of over 700,000 employees[2] and revenues of

---

1. UNIVERSAL POSTAL UNION, SURVEY OF POSTAL ADMINISTRATIONS 3 (1993).

2. For the year ended September 30, 1993, the Postal Service had 691,723 career employees and over 120,000 noncareer employees. 1993 U.S. POSTAL SERV., ANNUAL REPORT OF THE POSTMASTER GENERAL 34.

approximately $50 billion.[3] Over the years, the Postal Service has changed from a department of the federal government to a public enterprise organization. While this evolution continues with the introduction of high-tech equipment and other changes, traditional postal service is facing competition not only from different types of delivery services but also from electronic communications.

In 1837, Rowland Hill originally recognized that the modern postal service presented complicated organizational problems.[4] It is a chain of activities consisting of collection, processing, transportation, and final delivery. Traditionally, these activities have been highly labor intensive, with horses giving way to vans, and the railroad being supplanted by the airlines for long-distance mail carriage. Such advances as occurred took place primarily in suppliers to postal service. Processing mail, especially sorting, remains a highly labor-intensive activity, with approximately 80 percent of the Postal Service's expenditures attributable to labor.[5] With technological advances, however, postal services worldwide have started to adopt high-tech methods of processing. These include coding, such as bar coding, which together with optical character recognition and remote video encoding devices, have the potential to speed the sorting and other processing operations.

In addition to coming to terms with the implications of technological innovations, postal administrations have to face increased competition. For example, mail may be "presorted," "pre-bar coded," or transported to the local delivery network by private firms, which are, in effect, competitors of the postal administration in providing these elements of postal service. Since such competitors save the postal system the cost of performing these tasks, they expect and should receive appropriate discounts for these activities. Efficient approaches and regulatory policy for determining these discounts, or prices paid to competitors for their inputs, have been an active area of recent research.[6]

Competition in postal services extends well beyond coproduction activities. Competition from courier services and facsimile transmission services has already had a substantial effect on postal service,

---

3. *Id.* at 27.

4. ROWLAND HILL, POST OFFICE REFORM (C. Knight & Co. 1837).

5. 1993 U.S. POSTAL SERV., COMPREHENSIVE STATEMENT ON POSTAL OPERATIONS 39.

6. *See* Michael A. Crew & Paul R. Kleindorfer, Pricing in Postal Services under Competitive Entry, Address before the International Conference on Postal and Delivery Services, Stockholm, Sweden (May 1994).

and private delivery services such as Federal Express, United Parcel Service, TNT, Airborne, and DHL are clearly strong global competitors. Similarly, facsimile transmission competes with both first-class letter mail and courier services, and it enjoys the added adv antage of being able to interface with computer terminals directly. An other area of growing competition is electronic mail (E-mail) and electronic data interchange (EDI). Significant cost savings can result from E-mail and EDI services over traditional mail services, especially in repetitive modes of interaction, such as between buyers and suppliers of industrial goods.

The indicated increases in technological complexity and competition will provide significant pressure for postal administrations to commercialize their operations, whether or not they or their regulators may be so inclined. Thus, it should come as no surprise that growing competitive pressure and movement toward commercialized operations are already quite evident in most industrialized countries.[7] The Dutch PTT has just announced that it will privatize operations, beginning with the public sale of about one-third of its equity in June 1994 and moving to majority private ownership in the future.[8] On May 19, 1994, the British government announced its intention to begin the process of privatizing the Royal Mail.[9] A similar legislative initiative is under way for posts and telecommunications in Germany.[10] Several other postal administrations have taken significant steps toward commercialization, including Canada, Sweden, and New Zealand.[11] Commercialization in these countries has resulted in major changes: increased attention to measuring customer service and value added of postal service; increased attention to management effectiveness and to productivity in all phases of the postal value

---

7. *See generally* REGULATION AND THE NATURE OF POSTAL AND DELIVERY SERVICES (Michael A. Crew & Paul R. Kleindorfer eds., Kluwer Academic Publishers 1993); MICHAEL A. CREW & PAUL R. KLEINDORFER, THE ECONOMICS OF POSTAL SERVICE (Kluwer Academic Publishers 1992); COMPETITION AND INNOVATION IN POSTAL SERVICES (Michael A. Crew & Paul R. Kleindorfer eds., Kluwer Academic Publishers 1991).

8. *Hitting the Mail on the Head*, THE ECONOMIST, Apr. 30, 1994, at 69.

9. Ronald Rudd, *Tories May Rebel on Post Sell-Off Plan*, FINANCIAL TIMES, May 19, 1994, at 8.

10. *Labor Pact Clears Way for Privatization of German Post*, A.P., July 2, 1994, *available in* LEXIS, Nexis Library, AP File.

11. *Dying Days for Canada Post*, VANCOUVER SUN, May 19, 1992, at A19; *World Wire: Sweden May Alter Postal Agency*, WALL ST. J., October 18, 1993, at A17; Elmar Toime, *Competitive Strategy for New Zealand Post*, *in* COMPETITION AND INNOVATION IN POSTAL SERVICES, *supra* note 7, at 275.

chain; the introduction of managerial incentive pay; the separation of postal services from other units, such as banking and telecommunications operations, to ensure clarity of cost and value measurement; the introduction of new products and services to serve various segments of the postal marketplace; and generally an increased attention to customer responsiveness, efficiency, and profitability of operations.

The European Community provides a number of examples of the recent trend toward commercialization of postal services. The origins of this trend in Europe began in the general movement toward harmonization and competition across the Continent envisaged in the Treaty of Rome and the subsequent restructuring of the European Community. In postal services, the European Commission summarized the basic issues facing the European Community in the latest draft of the *Green Paper on the Development of the Single Market for Postal Services*.[12] The *Green Paper* is expected to be the basis of directives and regulations to implement its primary recommendations, including:

- establishment of independent regulatory authorities at the national level with some coordination by the European Community
- achievement of a single market, particularly with respect to service delivery standards
- definition of the so-called reserved area, services to be provided solely by national postal administrations, as distinguished from competitive service areas, where other qualified entrants may offer the services

While it is still too early to discern where the European Community will end up in the reorganization of its postal services, the discussion and directives resulting from the *Green Paper* give clear indications of more commercialized operations. The forces driving for this commercialization are competitors that offer express carrier service, some of the more innovative postal administrations (such as the Dutch PTT), and organized consumer groups representing industrial mailers.[13]

---

12. COMM'N OF THE EUR. COMMUNITIES, GREEN PAPER ON THE DEVELOPMENT OF THE SINGLE MARKET FOR POSTAL SERVICES (1992).

13. The conduct of the Dutch PTT, for example, would have been unthinkable in a previous era. In addition to providing fee-for-service consulting services to other postal authorities and private carriers, the Dutch PTT has capitalized through extensive remailing on regulatory-induced imperfections in "terminal dues tariffs." For example, mail destined for country *B* and mailed in country *A* is routed through country *C* in order to take advantage

For example, express carrier service operators are likely to achieve their efforts in having nonreserved or competitive services specified by a very low weight or postage limit. Anything weighing more than four ounces or requiring postage in excess of $2.00 could be open to competition. Similarly, customer groups and private consolidators have already achieved assurances in principle that the European Community will monitor service standards and costing for downstream access, both for in-country drop-shipments as well as for cross-border consolidated drop-shipments.[14]

These changes have brought about a new awareness in postal administrations of the importance of not only accurate and service-specific cost accounting, but also market knowledge—product usage, quality preferences, and price sensitivity of various customer segments.

A parallel development has been the clarification of cost-of-service elements. We have seen the divestiture of banking and telecommunications operations from postal operations, including the separation of British Telecom and the Royal Mail and the 1989 case of the Deutsche Bundespost[15] and the current evolution in Poste Italiane. A new sense of urgency and of customer and competitor awareness is apparent in many European postal administrations. This increased focus on the value added by postal administrations is further enhanced by changes in postal management systems to measure service quality, revenue, and cost by service and customer segment.

This increased commercialization is also apparent in Scandinavia.[16] For example, Sweden Post was recently reorganized as a private corporation, albeit with all shares still owned by the Swedish govern-

---

of inefficiently low rates (in the form of terminal dues payments) between countries C and B. The Dutch PTT, for example, would consolidate mail in country A, transport it to country C, and mail it from there to country B. The cost differences between this more complicated "remailing" routing and the apparently simpler AB route can be quite significant. *See* Philip Dobbenberg, *The International Mail Market in the 1990s*, *in* REGULATION AND THE NATURE OF POSTAL AND DELIVERY SERVICES, *supra* note 7, at 207.

14. *See, e.g.*, Colin J. Mitchell, A Consumers' Groups' View of New Services, Quality and Regulation, Address Before the International Conference on Postal and Delivery Services, Stockholm, Sweden (May 1994).

15. Katie Hafner, *German Phone System Is Taxed by Unification*, N.Y. TIMES, Dec. 10, 1990, at D8.

16. For a discussion of some of the service quality initiatives in Scandinavia, see Christian Bruun, *Nordic Measurements 1991: Service Performance and Terminal Dues Settlement*, *in* REGULATION AND THE NATURE OF POSTAL AND DELIVERY SERVICES, *supra* note 7, at 53.

ment.[17] This implies, however, that Sweden Post will be operated as a commercial venture, paying the value-added tax, providing profit and value-added accounting, and generally facing a number of reporting requirements and incentives that will move its operations to commercial status. In the beginning of 1994, Finland also reorganized its postal service into an arms-length, government-owned company.[18] These changes clearly underline the new spirit of commercialization apparent in Europe.

In Asia and Oceania similar commercial stirrings are becoming apparent. Best known is the New Zealand Post, which was incorporated in 1987.[19] The law and associated regulations have encouraged the commercialization of New Zealand Post by allowing and promoting competition from privately operated mail consolidation and mail-service centers and by requiring management reforms directed at profit and value-added measurement for the enterprise as a whole and for its separate lines of business. Coupled with new service offerings (such as downstream access, contract services to industrial clients, innovative billing procedures for large-volume mailers), and a strong service-quality orientation, New Zealand Post has clearly signaled its intent to operate and compete as a commercial enterprise.

In the United States, the Postal Reorganization Act of 1970 was intended to be a first step in moving the Postal Service toward commercialized operations. The establishment of the Postal Rate Commission and the cost and service arguments that have formed the core of service pricing in the commission hearings and decisions have arguably provided the informational foundation for commercialized operations. But it is also clear that, at least until recently, the Postal Service has been protected from the competitive pressures necessary to move it toward a commercial and competitive culture. The Postal Service provides an exceedingly basic universal service. It attempts to be responsive to its main customers—large business mailers—through its marketing and the regulatory process. Much of what it does now it would continue to do if moved to more commercialized operations through increasing competition. But the Postal Service will clearly have to move much farther in several areas if it is to be an effective competitor:

---

17. James Fryckland, *Private Mail in Sweden*, 13 CATO J. 69 (1993).

18. *Finland: Posti Ja Telelaitos Prepares for Incorporation of Tele and Posti*, KAUPPALEHTI, July 28, 1993, at 8.

19. *See* Elmar Toime, *Service Performance in the Postal Business, in* REGULATION AND THE NATURE OF POSTAL AND DELIVERY SERVICES, *supra* note 7, at 273.

• Cost, including capital costs, and value measurement systems must be mutually aligned with services and underlying processes so that postal management can understand whether they are earning profits from particular services and customer segments.

• New services must be devised for a variety of customer segments, including date-certain delivery services, service guarantees, better commercial billing practices, and contracting services.

• The Postal Service must develop market-driven orientation to understand and compete for the changing combination of demands for information-forwarding services, including both electronic and letter services, to and from industrial customers.

• A different (competitive) mind-set with significant effects on organizational decision processes and labor-management relations must evolve.

The most important ingredient in moving the Postal Service toward such commercialized operations will be the regulatory governance structure that will determine the nature and strength of competitive forces shaping its incentives, the potential entrants into the industry, and the customers of the Postal Service. This governance structure, the subject of the remainder of this chapter, will need to be changed from its current form if commercialized operations are to become a reality in the United States.

Regulation of a Commercialized Postal Service

In designing a regulatory regime for a commercialized postal service, we have a number of principles in mind. First, the regulator should be independent and be seen as independent. Second, the regulator should not micromanage the Postal Service. Third, efficiency should be a significant and explicit concern of the regulator. Fourth, the regulator should be able to make and be seen to make credible commitments. And fifth, the regulator should balance the interests of consumers and the Postal Service.

The Postal Rate Commission is nominally not independent of the Postal Service. Its decisions can be overruled by a unanimous vote of the Board of Governors of the Postal Service, provided that the board can show that the revenue requirement is not adequate for the financial viability of the Postal Service.[20] In practice, this statutory framework does not compromise the independence of the commission, which has a well-deserved reputation for making its own deci-

20. 39 U.S.C. § 3625(d).

sions based upon the evidence presented. The commission is in no way a rubber stamp for the Postal Service. A commercialized Postal Service, however, would have a board of directors, equivalent to that of commercial companies, thus making it improper for the Postal Service to have even the slightest oversight of, or influence over, the postal regulator. Such a change would further strengthen the commission's independence. The commission would continue to be subject to presidential appointment and Senate confirmation.

Although our view of the organization of regulatory governance to promote commercialization of the Postal Service would not require major changes, the nature of the regulation to encourage and sustain commercialization would differ considerably from the current regime on both practical and theoretical grounds. We propose that the new regulator not employ cost-of-service regulation[21] and not regulate all aspects of the postal business. The regulator would directly regulate only part of the business. The mode of regulation would be price-cap regulation, rather than the cost-of-service regulation currently employed. To understand how such regulation might be instituted, we consider the commission's current decision process and how this would be changed to institute price-cap regulation.

The commission now regulates all the services supplied by the Postal Service, except international mail, using cost-of-service regulation. The system of regulation currently operating is very similar procedurally to regulation of public utilities by state commissions and to regulation by federal commissions, such as the Federal Communications Commission and the Federal Energy Regulatory Commission. The procedure is adversarial. It is also complex and replete with transactions costs, as may be sensed from our brief description and commentary below.

There are two major types of postal cases, rate cases and classification cases. Rate cases consider applications to increase rates. Classification cases consider the grouping of mail into categories for the purpose of changing rates—for example, establishing new presort discount categories within a class of mail. Rate cases are usually initiated by the Postal Service, although they can be initiated by the Postal Rate Commission following a justifiable complaint from an interested party, such as a competitor or a mailer. Classification cases may be initiated by the Postal Service, or the commission may launch a classification case on its own initiative.

The commission also has jurisdiction in a number of other areas.

---

21. Cost-of-service regulation is also known as rate-of-return regulation in public utility regulation.

When the Postal Service wishes to change the terms and conditions of a particular service it must seek an "advisory opinion" from the commission[22]—which the Postal Service is then free to disregard.[23] A recent example of such an advisory opinion was when the Postal Service sought advice on changing the overnight delivery area for first-class mail.[24] The commission also hears appeals and rules on the issue of closing small post offices.

A rate case begins with the filing of a request by the Postal Service. The commission must render a "recommended" decision within ten months from the date of filing.[25] On receiving the commission's decision, the postal governors may accept it, accept under protest, or reject.[26] By accepting under protest, the new postal rates are allowed to go into effect, while the governors request a modification or explanation. After their request to the commission, the governors may modify the decision themselves by unanimous vote, provided that they can show that the revenue requirement in the commission's decision was insufficient to allow the Postal Service to break even.[27] However, only once have the governors modified the commission's decision.[28]

The litigation process is complicated and must comply with the Administrative Procedures Act, so as to provide due process.[29] Initially, the Postal Service files written testimony comprising its case. Typically, dozens of mailers and competitors intervene and respond with discovery requests. Intervenors may also orally cross-examine Postal Service witnesses and file written testimony, which the Postal Service cross-examines. There is a final opportunity to rebut intervenor testimony and cross-examination. Legal counsel for all parties file briefs and make oral arguments before the commission makes its decision.

---

22. 39 U.S.C. § 3661(b).

23. 39 U.S.C. § 3625(d).

24. *See* Testimony by John Potter and Seymour Lazarowitz, Request of the United States Postal Service for an Advisory Opinion on a Change in the First Class Delivery Standards, Dkt. No. N89–1 (Postal Rate Comm'n, Sept. 29, 1989).

25. 39 U.S.C. § 3624(c)(1).

26. 39 U.S.C. § 3625(a).

27. "Revenue requirement" is another way of saying "allowed revenues."

28. This happened in the 1980 rate case (R–80).

29. Judicial review of decisions of the Postal Rate Commission is to be conducted in accordance with the Administrative Procedure Act on the basis of the record before the commission and the Postal Board of Governors. Mail Order Ass'n of Am. *v.* United States Postal Serv., 2 F.3d 408 (D.C. Cir. 1993).

The procedures used by the commission to determine the revenue requirement involve the use of a "test year." The test year must begin not more than twenty-four months after the date of filing. Required revenues are calculated by estimating the volume of each class of mail and then estimating the costs in the test year based on assumed inflation rates. If existing rates would result in an excess of costs over revenue in the test year, a rate increase is allowed. The rate increase includes a contingency allowance, normally 3.5 percent of costs, and an allowance for the recovery of equity diminished by losses in prior years. The reduction in volume arising from the increase in rates, based upon demand elasticity estimates, is considered in arriving at the break-even rates.

In addition to determining the revenue requirement, a rate case will determine the rates. Thus testimony on rate design and cost attribution will be included in a rate case. Costs are divided into attributable costs and institutional costs. Each class of mail has to cover at least its attributable costs. Institutional costs, which are approximately one-third of total costs, are distributed to the different classes of mail, usually with first-class mail carrying a larger proportion.[30]

Although both postal and utility regulation are based on cost of service, the process of postal regulation differs significantly from rate-of-return analysis used in public utility regulation. The Postal Service is not a for-profit entity; unlike most utilities, it is highly labor intensive (over 80 percent of its costs are labor). Thus, rate-of-return regulation by no means takes on the importance that it does in utility regulation. The testimony on the allowed rate of return, which is paramount in traditional utility regulation, is not part of postal rate hearings. If the utility regulator allows a higher rate of return, the stockholders potentially stand to benefit. In postal service regulation, however, there is not the same direct concern with rate of return. The Postal Service has a break-even requirement, which includes covering interest payments on its borrowing. The requirement to establish an opportunity cost of capital, the basis of most rate-of-return testimony in utility cases, is not present in postal rate cases.

The current system of postal regulation emphasizes due process. As a result, it is inflexible and would prevent many of the potential benefits of commercialization from being achieved. Cost-of-service

---

30. For a discussion of how such costs are distributed and whether Ramsey principles are employed, see Roger Sherman & Anthony George, *Second Best Pricing for the United States Postal Service*, 45 S. ECON. J. 685 (1979); Frank A. Scott, Jr., *Assessing United States Postal Ratemaking: An Application of Ramsey Pricing*, 34 J. INDUS. ECON. 279 (1986).

regulation would destroy incentives for efficiency and, by continuing to subject the Postal Service to rate regulation of its competitive services, would increase the Postal Service's costs and place it at a serious competitive disadvantage. A more flexible approach to regulation is required if commercialization is to be accomplished.

Our basic proposal is simple: only services where there is any significant monopoly power would be subject to regulation and, for these services, the mode of regulation would be price-cap regulation rather than cost-of-service regulation.

We choose price-cap regulation for a number of reasons, the most important being that it breaks the link between cost and price that exists with cost-of-service regulation. Rate-of-return regulation caps the return on capital that the regulated firm is allowed to earn. For the Postal Service, with no shareholders and the absence of a profit motive, rate-of-return regulation does not have the same relevance. However, while rate-of-return regulation and cost-of-service regulation are synonymous, cost-of-service regulation better describes the situation faced by the Postal Service than rate-of-return regulation does. Under the current system of cost-of-service regulation, the only reason for granting a rate increase is that the Postal Service can show that it can no longer cover its costs or that it is in danger in the near future of not being able to cover its costs. The more the Postal Service can show that its costs have increased, the greater the total increase in revenue requirements it can seek (and obtain). As with all systems of regulation that condition revenues on costs in this way, cost-of-service provides no incentives for cost economy or intertemporal efficiency.

By contrast, under price-cap regulation, costs and revenues are decoupled. The basic idea of price-cap regulation is very simple. For the period of the price cap, changing prices no longer requires the explicit permission of the regulator. The price cap is set for the base year and is allowed to increase as a simple function of the rate of increase in the consumer price index, the GNP deflator, or some such economywide measure of price inflation.

Price-cap regulation has been employed to regulate a number of industries. The United Kingdom has used price caps to regulate gas, electricity, telephony, water, and the British Airports Authority. In the United States, price-cap regulation has been used extensively in telecommunications. AT&T is subject to the Federal Communications Commission's price-cap regulation for interstate traffic.[31] The regional

---

31. AT&T is also subject to state regulation for its intrastate traffic. In some jurisdictions, price caps apply to such intrastate traffic as well.

Bell operating companies (RBOCs) are subject to price-cap regulation in some jurisdictions. The form that price-cap regulation may take varies. All schemes start with a base of automatic price increases less an "X factor," for example, CPI − X. Such a scheme implies automatic rate increases at less than the rate of inflation for a fixed period, normally five years.[32]

Price-cap regulation was first proposed by Stephen C. Littlechild in 1983 as the regulatory scheme for British Telecom (BT).[33] The plan allowed BT to raise its rates automatically each year during a five-year period using the formula RPI − X.[34] On the expiration of the five-year period, the formula would then be revisited by the regulator. BT is a multiproduct firm; its products fall into three main groups: local, long-distance, and international. The price cap is applied to a Laspeyres index of all of these products. BT is allowed to raise the index of its products by the RPI − X formula each year.[35] Thus, within the constraint of the index, it has considerable flexibility to change prices. Although the freedom is apparently unlimited in practice, BT cannot raise local rates by a large amount and balance the index with a very large cut in long-distance or international rates, for fear that public outcry might result in unfavorable action being taken by the regulator. Unlike the case of AT&T and the RBOCs, there is no explicit limit on the rate of return that BT may earn on its capital within the period of the price cap.

The scheme for BT differed in one major respect from the plan originally proposed by Professor Littlechild.[36] He had argued that the plan would apply only to the natural monopoly services—basic service, primarily local residential and small business local service—which is sometimes known as "plain old telephone service" or POTS. He argued that his plan would provide protection against monopoly

---

32. The X factor is sometimes referred to as a productivity offset, the idea being to pass on some productivity gains to consumers. However, it is not, and should not be, directly related to productivity. It is best conceived of as a "give-back" for the freedom to change prices allowed in price-cap regulation.

33. STEPHEN C. LITTLECHILD, U.K. DEP'T OF TRADE & INDUS., REGULATION OF BRITISH TELECOMMUNICATIONS PROFITABILITY (1983). Littlechild was professor of commerce, University of Birmingham, when he made his proposal for price-cap regulation. He subsequently became the first director-general of the Office of Electricity Regulation (OFFER) in the United Kingdom.

34. The retail price index (RPI) is the United Kingdom's equivalent of the CPI.

35. See, e.g., JOHN VICKERS & GEORGE YARROW, PRIVATIZATION: AN ECONOMIC ANALYSIS 206–07 (MIT Press 1988).

36. See Littlechild, supra note 33.

because the "tariff reduction is focused precisely on the services of monopoly concern."[37] The scheme actually implemented included the whole range of BT services, however, including competitive services such as international services.

Regulators of commercialized postal services can learn from Littlechild's proposal and BT's experience. Under our proposal, services provided by the Postal Service would be divided into two baskets. One basket would consist of all regulated, or "reserved," services; the other basket would be the unregulated, or "unreserved," services. The regulated basket would consist of only those services over which the Postal Service had monopoly power, and price-cap regulation would apply only to this regulated basket.[38]

How would services be identified for each basket, and what would be the nature of the monopoly? In view of its universal-service obligations, a commercialized Postal Service would expect to have some monopoly protection. For example, a post office may have a legal monopoly for all letters requiring less than $2.00 postage. This is "monopoly limit." Currently the limit is $3.00, or twice the applicable first-class postage.[39] Under our commercialization proposal, the limit would instead be set at a multiple of the basic first-class rate. This multiple might initially be set at ten times the rate and then be reduced by one each year over the term of the price cap. Thus, the items in the regulated basket would all be services below the monopoly limit. Thus the monopoly limit would cover all traditional mail at present plus the rate for access to the local delivery network.

The price-cap index that we propose would be simple. The regulator would set the price of basic first-class postage and the price of access to the local delivery network for the first ounce and each subsequent ounce.[40] In addition, the price of special services and services mandated by Congress (such as material for the blind, certified mail, and registered mail) would fall within the price cap. The Postal Service would be free to raise rates by the rate of general inflation over the period of the price cap. With only two principal products, the Postal Service would have to decide how much to increase the price

---

37. *Id.* at 34.

38. Our regulated basket is quite small, consisting of only access and first-class service. This is to deter cross subsidy and predation within the basket.

39. 39 C.F.R. § 320.6 (c).

40. We discuss only what we believe is the strongest implementation of price-cap regulation. Other possible implementations include applying price-cap regulation only to access with a universal first-class service requirement and applying price-cap regulation to both access and first-class service, but without a universal first-class service requirement.

for each product so as to keep the index of the two products within the allowable rate of increase.

The commercialized Postal Service would be allowed to set all other prices without regulation. Thus, second-, third-, and fourth-class mail would be unregulated. Discounts for bar coding and quantity would not be subject to regulation. Would this structure enable the commercial Postal Service to exploit monopoly power or practice other anticompetitive behavior? As we have argued elsewhere,[41] the Postal Service should set discounts equal to its long-run avoided cost for the activity concerned. If it provides a lesser or greater discount, it will discourage efficient or encourage inefficient entry or "worksharing." Will there be an incentive to set such discounts efficiently?

Discounts for worksharing might include presorting and bar coding. With increases in automation, bar codes will assume greater significance while presorting will become much less valuable. A commercialized firm subject to price-cap regulation does not have incentives to cross subsidize its own bar-code operations.[42] It does not follow, however, that it will price bar coding exactly at marginal cost. The most likely scenario is that it will operate as a dominant firm. If the Postal Service behaved as predicted by the simple traditional model of price leadership,[43] then it would not set bar code discounts at marginal costs. Unless competitors' costs were dramatically higher than the Postal Service's, however, the distortions that might result from this kind of price leadership are not likely to be major.

Although our proposals represent a significant departure from the current practice of postal regulation, and even public utility regulation generally, they are consistent with Professor Littlechild's price-cap proposal. As such, they carry all the well-known advantages and disadvantages of price-cap regulation. The advantages are that price caps provide incentives for cost economy and efficiency, reduce transactions costs by avoiding rate hearings, and permit pricing flexibility in competitive markets. In addition, our plan provides protection against monopoly exploitation and a regulatory governance structure for resolving disputes. The disadvantages of price-cap regulation are that it does not answer the question of how to set the initial level of the price cap and does not necessarily maintain quality of service. In

41. *See* CREW & KLEINDORFER, THE ECONOMICS OF POSTAL SERVICE, *supra* note 7; and Crew & Kleindorfer, Pricing in Postal Services under Competitive Entry, *supra* note 6.

42. *See* Ronald R. Braeutigam & John C. Panzar, *Diversification Incentives under "Price-Based" and "Cost-Based" Regulation*, 20 RAND J. ECON. 373 (1989).

43. *See, e.g.*, ROBERT S. PINDYCK & DANIEL L. RUBENFELD, MICROECONOMICS 454 (Macmillan Publishing Co. 1992).

contrast to cost-of-service regulation, a price-cap regulated firm has an incentive to reduce quality of service in an effort to reduce costs and increase profits.

Setting the initial level of the price cap is normally problematic in telecommunications. Because of the existence of significant cross subsidies, merely setting the existing prices is difficult. With postal service, however, the main cross subsidies are not between products but within product classes. Thus the main cross subsidy of first-class mail customers in outlying areas is derived from the other first-class mail customers. Similarly, the cross subsidy that is provided to mailers of hard-to-read addresses, addresses without zip codes, and other problems are the other members of the class. Setting a monopoly limit is intended to address this problem. The initial level of the price cap is not expected to be very different from the structure of current rates. Some one-time individual adjustments may have to be incorporated into the initial price cap to take into account, for example, the problems of underfunding of pension benefits and the setting of a target rate of return on capital.

Under price-cap regulation, an important change takes place in the regulator's duties. The regulator has to become more concerned about quality of service. Currently the United States Postal Service and the United Kingdom Post Office employ independent consultants to monitor service quality.[44] Such efforts could continue with the consultants' reports being made available to the regulator as well as the postal service. Continuation of such efforts would be relatively more straightforward. More complicated would be situations where the Postal Service wants to modify its existing services. For example, the Postal Service recently proposed modifying its overnight delivery areas for first-class mail. Within existing areas, some places are much more difficult, and therefore more costly, to serve on an overnight basis than others. Indeed, recently, the Postal Service has addressed this issue with testimony before the Postal Rate Commission.[45]

---

44. The Postal Service, for example, recently reported that it had "expanded the range of the independent customer satisfaction and service performance measurement systems in 1993 through the award of two major contracts." 1993 U.S. POSTAL SERV., COMPREHENSIVE STATEMENT ON POSTAL OPERATIONS 1. Gallup will sample a full range of business customers on a set of service attributes critical to their business to measure how well the Postal Service is meeting business customer needs. Id. Price Waterhouse will conduct an independent measurement of service performance for third-class mail. Id.

45. See Testimony by John Potter and Seymour Lazarowitz, Request of the United States Postal Service for an Advisory Opinion on a Change in the First

Under price-cap regulation, the issue of service quality would take on increasing importance as the Postal Service seeks further ways of reducing costs as a result of the incentives created by the price cap. Such changes in service standards would require the permission of the Postal Rate Commission. Under our proposal, the commission would no longer give advisory opinions on such matters. Such decisions would now be binding (subject to the same rights of appeal from the decisions of other federal regulatory commissions). In making his decision, the regulator would take into account the change in benefits relative to costs. If the regulator were convinced that a substantial cost saving results from a service change that produced relatively few benefits, it would consider approving the change. Similarly, the regulator might allow a reduction in service standards in one area if this reduction accompanied an increase in another area, provided that the regulator judged the benefit-cost ratio to be favorable. The basis on which the regulator made his decision might be fairly complicated, a necessary condition being the demonstration of a favorable benefit-cost ratio.

A related issue would be the product combination. Under our proposal, if the Postal Service wished to introduce a new service, that service could remain unregulated for at least three years or until the end of the period of the price cap, whichever were longer. Following that, the regulator, if petitioned by an intervenor or on his own initiative, could undertake an inquiry to determine whether the product should continue to be unregulated or placed in the regulated basket. This arrangement would provide the opportunity for the development of many new services, not just variations on the Postal Service's unregulated services, but variations on its regulated services as long as the existing regulated services remained intact. (If a new service were to replace an existing regulated service, the regulator's permission would have to be sought.) All kinds of product innovation would be possible. For example, the local delivery network might offer package delivery so that existing carriers, such as UPS and RPS, and any new entrants might take advantage of this service. Similarly, the Postal Service might act as agents for express carriers by allowing express customers to drop off their express letters or packets at postal windows or in special postal drop boxes. Other possibilities would be for new products in traditional letters markets. One possibility might be a new class for business mail, which would replace some of the first-class mail currently used by business. This product might offer

Class Delivery Standards, Dkt. No. N89–1 (Postal Rate Comm'n, Sept. 29, 1989).

delivery standards that were slower than existing first-class mail but faster than existing third-class mail. It might be highly standardized—perhaps requiring only one kind of standard envelope—and would obviously have to be bar coded. This product might require drop off, either at the local delivery network or at the originating office, during particular hours of the day, and it might not be offered during the Christmas rush. We would expect such a product to offer a significant discount over existing first-class mail.

It is important for the Postal Service to be innovative in the current situation of competition and technological change, and the foregoing kinds of procedures would give the Postal Service an incentive to promote cost economy and to develop new services. By being guaranteed at least three years without regulation for new products that did not replace existing regulated products and by therefore being allowed to keep all the benefits of the new product for this period, the Postal Service would be encouraged to develop new products. Nevertheless, postal customers would be protected from abuse of monopoly power by these procedures.

New legislation would be necessary to establish a commercialized Postal Service that incorporated the regulatory changes that we propose. The statutes would not only define the nature and scope of the new regulatory regime, but also expressly address the relationship between regulation and antitrust, including the extent to which a commercialized Postal Service should have immunity from the antitrust laws. Given the state of knowledge, it would be irresponsible not to write the statutes with great care to address such issues. Although it is beyond the scope of this chapter to address these issues, the principles are clear.[46] In the monopoly market segments, the regulatory authority should be paramount, subject to appeal to higher tribunals. These procedures should provide immunity from litigation on antitrust grounds in the trial courts.

Organization and Ownership Structures

Many economists have sung the praises of price-cap regulation in the context of utility regulation.[47] The question that arises is whether these advantages would also occur in postal service. Under the current governance structure for the Postal Service, it is not very likely

---

46. Such issues are expected to be addressed at length in William Kovacic's study commissioned by the American Enterprise Institute.

47. *E.g.*, Ingo Vogelsang, *Price Cap Regulations of Telecommunications Services: A Long-Run Approach, in* DEREGULATION AND DIVERSIFICATION OF UTILITIES 21-42 (Michael A. Crew ed., Kluwer Academic Publishers 1989).

that many, if any, of the claimed advantages of price-cap regulation would materialize. This is because the incentives under the current system of public enterprise may override the efficiency incentives provided by price-cap regulation. Residual claimants are a primary condition if price-cap regulation is to promote efficiency. Under the current public enterprise system, the residual claimants are so ill defined—they are the entire population of the United States—as to be effectively nonexistent. Indeed, the system seems to be designed to eliminate residual claimants. For example, it is not clear that managers have any residual claims, because their salaries are subject to an upper limit. This absence of residual claimants may explain the compensation arrangements of the union personnel and their relatively high compensation.[48]

It would be possible for a privatized Postal Service to respond to the appropriate incentives for efficiency under a system of price-cap regulation. Could a commercialized but publicly owned Postal Service respond equally well? The answer would depend to a considerable extent on whether the board of directors acting as agents for the shareholder were truly independent of the political process and had duties and obligations that were no different from those of the board of any other privately owned company. This would mean that the Postal Service could no longer borrow from the Treasury but would have to go into the commercial market. If the board did indeed behave in these ways, it would change the rules for tenure of employment and set up widespread incentive compensation mechanisms for postal managers based upon productivity, financial performance, and customer satisfaction. Simultaneously, changes would be required in the system of compensation and tenure for rank-and-file employees to provide them with an incentive (perhaps profit sharing) to work to achieve commercial operations. For a commercial concern to operate within the current system, where the right to strike is replaced by compulsory arbitration and where certain benefits are mandated, would be exceedingly difficult. The probability of making these kinds of changes while remaining under public ownership would be exceedingly low. Labor and others would constantly be lobbying Congress to intervene, complicating the task of the board and management in attaining the goals of commercialization. Similarly, although the Postal Service no longer borrows from the Treasury and

---

48. *See* Michael L. Wachter & Jeffrey M. Perloff, *A Comparative Analysis of Wage Premiums and Industrial Relations in the British Post Office and the United States Postal Service*, *in* COMPETITION AND INNOVATION IN POSTAL SERVICES, *supra* note 7, at 115.

no longer has the U.S. government guarantee the bonds of the Postal Service, as a practical matter bondholders would recognize that the government would not allow the Postal Service to go bankrupt as long as it was the only shareholder.

On balance, it is difficult for the Postal Service to be truly commercialized under its current structure. In the long term, establishing credible residual claimants will require a move toward substantial privatization of the Postal Service. In the interim, commercialization could be initiated by moving to a corporate structure with a profit-oriented mission, subject to well-defined social obligations, such as universal service for letter mail. This corporatization could then be followed, as in the case of the Dutch PTT, by a gradual privatization through public offerings of stock. To initiate this process, an inquiry into the mission, organization, and ownership of the Postal Service should be initiated by Congress with due attention paid to the experience of other postal administrations currently undergoing privatization.

The evolution to privatization is likely to be a difficult one with many political obstacles in its way.[49] Progress in this direction may require that the Postal Service first incur significant losses under the current system. As this evolution occurs, however, it should be emphasized that the Postal Service will require a very different regulatory governance scheme in order to keep pace with pressures for commercialization arising from competition and technological change. The regulatory framework that we have sketched above offers the possibility of such incentives both within the current governance structure and for the evolving structure of a commercialized and privatized Postal Service.

Conclusion

In this chapter, we have argued that increases in competition and technological complexity will require commercially minded postal administrations. Sticking to more traditional public service or cost-of-service regulatory approaches cannot survive in the long run in this environment. Thus, the key question we have posed is not *whether* but *how* to assist in the process of encouraging the necessary transforma-

---

49. It is encouraging that others are currently examining changes in the organization of the Postal Service. *See, e.g.*, Kathy M. Rogerson & David E. Treworgy, Competitive Analysis of Vertical Integration in the United States Postal Services, Address before the International Conference on Postal and Delivery Services, Stockholm, Sweden (May 1994).

tion of postal services and regulatory governance structures to commercial operations.

The key ingredient is to encourage competition to provide the needed incentives and discipline for productivity improvements and service innovation. This also implies allowing postal administrations to compete and be as free as possible of the inflexibilities of regulation. At the same time, end-to-end, universal service must continue to be available to all citizens as a basic ingredient of the modern nation-state. The appropriate balance between these dictates of promoting competition, decreasing regulatory transactions costs, and maintaining the backbone of a universal network can be accomplished by a well-delineated price-cap regime.

What remains to be accomplished is to work out the details of the regime we have proposed and to move to implement this scheme as quickly as practicable. In the process, the following issues are likely to arise:

• fine-tuning the initial setting of the price caps to ensure viable cash flow and to "true up" the organization's balance sheet relative to competitive requirements, as in the case of accounting for unfunded pension liabilities

• the problems of adjusting for capital recovery requirements that were inherited from historical depreciation methods or that may result from "stranded commitments" that are not competitively viable

• agreeing on costing systems and service standards to ensure that costs are transparent, that continuing commitments to monopoly customers are met, and that cross subsidization of competitive services is minimized (especially where common facilities are employed)

In short, the normal transition pains associated with any major regulatory change can be expected.[50] These will be significant departures from the status quo. But judging from the benefits of commercialization achieved in other traditional network sectors, moving the Postal Service toward commercialized operations and encouraging stronger competition in postal services should be well worth the costs.

Commentary by Paul H. Rubin

Professors Crew and Kleindorfer have written a chapter at war with itself. Much of it addresses price-cap regulation, how it would work

---

50. For a more detailed discussion of some of these difficulties of changing to price-cap regulation, see CREW & KLEINDORFER, THE ECONOMICS OF POSTAL SERVICE, *supra* note 7.

for the Postal Service, and how it would be optimal. I have no particular problem with that analysis. But only the third section of the chapter confronts the important question, How do we accomplish postal reform?

As Professors Crew and Kleindorfer acknowledge, reforming the Postal Service would require major changes in labor relations. The probability of the Postal Service's making these changes while remaining under public ownership would be exceedingly low. Labor and other groups would constantly lobby Congress to intervene. We are left with a situation in which Professors Crew and Kleindorfer are in effect saying, "This would be the way to commercialize the Postal Service, if we could do it; but we probably can't do it this way." That may be right.

Professors Crew and Kleindorfer never define the relevant constraints. Theirs is almost an engineering approach. The constraints are clearly political constraints. What are they? In particular, is there any political condition that would make it possible to commercialize the Postal Service and impose efficient regulations? I suspect that there is not. If there *does* exist a set of conditions that would let us commercialize the Postal Service and run it efficiently, then those same conditions would probably let us either privatize the Postal Service entirely or repeal the Express Statutes and let firms compete with the Postal Service and probably starve it to death. I believe that it would be superior to commercialization of the Postal Service to pursue either complete privatization or repeal of the Private Express Statutes and free competition. If we have the political ability to accomplish what Professors Crew and Kleindorfer recommend, we might also have the political ability to accomplish what I recommend, and that would be clearly superior.

Consequently, I recommend that we examine reform of the Postal Service with a much more explicit public choice analysis. David Sappington concluded his remarks by saying that political constraints are important. I would start there and ask, Who are the interest groups with power, what power do they have, what kinds of reforms can we get past them? Perhaps more important, we should ask ourselves as economists whether there is any way to design a change in policy that would take account of the existence of the political constraints.

We economists talk about Hicks-Kaldor efficient changes in policy, where it is possible for the gainers to compensate the losers. On occasion, though not often, we can actually devise schemes under which the gainers *do* compensate the losers—for example, the proposal mentioned earlier that we give postal workers a share of the value of the Postal Service. Giving postal workers a share of the value and allowing them to trade those values may be a way to get around one of the political constraints. Similarly, is there a way to buy off major customers? I question the benefits of universal service; if people want to live in places to which mail delivery is expensive, they can pay that cost. But if rural people do have the political power, then is there any way we could buy them off—for example, by giving them each a modem so that they can send and receive their mail electronically? We must identify the interest groups and find ways to change their resistance to postal reform.

Professors Crew and Kleindorfer recommend a comprehensive inquiry into the mission, organization, and ownership of the Postal Service. Economists, of course, are notorious for recommending inquiries. In the worst case, we can use the results of the inquiries for further research; in the best case, we get hired to do the research. I will not violate the requirements of the guild. I too recommend an inquiry, but mine would be different in focus and could be described as follows:

> A comprehensive inquiry to determine who must be paid off, and how much they must be paid, to allow reform of the Postal Service.

Alternatively, if we want to have a mission statement for the inquiry that is more politically acceptable, we could say:

> A comprehensive inquiry into the equitable reform of the Postal Service, taking account of those parties with a legitimate interest in the functioning of the system.

Under either choice of wording, my proposed inquiry would be a public choice analysis of the actual interest groups involved. It would start with the political constraints rather than envision the technology that the Postal Service should aspire to achieve. I think we know roughly what a reformed Postal Service should look like. The real question is how can we get the political muscle to achieve it and whether there is any set of payments that we can devise that will help us to accomplish postal reform.

Discussion

WILLIAM TY MAYTON, Emory University School of Law: Concerning postal methods, I am struck by the fact that in 1995 labor costs will be approximately 85 percent of total postal costs. Most postal revenues come from first-class mail. With a work force of 800,000 employees, what can be done to improve the operating efficiency of the Postal Service? How are you going to get rid of the monopoly?

COMMENT: The common procedure in the private sector for downsizing a firm's labor force is to paint a picture of what will await the uncooperative employee in three to five years. Whether an employee sees his own layoff within that period depends on whether he sees himself as sufficiently powerful to be the last one on the ship.

PROFESSOR MAYTON: There was a buyout at one time. The 1970 reorganization was accomplished on the basis of a 14 percent pay raise. Further reorganization could be accomplished with a buyout, as well as collective bargaining and binding arbitration, with rates set according to what prevails in the private sector.

PAUL R. KLEINDORFER, Wharton School, University of Pennsylvania: In some ways the 1970 reorganization was better for postal employees than one may believe. One of our books suggests that the union premium—the amount above the competitive wage rate, adjusting for various kinds of skill—enjoyed by postal employees is approximately 20 percent.[1] Postal workers achieved most of the premium during the 1970s, just after the Postal Reorganization Act.

On the issue of price caps, we need to have a clear focus. Our discussion has provided a vision for a privatized, commercialized operation. We must realize, however, that any reorganization must maintain the viability of first-class mail. Postal reorganization must not be thrown open for a winner to take all. Rather, our goal should be to achieve a more efficient service, without a headlong rush to eternity, but with a bit of grandeur and stability. This will allow the citizens of this country to understand what the rules of the game are and how to make wise and prudent investments that are not going to be appropriated by the regulatory process.

Although we agree on privatization, the issue of setting up residual claimancies remains. Once the network is privatized with a single owner, a major regulatory scheme must be implemented. Our

---

1. Michael L. Wachter & Jeffrey M. Perloff, *A Comparative Analysis of Wage Premiums and Industrial Relations in the British Post Office and the United States Postal Service, in* COMPETITION AND INNOVATION IN POSTAL SERVICES 115, 130 (Michael A. Crew & Paul R. Kleindorfer eds., Kluwer Academic Publishers 1991).

sketch provides the basic guidelines for how that system might work.

QUESTION: I have a question about the relationship between the provision of competitive and monopolistic services of a reorganized Postal Service. On one side, we want to give the Postal Service more freedom to compete, innovate, and price. Maintaining an insulated monopoly in other services, however, poses problems for those wishing to compete in the provision of competitive services. If the monopoly services are regulated under a price cap, what rules will govern the relationship between monopoly services and competitive services?

PROFESSOR KLEINDORFER: I prefer a regulatory standard based on long-run incremental cost. With incentives and residual claimancy aligned properly, there is no reason for the Postal Service to do anything but compete.

COMMENT: The price cap or the residual claimants within the foreseeable future will not solve the problem. The fact that the services provided as a monopoly can pay for one-third of the Postal Service's costs for free, so to speak, distorts the costs faced by the branch that provides competitive services. Consequently, the Postal Service can price the whole range of competitive products without regard to costs and thus achieve a considerable advantage. The economies of scale or the economies of scope achieved by the reorganized Postal Service do not negate the danger of a firm with the power to distort a large portion of the competitive market.

MICHAEL A. CREW, Rutgers University: If the Postal Service is a profit-maximizing business, then, in the unregulated area, it will presumably try to price to maximize profit. Therefore, in the competitive area its profit will not exceed a normal return.

QUESTION: I understand the positive incentives associated with privatization. I am confused, however, as to how positive incentives result by making the government the sole residual claimant. How does a government agency receive incentives by transferring funds to the Treasury at the end of the fiscal year?

PROFESSOR KLEINDORFER: This is a very important point about how residual claimancy is structured to provide the necessary incentive to both the top line of revenue generation and to the bottom line of cost and efficiency issues. The Dutch PTT provides a good example of what we envision to be the role of a government holding company. As ownership in the Postal Service is gradually transferred through equity markets in a long-run privatization scheme, the government must maintain some control to protect the public interest. With as much as two-thirds of the firm's shares privately owned and openly traded, would you still have concerns about the pricing of competitive services?

ANSWER: Yes.

PROFESSOR KLEINDORFER: Tell me why, now that we have a question free of the residual claimancy issue.

COMMENT: The issue still depends upon what the Postal Service can get away with in monopoly services. If it has the ability to cross subsidize, there is a real danger. I doubt that the price cap prevents cross subsidization.

QUESTION: Under price caps, the Postal Service would not have the incentive to cross subsidize. How could the firm cross subsidize competitive services if the income from its monopoly services is price capped at a rate lower than the increase in inflation?

PROFESSOR KLEINDORFER: The ability to cross subsidize depends on the firm's initial position. British Telecom, for instance, had such low productivity and so much waste in its system that it remained immensely profitable even after a 3 percent price reduction and then a 4½ percent price reduction above the general rate of productivity increase in the economy.

COMMENT: Setting a good price cap is a cost-of-service problem. One does not avoid cost of service.

PROFESSOR CREW: Note that included in cost-of-service calculations would be any pension deficit.

COMMENT: If the firm kept high costs in the reserve area, it could still profit by cutting prices. Rather than lowering price, however, it may choose to cross subsidize competitive services and keep employment high. Because the firm could avoid the difficulties associated with layoffs, it may have an incentive to cross subsidize.

COMMENT: If the firm has large cash reserves and has already paid for its fixed costs, it can force other competitors out of the market. Such a firm can immediately produce at marginal cost. If its only constraint is to meet long-run marginal cost for all its competitive services, then it can price below marginal cost in any single service. A firm has an incentive to monopolize a market, force out competitors, and recoup higher profits later. First-class mail service is not a perfectly competitive market. Competitors need years to set up, to establish customer loyalty, and so forth.

PROFESSOR KLEINDORFER: The extent to which, in a joint-product market, a price leader with one product, like delivery service, has strong incentives to engage in predatory pricing depends on the structure of the specific market in question. The price-leadership models of oligopoly service provide very little room for predatory pricing unless quite unusual costs and demand curves exist. We do not believe that such circumstances exist here. The question of predatory pricing is an empirically testable issue, however. Whether the cost and demand conditions exist for the incumbent to engage in predatory pricing is something that we have not studied in detail. We have relied on the normal economics literature to make our statements.

QUESTION: Unless there are economies of scope, one might go to Professor Rubin's solution and privatize the Postal Service. If there are economies of scope, then even under price caps one encounters cost shifting onto the regulated side. Still, we are ducking the key issue that Professor Rubin has raised: if one can get to the Crew and Kleindorfer solution, then why not go farther and minimize regulatory problems through outright privatization?

QUESTION: What services are we regarding as regulated (monopoly) services, and what services are we regarding as unregulated (competitive) services? At some points, the chapter suggests that first-class mail would be regulated, and that second-, third-, and fourth-class mail would be unregulated. At other times, your chapter states that the delivery function would be regulated as a monopoly and that work-sharing discounts would be unregulated. Instead of selling second-, third-, and fourth-class mail, would it make more sense for the Postal Service to sell a regulated delivery function, a regulated presortation function, and an unregulated transportation function?

PROFESSOR KLEINDORFER: That is exactly what we have in mind. To correct any misunderstanding, the end-to-end service would be regulated as first-class service. Access for first-, second-, third-, and fourth-class to the local delivery network would be regulated also. That includes all of the regulated services.

QUESTION: Why do you want to regulate the end-to-end service?

PROFESSOR KLEINDORFER: Do you mean the first-class service? For one thing, it provides some information. Unless the government is going to relax the private letter-carrier statutes to allow competitive entry into the marketplace, then what will get rid of the exploitation of monopoly power? The only thing that will stem monopoly power is price-cap regulation or competitive entry.

COMMENT: Yes, competition. You just reserve the delivery end for the Postal Service. From the origin to the delivery end, service could be unregulated.

QUESTION: If one is going to regulate the delivery function, which serves second- through fourth-class mail, what part of second-, third-, and fourth-class mail would be unregulated? It is not clear from your chapter what will be regulated and what will be unregulated.

PROFESSOR KLEINDORFER: First-class, end-to-end, and local access for all services would be regulated.

PROFESSOR CREW: First-class end-to-end would be regulated up to a price of two dollars, possibly with a decline in this limiting price over time.